For Joa quín, se eker of knowledge
E. M. C.
For my Jaan, *who makes my life possible*
A. J.

BODIES WITHOUT BORDERS

Also edited by Afshan Jafar and Erynn Masi de Casanova:
Global Beauty, Local Bodies

BODIES WITHOUT BORDERS

Edited by

ErynnMasi de Casanova
and
Afshan Jafar

palgrave
macmillan

BODIES WITHOUT BORDERS
Copyright © Erynn Masi de Casanova and Afshan Jafar, 2013.
Softcover reprint of the hardcover 1st edition 2013 978-1-137-37218-5

First published in 2013 by
PALGRAVE MACMILLAN®
in the United States—a division of St. Martin's Press LLC,
175 Fifth Avenue, New York, NY 10010.

Where this book is distributed in the UK, Europe and the rest of the world,
this is by Palgrave Macmillan, a division of Macmillan Publishers Limited,
registered in England, company number 785998, of Houndmills,
Basingstoke, Hampshire RG21 6XS.

Palgrave Macmillan is the global academic imprint of the above companies
and has companies and representatives throughout the world.

Palgrave® and Macmillan® are registered trademarks in the United States,
the United Kingdom, Europe and other countries.

ISBN 978-1-349-47603-9   ISBN 978-1-137-36538-5 (eBook)
DOI 10.1057/9781137365385

Library of Congress Cataloging-in-Publication Data is available from the
Library of Congress.

A catalogue record of the book is available from the British Library.

Design by Newgen Knowledge Works (P) Ltd., Chennai, India.

First edition: December 2013

10 9 8 7 6 5 4 3 2 1

CONTENTS

BODIES, BORDERS, AND THE OTHER: AN INTRODUCTION

ErynnMasi de Casanova and Afshan Jafar

BODIES IN TRANSNATIONAL PERSPECTIVE

What is the meaning of this book's title, *Bodies without Borders*? Human bodies obviously have some physical boundaries that separate them from the world outside, but these boundaries can also have points of entry or exchange connecting the body with this exterior space. Just as virtual reality and new forms of body modification have problematized the boundaries of bodies, empirical studies of globalization have shown that borders between nations have not been erased, but have become increasingly porous in the last few decades. As scholars have demonstrated, borders and nations still matter, but the rate and speed of cross-border interactions—at the microlevel and the macrolevel—have increased (Appadurai 1996; Harvey 1991; Moghadam 2005). In this volume, we focus on the role of bodies in the flows of people, money, commodities, and ideas across national borders. In other words, we are concerned with bringing the body into examinations of transnational processes such as migration, economic globalization, and cultural globalization.[1] Many of the people portrayed here are engaged in "transnational body projects," defined as "a (re)fashioning of individual bodies that makes use of resources that stretch across national borders" (Casanova and Sutton 2013, 60).

Part of the impetus for compiling *Bodies without Borders* came from our realization that most studies of globalization remain at the level of abstract theory, or focus on interactions and exchanges between massive macrolevel entities, for example, nation-states, multinational corporations, or international aid agencies.[2] Although these types of studies are necessary for understanding large-scale processes of globalization, as we read we noticed that it was nearly impossible to find any actual people in them! And when individual people do appear, it's often difficult to learn anything about how bodies are involved in transnational activities; most globalization scholars are not analyzing or considering embodiment. Yet bodies are obviously already there. The people who work for transnational financial institutions like the International Monetary Fund have and are bodies, and think about other people's bodies (e.g., the citizens of countries who are given loans or bailouts) when they make their funding allocations and other decisions. The people who create international media products, say, the news producers on the *Al Jazeera* network, also have both minds and bodies. Despite the somewhat obvious observation that all individuals have/are bodies, and thus all social groups and organizations are collections of bodies, discussions about bodies in the literature on globalization are scarce. It is more common to see bodies in research that begins with a specific local (or national) case study, which is then seasoned with the spice of globalization or transnational links (Dewey 2008; Edmonds 2010; Sutton 2010; Wilson 2004). In general, however, it is safe to say that most studies of globalization are disembodied.

Studies of the body and embodiment are similarly limited. They set "the" body—or more accurately, bodies, bodily practices and experiences, and ideas about bodies—at the center of their inquiry. The excellent anthologies that we use in our courses on the body all focus almost exclusively on the United States and Western Europe.[3] The problem with this focus is that only about 10 percent of the world's population lives in the United States and Western Europe. What about the other 90 percent, whose bodies and embodied experiences are also worth considering? And what about people who have moved from the home of the 90 percent to the home of the 10 percent, or those who have moved in the opposite direction? What can their migrating bodies teach us about global political economy and transnational connections or disconnections? Globalization processes influence the bodies and embodiment of all people, not just those who physically cross national borders. The empirical chapters in this book, and those in our complementary volume (*Global Beauty, Local Bodies*) represent an invitation to scholars of embodiment to consider the role of bodies in globalizing processes, and an initial effort to begin to globalize body studies.

As the title suggests, the research in this book explores embodied experiences that trouble strictly defined borders between countries, or between the global and local. While elaborating their particular case studies, the authors of these chapters do not lose sight of two key dimensions of globalization: (1) the material conditions of people's everyday lives; and (2) transnational connections. By material conditions, we mean the social, political, and economic structures that directly constrain or improve individuals' life chances. Even if we as researchers are most concerned with bodies or "culture" (however defined), these structures matter for understanding what is happening on the ground—in people's experience of quotidian interactions or in the diffusion of media or consumer products. In fact, examining people's embodied experiences without giving sufficient weight to these material conditions is dangerous, as it assumes that all members of a society or social group have equal access to resources. As some of the cases presented here show, our bodily practices and ideas about bodies are tangled up with and constrained by social class distinctions.

Transnational connections are based on the movement of people, money, products, and ideas across national borders, which is not a unidirectional or permanent move. When people cross borders, they do not leave behind all of their beliefs about bodies or habitual embodied practices. The circulation of media images of bodies and products designed for bodies also involves the geographic mobility of ideas about bodies that emerged in a specific time and place. Such images and objects are then interpreted and used in new local settings, allowing for a complex and sometimes unpredictable interaction between global, local, national, and transnational ideas and practices. Rather than privileging either the global or the local in analyzing how bodies are used and conceived of, the studies in this book document multidirectional movement across these scales, or people's simultaneous invoking of different scales. The resources for individuals' border-crossing corporeal practices may be economic, cultural, or social, but the bodies described in *Bodies without Borders* are always most legible through the lens of the transnational.[4]

Our primary goal in this work is to bring together two largely separate fields of scholarly inquiry: the study of globalization and the study of bodies and embodiment. While this introduction does not provide a comprehensive overview of the relevant literature in these two interdisciplinary areas, readers will find useful references to key texts throughout the chapters. The bibliography at the end of this book is unique in that it focuses relatively equally on globalization and the body. In a departure from previous studies, the research compiled here takes as its starting point the *intersection* of bodies and globalization. The chapters in *Bodies without Borders* include both empirical research and personal reflections, in the recognition that telling the story of what it means to have and be a body in a globalizing world is just as interesting and important as systematically documenting how embodied individuals and groups navigate their globalizing societies.

In this introductory chapter, readers will also find multiple voices, as we (the editors) alternate reflections on our subjective embodied experiences with theoretical questions and descriptions of the book's themes.

* * *

BORDERLESS DANCE, BOUNDED BODIES

Ras. Dva. Tri. Chetiri.

The only Russian words I know are the numbers one, two, three, four. I learned them as an adolescent in warm-up classes before performances of the *Nutcracker*, in which my local ballet company was joined by guest artists from Russia's Kirov Ballet. Allowing muscle memory to guide me through the typical exercises done at the barre, I began to repeat these numbers in my head along with the instructor. My body reacted frantically to faster, more emphatic counting once the portable barres were cleared away and we occupied the center of the stage facing the darkened auditorium. *Ras! Dva! Oh-shit-I-am-messing this up! Tri! Chetiri!*

* * *

Though I'd guess that dance has always been a part of the human bodily experience, ballet is a unique form of art (some would say torture) that emerged in a specific historical period and geographic and cultural space: the royal courts of Renaissance Italy. Ballet quickly made the jump to France, where it was codified in a form somewhat recognizable to today's dance enthusiasts. From the beginning, this was a transnational bodily practice.

* * *

As a pre-professional student of dance, I was part of this transnational social and cultural world. The teachers who taught me were not only from the United States, but also Russia, France, Denmark, Finland, Germany, Egypt, the Philippines, Japan, and Cuba, among other places. Distinct identifiable styles of ballet include the Italian (Cecchetti) technique, and also the Russian (Vaganova) and Danish (Bournonville). Learning to move between these different corporeal vocabularies was akin to what linguists call "code switching"—slipping in and out of languages and dialects. The international languages of ballet require dancers to align their bodies with different norms, sometimes within a single performance. The stylized arabesque position I would be trained to use as a sylph in one ballet was not the arabesque needed in a piece choreographed by the late George Balanchine (a truly transnational figure: born in Russia, he became a star in France, and then created a ballet technique seen as uniquely American). Dancers rely on muscle memory—literally the embodiment of experience—to help them replicate movements, but this memory needs to be polyglot and flexible.

*   *   *

There is a certain "look" that female ballet dancers' bodies are supposed to have. It is difficult for young women not to become obsessed with this body ideal, which is much the same no matter where in the world you are stepping into a ballet classroom or onto a stage. I remember a time in my early teens when I had read some treatise on this ideal dancer's body and I could not stop asking myself—and a few long-suffering friends—whether I had the required combination of a long neck and small head. Long compared to what? How small is small enough? As my adolescence progressed, I was repeatedly told I should lose weight (so that I could jump higher, as one teacher put it). I was not obese or even overweight by non-ballet standards. When I took a deep breath, I could feel each one of my ribs, and I could make a bracelet around my wrist with my thumb and index finger. Nevertheless, I grew fixated on trimming my hips, backside, and thighs, until one day a fellow dancer snidely told me it was really my *upper* body that was too heavy! Ballet dancers should also not have a bust, it seemed. The body demanded in this social world is almost asexual, all straight lines and none of the softness associated with post-pubescent women.

*   *   *

The *corps de ballet* (literally, the ballet body), the anonymous women who must form straight lines and whirling patterns on the stage, is usually characterized by racialized uniformity. In the ballet world, a *corps* made up of similarly thin bodies of equal height and proportions is idealized—and faces and limbs whose colors match are standard. The transnational, globally interconnected ballet world demands a particular type of body, one that is stereotypically white or "Caucasian" in its thin curve-less-ness. Although women who are classified as white in US society evince a range of body types, thicker, more voluptuous bodies tend to be associated with black and Latina women. As scholars and pop culture tell us, there is also greater acceptance of fleshier bodies in some minority communities. When it comes to the flat-chested, flat-bottomed, inner-thighs-not touching body ideal propagated globally in the sociocultural world of ballet, even some white women's bodies are not white enough. I know, because I was one of those women.

—Erynn Masi de Casanova

*   *   *

EMBODYING THE MODERN

As a child growing up in Pakistan, I was scrawny. My parents were always concerned about me because no matter how much I ate, I never put on any weight. Most of their concern was for my health. My father, having been even scrawnier than I was, and not having had access to plentiful food once his family migrated to Pakistan (during the partition of the Indian subcontinent in 1947 upon gaining independence from British rule), was always concerned that I was somehow malnourished. I was far from it—my mother made sure of that. Yet, I remained scrawny. I wasn't unusual, though. I had many friends who looked like me. So why did people worry so much about my body?

As I grew older, I started to realize that there was something more to people's worry than just my health. I did not fit the image of an ideal body. An ideal female body, I was told, was one that had some "meat" on it, some softness, some extra flesh. That is what made it beautiful and womanly.

This image of the ideal female body coincided with the images we saw in the media—both in Pakistani media (models and actresses both) but perhaps even more importantly, in Bollywood. I grew up surrounded by images of soft, rounded, women as top Bollywood actresses. Rekha, Sridevi, Madhuri Dixit, Dimple Kapadia, and Raakhee, were all women who were on a spectrum of curvaceous bodies. Sridevi was known as "thundering thighs" and even though I remember criticism of her weight (she was probably the heaviest of all the actresses listed above), it didn't stand in the way of her success. Madhuri Dixit did one of her most famous "dance numbers"—"*Choli Kay Peechay Kya Hai*" ("What's behind the blouse?")—as a much heavier woman than when she started acting. And yet she was considered beautiful.

But something changed from the time that I was a young girl watching these actresses to the present day when I visit Pakistan. As I pick up one of today's fashion magazines and skim through it, I am struck by how different the models look. They are truly emaciated. Their bodies are no different from the models I see in fashion magazines here in the United States. I turn on the TV and catch an interview with a top Bollywood actress about her "sexy dance number." The actress and her dance choreographer can't seem to stop talking about her dedication as an actress. The choreographer then goes on to say that prior to shooting this video, the actress had given up all desserts and was working out at all hours of the day and night in order to "look her best" for this video. The actress then reveals, laughingly, that the minute they were done shooting the video, they ordered Danish pastry for her to celebrate.

I am puzzled by this and decide to do a Google search for the actresses from my childhood. I am stunned to find that most of them don't look anything like what I remember. They are slimmer now than they ever were at the peak of their careers and look…younger almost. *Are my memories false?* I keep digging and after several minutes I find them—the actresses how I remember them. The reason why my Google search was finally successful in finding these old images (instead of the newer, slimmer, younger version)? I added the word "fat" before their names.

In yet another experience in present-day Pakistan, I watched a morning talk show in which a woman gets a Botox shot in her forehead. All the while the host proclaimed proudly and almost deliriously, how wonderful it is that such "treatments" are readily available in Pakistan! All I had planned on consuming for breakfast that morning was my omelet and *paratha* (flatbread). Who knew I'd also be fed a steady diet of a pseudo-scientific campaign about self-improvement? All before nine in the morning!

What happened between the time I was growing up in Pakistan and now? One of the most profound changes was that the global media became a lot more powerful and visible in Pakistan. When I was a child, Pakistani television consisted of one, government-run, channel. By the 1990s, satellite television was streaming *Santa Barbara*, *The Bold and the Beautiful*, E!, and MTV right into our living rooms. And we devoured every minute of it. Long starved of global media, we overindulged in the calorie-free diet happily. As Pakistan cast off the shackles of a military dictator and his religious reforms, the notions of progress and modernity as symbolized by the entry of Western media and their concomitant ideals of self-improvement, commodification of the body, and insatiable consumerism became ever more salient in a nation experiencing a rebirth.

—AfshanJa far

* * *

BORDER CROSSING, BODY MODIFICATION, AND ENCOUNTERING THE OTHER

It would be shortsighted of us to believe that the obsession with physical appearance is simply the globalization of a Western idea. Indeed the Indian subcontinent has its own long history of traditional herbs and medicines used to beautify and modify the body. Women's bodies are openly scrutinized and criticized in India (Dewey 2008) and Pakistan. What we are seeing though is that the ideal body has become far leaner, far skinnier, far more toned, and the range of acceptable body types is shrinking. And it isn't just women's bodies. Men's bodies too have become the object of much management and disciplining. For instance, Bollywood's male actors' bodies have changed drastically too. They are now bulkier, and far more muscular than the previous generations of men in Bollywood. This may be one example where we do see an acceptance of a particular Western ideal of body modification. However, globalization is not Westernization, nor is it a homogenization.

While people may think only of the more "permanent" forms like tattooing and surgical interventions when we discuss body modification, there are many ways that our bodies can be modified. A fitness workout, martial arts practice, or an item of clothing modifies our appearance. In what ways, and to what end? These are some of the questions that this book explores. One of the things that we caution the reader against falling into is a traditional versus modern dichotomy when studying body modification. That is, we often classify some forms of modification as "modern" or "progressive" while we see others as "traditional," "backward" or even threatening and upsetting. These classifications tell us more about our own anxieties regarding certain cultures and practices, as they come into more frequent contact with one another through globalization, and our encounters with the Other, than any inherent reality about the practice itself.

We now discuss an example briefly as it illustrates the false nature of these dichotomies so well. The example that we discuss here is the *hijab* or the headscarf that some Muslim women adopt. Often a lightning rod in European politics and debates on immigration, this item of clothing represents the intersections of globalization and the individual body very well.

The hijab, often seen as a traditional item of clothing or the choice of ultrareligious Muslim women, defies any such label when studied more closely. The history of the hijab is very diverse. Historically, in some Arab countries, the hijab was adopted by the wealthy Muslim, Christian, and Jewish women (as a status symbol), whereas in other places, like Pakistan, the hijab was not common at all. In fact, the 1950s, Leila Ahmed notes, "[was] an era when being unveiled and bareheaded had become the norm in the cities of Egypt, as well as in those of other Muslim-majority societies (2011, 10). In some countries veiling was imposed by the state (as in post-Revolution Iran) and resisted by women, and in some countries women adopted it as a symbol of their struggle against Western colonization, as in the case of Algerian women's resistance to their French colonizers (Winter 2008).

As the global migrations of people continue and the boundaries that separate people and nations continue to blur, we are faced with encountering the Other in our homelands. Of course, colonized nations had not only encountered the Other, but been ruled by them. It is only when brown-skinned Others start to enter the lands of their former rulers that nations start to worry about immigration reform and the "threat" of globalization. As Edward Said (2001) stated in his famous essay, "The Clash of Ignorance": "Think of the populations today of France, Italy, Germany, Spain, Britain, American, even Sweden and you must concede that Islam is no longer on the fringes of the West but at its center." As Islam moves into the heart of Europe and North America, we see that anxieties about the practice of "veiling" become reinvigorated. That the hijab is now seen in Muslim countries, like Pakistan, where previously it was a rare sight, or in countries like Egypt, where it had been abandoned by the 1950s (Ahmed 2011), is evidence of the power of globalization and the flow of ideas and practices from one place to another. Further, that the hijab is often adopted by second- or third-generation immigrants (even to their parents' dismay and consternation) speaks to how much of a modern, global phenomenon it really is. As Caitlin Killian (2003) shows in her research, *young, educated* Muslim women in France are much more likely to support the wearing of the hijab *as their right in a democratic society* than the older, less educated generation of immigrants.

Thus we see that while globalization has facilitated a movement of bodies from one place to another, not all bodies are welcomed equally and not all practices are considered acceptable. In our encounters with the Other comes a need to define, and redefine, ourselves and the Other. We may do so by absorbing and accepting certain practices or we may do so by rejecting and resisting them. But the more we label a practice as unacceptable, the more important it becomes as an identity signifier to the rejected group. We are never more aware of or attached to our identity than when we believe it to be under attack. This is certainly the case with the popularity of the hijab. Is it a coincidence that the hijab has gained popularity during a time when it has also gained world infamy?

And so it is that through analyzing bodies, we see the contradictory nature of globalization: it involves an increasing flow of bodies, ideas, and practices but that does not always lead to an acceptance of those bodies, ideas, and practices. Nor does it always lead to a homogenization in terms of culture or shared ideals and practices. In fact, it may very well lead to a reentrenchment or revival of particular practices or ideals. Thus, some borders dissolve and disappear, but new borders are erected. And our bodies are often the terrain on which the fight for these borders takes place.

SCOPE AND PLAN OF THE BOOK

It is difficult to list the number of countries, nationalities, and ethnic groups covered in the empirical research compiled in this book, because many of the phenomena discussed are truly transnational. At the least, the research-based chapters draw on experience in and documentation from more than a dozen countries, including Thailand, Singapore, Germany, Mexico, and the United States. They reflect on the meanings of concepts such as fitness, whiteness, blackness, fashion, and security in globalizing societies. The personal reflections included here are similarly diverse, exploring how individuals deal with experiences of racial difference, body modification, and gender identity as their bodies cross borders. While most of our chapters, in keeping with trends in the scholarly and popular literature on bodies, focus on the ideals and practices associated with women's corporeality, three of the selections in this volume also address men's bodies and ideas about masculinity in various sites. This small number, while an important contribution, points to one limitation of this book: its disproportionate focus on women and femininity. The interdisciplinary field of body studies still tends to follow ancient distinctions in Western society that see women as more embodied and men as more cerebral. To some degree, our inclusion of chapters on men's bodies works to counter this tendency. Despite gaps in coverage, *Bodies without Borders* provides an inclusive, transnational collection of writings on embodiment in the age of globalization.

The chapter by Lionel Loh Han Loong draws on embodied participant observation, or "performance ethnography"—meaning that he used his own body as a data collection instrument—to explore the transnational body projects of men who travel from around the world to train at a martial arts gym in rural Thailand. While simultaneously describing the internationalization of martial arts in recent years, Loh details how these students of various fighting techniques manage the embodied code-switching required to master styles that originated in specific cultures yet are now geographically unmoored and globally popular.

In her chapter, Kamille Gentles-Peart follows the migration of both women's bodies and ideals of women's bodies from the Caribbean to the United States. She allows the voices of the black West Indian women she interviewed to tell their own stories of navigating distinct concepts of beauty "back home" in their islands of origin and in their new home of New York City.

The personal reflection by Mónica G. Moreno Figueroa also addresses the situation of the African diaspora, narrating moments in which her racial self-identification (or desire not to identify with just one racial group) was challenged. We see how, in a variety of social situations, individuals tend to classify each other by skin tone and racialized features. She shows how the acts of seeing and being seen are never neutral, but always highly charged with cultural ideals, local interpretations, and ultimately, moral evaluations.

Joel Gwynne takes on the transnational space of the Internet in his analysis of two popular fashion blogs created by and for young women in Malaysia and Singapore, and available to Internet users around the globe. The act of blogging is an assertion of selfhood and autonomy, yet many of the goals and pastimes represented in the blogs fit with stereotypes of traditional femininity. The blogs' foregrounding of consumption and the fetishizing of particular products as ways of "doing" individual identity in rapidly globalizing Asian societies shows the influence of economic development and its relation to culture and microlevel processes.

In her chapter on one Colombian company's transnational marketing of "bulletproof fashion," Barbara Sutton shows the theoretical underpinnings of current obsessions with protecting elite bodies in uncertain and violent settings. Sutton explains the appeal of bullet-resistant clothing in a globalizing world, in which national and other borders have become hyperregulated, and in which not all bodies' safety is equally valued.

Nahed Eltantawy's personal reflection picks up this theme of safety and danger, as she describes how the hijab or headscarf and its wearers are viewed by non-Muslims in countries in which Muslims are a minority, such as the United States. She also narrates her conflicted feelings on the meaning of this dress practice as a Muslim woman who does not wear hijab, but who tries to understand the perspective of her friends and family members, some of whom do participate in this custom.

In his personal reflection, Thomas J. D. Armbrecht reflects on a series of body modifications that he has undertaken in a number of countries. He shows how literal border-crossing and cross-cultural experiences relate to the breaching of the body's physical boundaries through practices of adornment and alteration such as piercing and tattooing. These transnational practices manage to be simultaneously seen as remnants of the past, while also being an indication of a modern individualizing body project.

Similarly, Verena Hutter argues against a notion of globalizing bodies as existing "out there" in the world; instead, she recognizes their location in the modern, developed West. Using Germany as a case study, she examines attitudes toward tattoos and tattooing over the past 150 years, arguing that these attitudes were wrapped up in ideas of national distinctiveness as well as fearful and curious encounters with various "others," ranging from non-European "natives" to US soldiers during wartime. Today, tattoos in Germany are a form of symbolically communing with otherness, and for this reason, the stigmatized practice has become something of a political punching bag.

While she also discusses the personal significance of tattooing, Anisha Gautam's essay highlights the displacement of migration and the challenges of being/having a racialized minority body in a majority-white society. Gautam connects her literal border crossing in migrating from Nepal to Australia with other types of corporeal border crossings, telling a hopeful story of reclaiming the abject body.

The final chapter, by Diana Brenscheidt gen. Jost, recounts the way that Zumba became arguably the most popular branded fitness practice on the planet. She explores the way that Zumba is marketed and perceived differently in different local settings, explaining how it can be both embraced as "authentically" Latin American (and even Mexican) in Mexico and as exotic and "other" in the United States and Europe. Brenscheidt links the rise of Zumba with the circulation of regional and local ideals of body and beauty that originate in Latin

America and are increasingly popular in non-Latin American societies, such as the appreciation for curvier figures and bigger behinds.

Though each chapter focuses on a different discrete topic, we trust that readers will see some thematic threads running throughout the book. The act of bodies crossing borders—that is, the transnational movement of people and ideas about bodies—our notions of the Other, and the boundaries of what constitutes a socially accepted body, are inextricably linked. In *Bodies without Borders*, we explore and explain these links, asking new questions that we hope will be answered by future research on globalizing bodies.

NOTES

1. For some useful definitions and general discussions of globalization, see Chossudovsky 2003; Lechner and Boli 2011; McMichael 2011; Stiglitz 2003; and Wallerstein 2000.
2. Examples of these types of studies include some of the essential readings on globalization, such as many of those included in Lechner and Boli 2011; also Harvey 1990; Ong 1999; Sklair 2000; Stiglitz 2003.
3. These books include Bobel and Kwan 2011; Lorber and Moore 2010; Malacrida and Low 2008; Moore and Kosut 2010; and Weitz 2009.
4. For more on transnationalism, see Moghadam 2005; Mohanty 2003; Ong 1999; Sklair 2000; and Smith 2005.

1

THE GLOBAL MARTIAL CIRCUIT AND GLOBALIZED BODIES

LionelL ohH an Loong

* * *

Already, bruises are starting to form on my right shin, the leg that I frequently use to execute roundhouse kicks. In a sense, I am modifying my body, making some parts of it, deemed by the martial arts community as essential to fighting, stronger and faster. I commented to Ivar, 39, Swede, security guard, whose shin is a whole mass of bruises how hard-core he is. He smiled and said, "At least you know you are hitting the right places."

Fieldnotes

* * *

In *Techniques of the Body*, Mauss (2006, 83) expounds upon how "the body is man's first and most natural instrument... man's first and most natural technical object, and at the same time technical means, is his body" and that "techniques are thus human norms of training" (2006, 85). Culture mediates the way individuals come to think about the world vis-à-vis bodily knowledge and the way they utilize their bodies. As a case study of an explicit somatic culture, this ethnographic study of a mixed martial arts (MMA) gym in Thailand examines how martial arts are embedded within transnational flows and practices. I argue that these processes of globalization impact the discursive construction and practice of martial arts. The flow of individuals, televised images, and particular techniques of the body (Mauss 2006) across transnational boundaries results in individuals drawing upon an eclectic array of martial disciplines. This in turn influences the transmission and modification of sensorial knowledge and the commercialization of martial arts.

METHODOLOGY AND RESEARCH SITE

Researchers on somatic cultures such as dance and martial arts often stress the materiality of the body as being central to understanding the lived realities of these practices, given that language alone is often inadequate to convey and transmit embodied knowledge (Leigh Foster 2003; Potter 2008; Samudra 2008). Practice, constituted by "shared skills and understanding," "tacit knowledge," and "embodied, materially mediated arrays of human activity" (Schatzki et al. 2000, 2–3), is thus central to my research methodology. A number of similar generic terminologies are often used for this, such as "performance ethnography," "practice-as-research," and "performance-as-research." In their review of the methodologies used in theater and performance studies, Kershaw et al. (2011, 63–65) argue that "practice-as-research" is characterized by "post-binary commitment to activity (rather than structure), process (rather than fixity), action (rather than representation), collectiveness (rather than individualism), reflexivity (rather than self-consciousness)," and the "unsustainable bifurcations between becoming and being." As embodied knowledge is not easily transmitted except through learning a skill for yourself, this methodology attempts to bridge the chasm between "practical" and "discursive" consciousness. Polanyi (1983, 10) argues that this form of tacit knowing, whereby one knows the proximal (practical consciousness) only by attending to the distal (discursive consciousness), reflects how individuals "can know more than we can tell" (1983, 4). For Giddens, the former refers to "recall to which the agent has access in the durée of action without being able to express what he or she thereby 'knows,'" while the latter refers to "recall which the actor is able to express verbally" (1984, 49).

Performance ethnography, as an embodied methodology, allows research to be conducted about and through bodies due to the embodied sensuous experiences that "create the conditions for understanding...[P]erformed experiences are the sites where felt emotion, memory, desire and understanding come together" (Denzin 2003, 13). Performance ethnography allows the researcher to comprehend how culturally specific meanings are generated and sustained through movements, the motivations by which particular movements are generated, and a yardstick by which to contextualize and situate these movements. Kaeppler (1999, 22) cautions against marginalizing the role of the audience because "movement sequences are analogous to utterances, and without knowledge of the movement conventions, a viewer will be unable to understand what is being conveyed." My methodology reiterates Kaeppler's (1999) advice because it captures the dynamics between the performer and audience. As a methodology in which my material body is intrinsically intertwined with the ongoing social processes, performance ethnography allows for the construction of experiential knowledge vis-à-vis my subjective experiences, observations, and perceptions (Dickson-Swift, et al. 2009; Okely 2007; Parker-Starbuck and Mock 2011; Seymour 2007). By subjecting my body to the rigors of the gym, by bodies interacting and communicating in the social drama that unfolds, at times nonverbally, important data are generated. The visual, verbal, sensual, olfactory, and kinaesthetic processes at the gym constitute important data sources (see Spencer 2013). As the way in which one's senses are directed to perceive selective aspects of reality is influenced by one's cultural, ontological, and epistemological paradigms (Howes 2003; 2004), self-reflexivity is necessary to translate that which is experiential and interpretive into the discursive dimension. Within this somatic culture, my body is "a tool of inquiry and vector for knowledge" (Wacquant 2004, viii).

For five weeks, I embedded myself in the social reality of Kwaan-saa-maat Gym [Might Gym], a Muay Thai (MT) and MMA gym in a rural province in Thailand, training, living, and interacting with the other participants at the gym. As accommodation is part of the training package, everyone stays and trains at the gym, making this field site one that is geographically bounded. While numerous martial arts gyms owned by both Thais and foreigners abound in places such as Bangkok, Phuket, Chiang Mai, and Koh Samui, I deliberately chose Kwaan-saa-maat Gym because of its relative isolation, situated far beyond these touristy locations. I was interested in the everyday realities of men who were passionate about martial arts and were willing to isolate themselves and devote their time to training. Unsurprisingly, individuals at the gym often attempt to differentiate themselves from other foreigners by vocalizing their disdain for the idea of training at gyms located near tourist hotspots. They prefer to subject themselves to the more strenuous martial arts training at Kwaan-saa-maat Gym, which is of a variety not found at those gyms. Michael is a Norwegian student, aged 18. His comment typifies the kind of responses given

by the participants when asked why they decided to come all the way
to rural Thailand to train:

> How I heard about Kwaan-saa-maat Gym? I just Googled it and type
> Issan and MT. I wanted to get away from everything and Issan is far
> enough, away from tourist traps! At the World MT Council at Koh
> Samui, it is much more tourist focused…they don't push you as hard
> likehe re.

A particular appeal of Kwaan-saa-maat Gym is the opportunity to
train with its owner, described by Stefan, 22, a German student, as
being "one of the top MT fighters. He was actually one of the best in
the world!" Another is the lack of distractions due to Kwaan-saa-maat
Gym's location far away from popular tourist destinations. Karl, 22, a
Scottish postgraduate, explains why it appeals to him:

> I also wanted to get out of way from the touristy place like Pattaya,
> Phuket, Koh Samui, it's just too much distractions. Too hectic and all.
> I wanted to be out here where it's relaxed. Hectic as in it is just party-
> ing and people hustling you? It is just more stressful. More traffic, more
> bars that people go to, girls, so many things to distract you, put you off
> MT. Cheap alcohol, the beaches and stuff. Out here there is less to do,
> enough to keep you entertained but you just train and that is what you
> do. Don't get to do anything else except train so it is good that way.

For the men, the relative isolation of the gym, away from tourists, is
perceived to be one of the characteristics of the "authentic" Muay
Thai experience. As the above extracts highlight, this is a point that
the men constantly reiterate to outsiders.

Martial arts gyms in Thailand that cater to foreigners constitute
a transient community. Most individuals, with the exception of the
instructors, stay at the gym from between a week to a few months.
Prior to my trip, I communicated with the owner of Kwaan-saa-
maat Gym and obtained his consent to conduct my fieldwork there.
Throughout my stay at Kwaan-saa-maat Gym, I became acquainted
with 22 men, the majority coming from Scandinavian countries like
Sweden and Norway. Excluding the Thai MT instructors, there were
only three other Asians there during my stay. The men are mainly in
their early twenties; the youngest is 18 and the oldest 39. Coming
from diverse occupations, from law undergraduate to security guard,
one commonality they share is their socioeconomic status and their
passion for martial arts. Some motivations behind the men's sojourn
in Thailand are to pursue a hobby, to be physically fit, and for the few

professional fighters at the gym, to recuperate or prepare for their upcoming fight. Most of the participants are of at least a middle-class background and so are able to afford the costs of training in Thailand for a prolonged period of time without worrying about their means of livelihood. I was informed that it is very rare for women to come and train at the gym.

In short, Kwaan-saa-maat Gym is a site where a community of individuals coming from diverse cultures and nationalities are united in their passion for martial arts, subjugating their bodies to the rigors of training. Communal moments are created when the guys talk about the fights they have seen or participated in. In addition, the training grounds have a dual functionality: they are at the same time a site where bodies get reconfigured as particular martial disciplines become embodied, and just a place to hang out. This sense of *communitas* is exemplified by Veron, 28, Indian, unemployed, who comments:

> Aside from discipline and focus, meeting up with amazing people, amazing fighters and understanding their reasons for fighting and learning MT is also impressive. People come from all walks of life, there are electricians, there are street fighters, there are university graduates who learn MT. So you try understanding what works for them [and that] inspire[s] me...these are people who have a past and they decided to channel their energies, channel their focus in the right way. In doing something good in their life, they focus on MT.

Turner (1969) conceptualizes communitas as existential or spontaneous social groups that are forged through a sense of collective purpose, communion, and emotional bonds. As the previous extract demonstrates, the shared experiences of the participants engaging in martial arts training allow them to bond, despite their different socio-structural positions and nationalities, and focus on martial arts. Above anything else, one's commitment to training hard and learning to be a good fighter is valued at the gym. The gym is a "short-lived society" (Foster 1986), where social interactions are intensified due to the men's limited time there, a structured training schedule, language barrier, and mobility issues. Kwaan-saa-maat Gym is located about 15 minutes' ride away from the town center and aside from a couple of restaurants and grocery stores, there is little in the way of entertainment. Unless one knows how to ride a motorbike and rents one from the gym, it is hard to partake in the province's nightlife or get to know people outside the gym. There is also a language barrier that needs to be traversed. Mobility (or the lack thereof) becomes an important factor in shaping communal life at the gym, as most individuals often spent their time either resting within the privacy of their rooms or talking with the other men at particular sites in the gym.

THE GLOBAL SPORTING AND MARTIAL CIRCUIT

Sport, "in its dual role as a long-term motor and metric of transnational change," provides a distinctive lens through which to analyze the forces of globalization (Giulianotti and Robertson 2007, 1). For example, sports historians analyzing the linkages between sports and globalization have shown how the globalization of sports is implicated in the colonial project. Sports such as cricket and football have been used as a medium to "civilize" indigenous people (Guttmann 1995; Mangan 1987) and both indigenous and nonindigenous sports have been subjected to the processes of adaptation, change, and commercialization (Appadurai 1996; Giulianotti 1999). Baseball in Cuba epitomizes how sports are linked to the maintenance of one's national identity in a globalized world. Initially introduced to Cuba by Americans, baseball has been discursively reconstructed as a source of nationalistic and anticolonial pride (González 1999; Jamail 2000; Pérez 1994). In today's milieu, sports have become institutions that are economically prominent, popular, and are able to unite and mobilize individual sentiments regardless of people's cultural differences (Eco 1987; Smart 2007). The rise of sports as an institution in the global arena is the result of commercial interests (Aris 1990; Harvey and Houle 1994; Houlihan 1994; Jarvie 2006; Klein 2001; Miller et al. 2001; Smart 2005; 2007), multinational media corporations investing in sports, the institutionalization of inaugural international sporting events, and the rise of governing bodies (Maguire 1999) that have sought to standardize and institutionalize sporting rules and regulations (Van Bottenburg 2001). The institutionalization of sports results in the transnational movement and migration of sports personnel, the use of the media to deliver sporting events on a global scale, the flow of finances generated by the sports industry and ideas about sports across the globe, the emergence of transnational regulatory bodies and organizations for sports and new ways in which sports are interpreted and consumed by diverse cultures (Jarvie 2006). However, to polarize this "global-local nexus" is unnecessarily to attribute hegemony to one pole and exclude the other (Andrews and Ritzer 2007). Robertson (1995) argues for the need to recognize the interpenetrative and complementary relations that characterize this nexus: the local is complicit in the creation and perpetuation of the global, and vice versa. In making its presence felt in the global arena, the institution of sports is simultaneously furthering globalization processes in areas such as politics, culture, and the economy (see Friedman 1994; Jarvie 2006; Maguire 1999).

Utilizing my informants' vignettes, I elucidate the ways in which these bi-directional global flows of ethnoscapes, mediascapes, technoscapes, financescapes, and ideoscapes (Appadurai 1996, 33) impact martial arts, paying particular attention to the relationship between techniques of the body and the commercialization of martial arts. I appropriate Appadurai's concept of "-scapes" and offer the term "martialscape" to describe the dynamic interaction between discursive constructions of martial arts and the manner in which individuals conceive of and experience martial arts at the global level. Divorcing himself from a paradigm that seeks to comprehend globalization "in terms of existing center-periphery models" (1996, 2), Apparadurai argues that "at least as rapidly as forces from various metropolises are brought into new societies they tend to be indigenized in one or other way" (1996, 295). Apparadurai's concept of "-scapes" is reflective of a deterritorialized, postmodern, and transnational milieu where myriad centers are involved in bidirectional processes of hybridization that calls into question an "authentic and original" culture. Similarly, martial arts traditions, having circumnavigated the globe, have been transformed into deterritorialized cultural practices. The term "martialscape" reflects these deterritorialized cultural practices, the hybridization process these cultural forms undergo by a receiving audience, and the transnational movement of fighters.

MARTIAL ARTS: A RECONFIGURATION OF THE SENSES AND KNOWING THE BODY

Through the men's vignettes and my ethnographic data, I illustrate how Muay Thai involves an embodied socialization process that contests the men's normative ideas regarding Muay Thai and how they have already been socialized by their own cultures or other martial traditions into using particular techniques of the body. These men are not only negotiating new ways to use their bodies but also new ways of thinking of and about their bodies. Individuals learn to visualize their knees and elbows as extensions of their selves. Perceiving one's body as having more than the normal four limbs may seem counterintuitive to nonfighters, but Muay Thai, often affectionately known as the art of eight limbs, calls upon neophytes to reconceptualize the way they view their own bodies. The men's initial normative ideas of what Muay Thai entails are challenged as their bodies are socialized into performing particular bodily techniques of Muay Thai taught and practiced at the gym. During training, individuals are also socialized to utilize visualization techniques. To be a successful fighter, one needs to reconfigure his senses and use them to gain an advantage over opponents:

> There will be attempts to maintain constant eye contact, watching *Ajarn* [teacher, in Thai] Lai's movements as he calls out for me to execute different punches or kicks. The quality of the punches I throw is not only measured by our eyes but the impact of the punches on the pads. This impact, experienced between the fighter and trainer, forges a temporary relationship between the two. After some time, Ajarn grabs hold of my leg and twists it in a particular position so that I will be forced to use my hips. Ajarn does this to me a couple of times, holding my body and forcing it into the correct position, forcing me to use the hip, and hand movement to accelerate the power of my kicks.
>
> Fieldnotes

When one is raining blows on a punching bag, one learns to view the inanimate bag as a living thing, and imagine that the blows are hitting vital areas of the body such as the liver, kidneys, ribs, and jaw. Ironically, while these visualization techniques attempt to embody the inanimate, individuals may deliberately disembody and dehumanize their opponents within the boxing ring. Similar to the way in which scientific knowledge dismembers the patient's body (Young 1997), rendering it vulnerable and malleable to scientific discourses (Foucault 1990) that circumvent the individual's agency, this disembodying of their opponent's bodies into discrete components projects a map of targets to punch. I suggest this visualization technique allows individuals to throw off the inhibitions of the civilizing process. Individuals thus learn to oscillate between embodying and disembodying other individuals, as well as objects, in the gym.

In *The Civilizing Process: The History of Manners*, Elias (1978) explores how civilization results in human behavior being transformed in a particular manner. Elias's historical analysis of etiquette books and textual accounts highlights how between the Middle Ages and the eighteenth century, there were radical transformations in what were previously seen as socially acceptable forms of human interactions in myriad areas such as table manners, the use of cutlery, natural functions, blowing one's nose, spitting, bedroom behavior, changing attitudes toward male and female relations, and aggression. Elias views such shifts in everyday life as indicative of profound transformations in basic human relationships, in which the boundaries of aversion and embarrassment were raised and heightened, and there exists an "invisible wall of affects which seems now to rise between one human body and another, repelling and separating" (2000, 60). This "affective wall" influencing the mental and social structures of individuals within society impacts spatial relations between one's body vis-à-vis other foreign bodies. Of particular relevance to the genre of martial arts is how the civilizing process entails the pacification of society at both the physical level and the psychological level of affect (Elias 1978). The "affective wall" has a crucial role in the diminishing of violence in everyday interactions over the last 500 years as individuals exert a greater degree of self-control at the subconscious level over their actions. Civilization is an ongoing process in which restrictions are placed upon the individual conduct with the purpose of attenuating excesses in violence, inequality, disorder, pleasure, and anarchy.

At the gym, the men's bodies are subjected to an ongoing socialization process where they learn to put aside the civilizing process. For participants who are professional fighters, their bodies learn to put aside these societal inhibitions against violence and they often talk about how their bodies know that they have an upcoming fight:

Paul, 34, American professional fighter: Do you know how many people, they work a nine to five job for 30 years, they eat breakfast every day same time, they go work exact same time, and they pick up their kid exact same time? Life is just a routine for them. For me, every three months [prior to a match], I get to go find something out of myself. That's intense, man! Really is intense! And you know you try, you try to deal with this in ways. When I was in Singapore [competing], you try to tell yourself, "I been doing this well. This is okay, just any other day, just any other week," but on the week of the fight your body just knows. Human beings fight for a million years, now it is for prize money but it's always been fighting, surviving, right? Your body just knows, you know, tells you something is gonna happen this week. As it gets closer and closer to the event, you hate that feeling? But you love it, you know, at this moment! What's gonna happen, your future is undecided. Maybe God knows what's gonna happen, maybe a higher being knows what's gonna happen, but I don't know what is gonna happen.

L.L: You said that your body just knows? Means what, your body tends to...?

Paul: Yeah you just wake up...your body will tell you on Monday that the fight is on Saturday. On Monday, your body is like, hey man, you wake up, you are a little bit more keen, a little more aware of things going on around you and your body just changes, man...That's kind of like excitement! Like I said, you don't know that...the future for this particular moment in your life, no one knows what is gonna happen. I love that feeling.

Paul's narrative of how his body "knows" when a match is coming can be seen as indicative of the arduous training that embodiment entails. Even before their arrival at Kwaan-saa-maat Gym, the bodies of the men have already been marked by their involvement in martial arts. Oates's (1987, 25) observation that "boxing is more about getting hit than it is about hitting" underscores the importance of scrutinizing the physical aspects of fighting. The muscular physique of the men, the broken bones, sprains, and bruises experienced by their bodies are not only reflective of the rigorous training to which they have subjected their bodies, but also narrate their trials and tribulations as fighters, a nonverbal testimony to the professional fights in which some of them have participated. The following interview excerpt highlights how the men's personal stories as fighters are imprinted on their bodies:

Stefan, 22, German, undergraduate: When are you going to fight again?

David, 33, Danish professional fighter: I don't know, man...my knee and this shit [points to his shoulders].

Stefan: How much time before you will recover from that knee?

David: Honestly? I don't know, man...I had so many broken bones from all my fights...my knees, ribs, hand, collarbone were all broken in my previous fights...I think I am having so many problems, like my current broken knee, because of cutting weight to meet the weight categories...cutting weight [is] really fucking me over.

Mauss (2006) notes that culture plays a role in mediating the way one uses one's body, detailing how growing up is an embodied process of socialization. Brooks originally used the term *storied bodies* to discursively examine the role that bodies play in literature, and how bodies are pieces of "work in progress...[The concept of storied bodies] concerns the relation of the body to narrative: how bodies come to be inscribed in narratives and narratives inscribed on the body" (1989, 1). This concept, as used by Brooks, examines the linkages between bodies and narratives. In this article, I alter this concept and utilize storied bodies not in the discursive sense, but to detail the centrality of embodiment within this somatic culture. Storied bodies become a lens for comprehending how encapsulated within the men's bodies are narratives of somatic experiences. Not only do the men learn how to embody martial disciplines by reconfiguring their senses and bodily movements, but also, the injuries sustained in the course of their training continue to remind them of their past experiences, and their mortality. Yet pain inscribed onto the body can be positive and reaffirming.

Pain, as a biological response to external stimulus, forces the individual to respond, or prevents further injury or suffering (Melzack 2001; Schiefenhövel 1995). Sensory feedback modifies adaptive responses in reaction to the changing environment. Within these lived spaces, the men deliberately attempt to increase their pain thresholds and normalize the pain experienced. One mechanism by which they normalize the pain is to perceive pain as temporary, telling themselves that the pain that they would have experienced if they had not been training hard would be multiplied. For example, when I asked David for advice on how to avoid flinching when a punch is thrown at my face, he said:

> You realize that a punch is less dangerous to you when you see it coming, versus closing your eyes pretending it is not coming. That could hurt you so much more. You have to see it. When I see the punch coming right at my face, I can put my chin down and absorb it with my body [raise his fists to his cheeks and tilt his neck downwards]. If you keep your chin down, then the body absorbs the shock. I can eat good shocks to my face and still not be taken [knocked down by one's opponents].

Pain arising from the utilization of particular muscles not used every day is also an important avenue by which individuals come to embody martial arts. This type of pain, as a form of body callusing (Spencer 2009), is embraced by fighters because it is a reminder of their progress, their journey into martial arts, and that they are becoming better by using the "proper" muscles (cf. Spencer 2012; 2013). Jack nonchalantly commented that when he was doing kickboxing in Sweden, he would get the guys to punch him in the forehead as a form of training. In an activity where injuries are the norm, what is of greater sociological interest is how the men deal with their injuries and manage their relationship with their injured, aging bodies.

My ethnographic data help to further elucidate the culturally specific and subjective experience of pain in the sporting realm (Allen-Collinson 2005; Hockey and Allen-Collinson 2007; Howes 2004; Loland, Skirstad, and Waddington 2006; Sparkes and Smith 2003).

Merleau-Ponty (1962) argues that individuals project their conscious-ness out from their bodies into the world around them. In contrast, pain is the catalyst that results in individuals focusing exclusively on the materiality and fragility of their bodies. Scarry (1985, 32–35) argues that in moments of intense pain

> as the body breaks down, it becomes increasingly the object of attention, usurping the place of all other objects...destroy[ing] a person's self and world, a destruction experienced spatially as either the contraction of the universe down to the immediate vicinity of the body or as the body swelling to fill the entire universe. Intense pain is also language-destroy-ing: as the content of one's world disintegrates, so the content of one's language disintegrates; as the self disintegrates, so that which would express and project the self is robbed of its source and its subject.

The men are constantly reminded of the injuries sustained during training as pain restricts and limits their range of movements.

> *L.L:* So how did you injure yourself in the first place?
>
> *Alvin, 22, Danish:* Actually I injured myself while I was practicing MMA back home in Denmark. So actually I have been injured for like five weeks now? More, actually...
>
> *L.L:* And yet you are still able to train?
>
> *Alvin:* Yeah. I can still do some techniques...I can't do push-ups but I can do the jabbing, punching and everything? So it depends on what move I have to make for my shoulder...As long as the pain doesn't flare up, I guess I should be fine? Maybe after my fight back home, I will take a break for a month or something if I can. [Laughs] I like to train, so it is hard not to train even if you are injured.
>
> *L.L:* So you know the injury is there, but you have to adapt after the pain?
>
> *Alvin:* Yeah, but sometimes I still have to know when to say stop because while I can take some [pain], I still got a limit for how much [pain] I can take. But shoulder injuries are fucked up, man...I mean if you break an arm, it heals, but dislocate a shoulder, it will always be a problem. Always going to be...this shoulder [pain] is always goingtobe w ithme .

Despite attempts to regulate, rationalize, and discipline the body, the body is able to defy such rational body projects through pain. Pain is a stark reprimand and reminder that our identities are constituted and restricted by the potentialities of the physical body. Bodily techniques are not only embodied, but pain, which has the ability to return to haunt the self many years later, will always be a visceral testimony to the carnal costs of training. The men often attempt to normalize the pain experienced by weaving it into an ongoing narrative about their identities as masculine, stoic fighters. Most of the men were adamant about continuing their training despite the injuries sustained and developed strategies, such as varying their exercise regimes, to work around the limitations of their bodies (e.g., Charmaz 1995; Messner 1990; Shilling 2005). This is exemplified by how Jack constantly reiterates the need to continue training even when one is injured:

L.L: How do you feel when you can't train because of your injury?

Jack: I believe you can always train something. Maybe not if you are really sick. If you are injured, you can always do some kind of training! You should always do some kind of training. I don't really believe you can't do any unless you are paralyzed or something.

L.L: I think it depends on the kind of injury? When I sprained my lower back, I really couldn't walk! I had difficulty walking down the stairs and everything.

Jack: But you can do those rubber band exercises. There is always some kind of exercise you can do. Unless it is that extreme, then of course you should not train. But if it is an arm or leg, you could do something.

The men's sojourns at Kwaan-saa-maat Gym highlight how learning Muay Thai entails a socialization process and rethinking about the ways in which one uses his body. The processes of globalization have facilitated these individuals' quests to learn a foreign martial art and the narratives of most informants are those of transnational travels. The acquisition of bodily techniques becomes a transnational process whereby each locale is perceived to hold some "authentic" martial tradition which they go to learn. This is typified by the two extracts below:

Sigurd, 27, Norwegian car mechanic: I guess you get more confident [from learning martial arts], but I noticed that I started to travel a lot more. Last year I went to Japan, Brazil, Italy, France, Sweden and England. And this year I am going to Thailand, Vietnam, Cambodia, and after Christmas I am going back to Brazil again.

Ivar, 39, Swede, security guard: In 1993, I started with Kendo and did that for about one semester and then karate for about eight years. The next couple of years I tried different martial arts, anything from kempo, jiu-jitsu and just stuff? In 2005, I started to do some Thai boxing. After coming back from training in Thailand, it was really hard to motivate me to continue with the Muay Thai in Sweden. There wasn't any good training...Then I started with Brazilian jiu-jitsu two years ago and mixed martial arts.

I will later elaborate on how the men come to embody different configurations of martial traditions.

THE RISE OF MT AND MMA

The spread of MT across the globe is fueled by a variety of factors such as its prominence in popular culture. Examples include the reality television show *The Contender Asia*, which first premiered in 2008 as an offshoot of the American boxing reality series *The Contender* (2005), action movies such as *Beautiful Boxer* (2004), *Ong-Bak: Muay Thai Warrior* (2003), and *Kickboxer* (1989), and the rise of martial arts gyms such as Singapore's *Evolve*, which hire Thai trainers to impart Muay Thai to foreigners. Sigurd's narrative illustrates how global flows have facilitated the men's decision to train in Thailand:

> *L.L:* So what started you on martial arts?
>
> *Sigurd:* I don't know. Probably the UFC [Ultimate Fighting Championships, founded in 1993]? I wanted to learn how to fight so I started with Thai boxing. And my gym, we had both Thai and BJJ [Brazilian jiu-jitsu]. I started doing both and after one year, the gym split. The Thai guys wanted to open their own gym so you had to pay for both the Thai and the BJJ. And I got BJJ. I had most friends in the BJJ community so I just became BJJ.

Unsurprisingly, Sigurd cited the UFC as one of the factors that sparked his interest in martial arts. This is because the UFC, a multi-million dollar MMA promotion company based in the United States, is responsible not only for the sportization process (Elias 1971) but also for facilitating the transnational flow of televised images that impact the discursive construction of martial arts and the lived spaces of the gym (see Krauss and Aita 2002; Mayeda and Ching 2008). For Elias, the term "sportization" refers to the process that started in the eighteenth century, whereby organizations begin to define the "rules of sport-like recreations more precisely, strictly and explicitly, orientated around an ethos of 'fair play' and eliminating, reducing and/or more strictly controlling opportunities for violent physical contact" (1971, 92). In addition, to regulate the sporting arena, new organizational structures and bureaucratic positions such as referees were established (Van Bottenburg and Heilbron 2006). As such, Elias views sportization as having the "character of a civilizing spurt comparable in its overall direction to the 'courtisation' of warriors where the tightening rules of etiquette played a significant part" (1986, 151). This comparison rings true given that sportization necessarily requires the strict cultivation of self-regulation and discipline among its participants. Commercial interests propel the sportization process. Through measures such as institutionalizing an official set of rules, fixed weight classes, and the use of protective gear, the organizers attempt to redefine MMA as a mainstream sport (Van Bottenburg and Heilbron 2006). Mainstream sports like football are legitimized partially through these structural features. Elias would argue that the transition of MMA from being perceived as a deviant activity, akin to "human cock-fighting" (Gentry 2001, 73) to a mainstream activity is due to the civilizing process, of which the sportization process is but one aspect. However, while it would appear that the structural evolution of MMA is characteristic of the sportization process, interviews with my informants suggest otherwise. At the gym, the men are actively socializing their bodies to throw off the inhibitions of the civilizing process. The men often speak of how they were initially hesitant to hit hard during the sparring sessions and individuals who vocalize how violent MT is are quickly socialized to view MT as a means of training the body. The liminal experiences of the men can be attributed to how the gym's regimes are constructed in opposition to this civilizing process. I draw upon Meyer et al.'s (1997) argument to provide an alternative explanation to account for the disparity between the structural similarities of MMA with the civilizing process and why the indoctrination of the men into MMA appears to be a decivilizing rather than a civilizing process.

Meyer et al. (1997, 153) theorize that the primary reason that nation-states and organizations possess similar structural features (such as bureaucracy) is premised upon their adopting the "model of the rational and responsible actor." The adoption of this model by organizations gives rise to structural isomorphism, resulting in organizations having similar characteristics in terms of their structures, policies, and conduct toward other actors at both the local and global stages (see DiMaggio and Powell 1983). The outcomes of structural isomorphism and the civilizing process are similar, but there exist differences in the way theorists explain these processes. Elias (2000) theorizes these developments as arising from changes in the way society and human relations are organized. On the other hand, Meyer et al. (1997) view structural similarities in social institutions as the result of emerging institutions attempting to legitimize themselves by imitating successful and established ones. Here, the success of structural isomorphism is due to current predominance of the civilizing and sportization processes. The UFC, mimicking the structural features prevalent in sports, confers on MMA an aura of legitimacy, allowing MMA to be recognized as legitimate sport. This accounts for why scientific discourses that attempt to rationalize, regulate, and discipline the body are increasingly prevalent in martial arts.

These scientific discourses result in some of the tensions and contradictions experienced by the fighters. For example, the daily physical regimes to which the men subject their bodies as they strive to master new bodily techniques and transform into better fighters come at a price. The men often talk about using scientific developments to improve their bodies. Scientific discourses, which the men internalize, are premised upon the principle of productivity and efficiency. The allure behind the use of scientific discourses is the promise of "limitless performance" (Hoberman 1992, 25) by "subordinating the body completely to the will of the rational mind" (Cashmore 1998, 84). Yet such training, which forces the body to operate at its limits to "elicit positive adaptational responses" (Shilling 2005, 110), marks the flesh. The body constantly treads a fine line between optimal performance and physical breakdown. There is a contradiction between discourses that inscribe ideals of wholeness and the body's integrity and the lived realties in which injuries contest these discursive constructions by rendering the body vulnerable and susceptible. In addition to injuries that may severely curtail the life span of a fighter, training regimes and strict schedules may force fighters to forgo activities such as birthday celebrations, weddings, and other occasions. These sacrifices may negatively affect their physical and psychological well-being (Evans et al. 2003; Flynn 1998; Hargreaves 1994; O'Toole 1998; Sparkes 1999). Paul's reflexive comments illustrate this:

> *L.L:* What opportunity costs that you incurred over your years as a professional fighter who travels constantly?
>
> *Paul:* The cost to your family life, your personal life is tremendous. I miss lots of moments. You know my only brother? He has a daughter and when she was born I was getting ready for a fight...I wasn't there when she was born...Moments like that. Well looking back now, would it been a big difference to have missed two days of practice to go see her? 'Cause she might be the only child in the family...She is now a wife, having kids...things like that. Where am I now? Where are we all at? Thailand. Away from my family, away

from my friends, but I believe somewhere someplace down the line, this will be the reason why I win. If you don't do that, won't do it, then you are not gonna make it unless you are born with superhumans kills.

The demands that the men subject their bodies to unveil the contradiction inherent within the discourse of the modern sporting body. Structural isomorphism is thus partially responsible for the increasing popularity of martial arts and the shifts in the way bodies are disciplined and manipulated. This is reflected in how MMA's popularity is due to the incorporation of rules and regulations found in other established sports and how the men subscribe to a particular version of "authentic"ma rtialtr aining.

THE TRANSNATIONAL FLOW OF BODILY TECHNIQUES

Sigurd's narrative highlights how UFC is one avenue through which individuals imbibe martial arts as a self-defense system, a form of popular culture, or even as a surreal fantasy. UFC is one medium that disseminates televised images of MMA practitioners who draw upon eclectic fighting styles to incorporate into their growing arsenal of techniques. These fighters actively modify their bodies and styles in order to excel in the ring. As individuals are concerned only about the efficacy of the techniques, this process of adaptation and hybridization results in techniques of the body being dis-embedded from their original martial traditions and cultures. Previously, fighters and fighting systems were rooted within a particular culture at specific geographical sites. The current martialscape, with individuals mixing and matching different fighting styles, defies attempts to simplistically categorize fighters as originating or appropriating from a particular culture. Paul, a professional fighter, summarizes the evolution of MMA through the years:

> *Paul:* MMA is finding the best of each martial art. Each martial art has a benefit…MMA is around for 15 years. Think about when it first started, what did it look like then? It was horrible. Even the champions from five years ago couldn't beat the champions of today and that is a short time, man. Previously it was one style versus another. You have like karate versus say BJJ. Now everyone does the same kind of training. Everyone does boxing, wrestling, jiu-jitsu, Muay Thai. Now is about who is [in] better shape, better conditioning, andmixinga ndma tching.

This extract highlights how in the previous era of MMA history, individuals were identified by their fighting styles. Implicit in this categorization is the assumption that fighting systems can be essentialized to particular cultures and nationalities. For example, karate fighters are often assumed to be Asians (see Hughes 2008). Due to the free market and capitalist organizations, global sport is de-territorialized, "making it more problematic for people to identify with it as an expression of their nation" (Hargreaves 2002, 34). In a global martialscape, with fighters of different nationalities competing and being exposed to different fighting systems, "mixing and matching" is thus an adaptive response. Fighters, whose bodies have already been socialized into utilizing particular bodily techniques, are now faced with the challenge of incorporating new bodily techniques in order to be successful in this new environment. However, as the extract below demonstrates, embodied techniques, reflective of arduous training, are not so easily forgotten:

> *Jack, 22, Swede, unemployed:* You have an excellent sense of stability and balance.
>
> *L.L:* What do you mean?
>
> *Jack:* Like the other day when I was grabbing your leg after you threw the roundhouse, you were still rather stable. I guess it must be your Aikido training? So how do you find Muay Thai?
>
> *L.L:* Well, it is rather difficult. Like I am not sure how to stand. It is totally different from Aikido and the *ajarns* keep correcting my footwork.
>
> *Jack:* I used to do kickboxing and I took some time to get used to standing in the Muay Thai stance. Guess I am too used to the kickboxing stance. My stance is more like MMA than Muay Thai. I guess you have to discover it for yourself and take time to discover whatw orksf ory ou.

This process of mixing and matching is reflective of a layering of body memory as fighters attempt to find the combination of bodily postures, movements, and techniques that suits them best. For them, this process takes place not only at the gym, but also throughout the rest of their fighting careers as they encounter new bodily techniques or learn to adapt their aging bodies to the rigors of being a fighter.

Extending my argument about how somatic culture involves a reconfiguration of the body and the senses, the mixing and matching of bodily techniques unifies spatial and temporal distances. In this global circuit, transnationally mobile individuals come to embody particular bodily schemata and dispositions, which they then transmit onto other bodies through training or the act of dominating their competitors. Fighters like Paul, Ivar, and Sigurd, who travel to places like Thailand and Brazil to hone their technical corpus in Muay Thai and BJJ respectively, are quite common. Spencer (2012, 98) argues that "the inscription of strategy on the bodies of fighters involves the training of specific body techniques for a future opponent, and in doing so, the fighter's body unites the past, present, and the future" in terms of bodily techniques. The fighter's body transcends not only temporal but geographical boundaries as fighters, professional or otherwise, travel the global martial arts circuit to refine their skills and compete. There is a constant circulation of individuals, ideas, and fighting styles as people travel across geographical boundaries to train, test, and reaffirm their mastery of their bodies. This is exemplified in the recently concluded *One Fighting Championships* held in Singapore, where fighters from diverse countries like South Africa, Denmark, Taiwan, South Korea, Japan, and the Netherlands were brought in to draw crowds (Lim 2011; *Manila Bulletin* 2011; *Today* 2011). The *One Fighting Championships*, an arena where fighters of diverse fighting styles have the opportunity to assert their bodily capital, testifies to the transnational and commercial nature of martial arts. Another avenue that perpetuates this transnational circulation of bodily techniques is when some professional fighters retire and set up martial arts gyms to impart the somatic knowledge they have gained from traveling and competing. As instructors, the lifelong acquisition of knowledge from their transnational travels gets transmitted to aspiring neophytes.

Bourdieu's (1977; 1984; 1990a; 1990b; 1998) concepts of "field" and "capital" provide a framework to understand the vocabulary of motivations and actions employed by the men at the gym. Within a particular field, different participants have different levels of involvement depending on what their stakes and interests are. As a theoretical tool by which to understand the practices and interactions of a particular group, participants in a field[1] often vie for capital to demonstrate their allegiance and competence to social others. The men's comments about almost every aspect of martial arts constitute one form of bodily capital, an idiosyncratic form of capital that has particular value within the field of the gym itself. Bodily capital, as a form of cultural capital, refers to possessing knowledge of pugilistic information such as the weight categories of various fighters and (as Wacquant noted of boxers in Chicago) the "diffuse complex of postures and (physical and mental) gestures that, being continually (re)produced in and through the very functioning of the gym, exist in a sense only in action, and in the traces that this action leaves within (and upon) bodies" (Wacquant 2004, 59).

At the institutional level of MMA, this mixing and matching of bodily/cultural techniques is subsumed within the larger discourse of effectiveness and efficiency. Promoters for MMA fighters often emphasize how deadly the fighters are, downplaying the cultural components embodied in their arsenals of bodily techniques. The men also appropriate these narratives when they analyze professional matches or their own sparring experiences. For example, in describing his first sparring match at the gym, Jack ignored how his opponent draws upon an eclectic array of martial traditions and focused on how "wicked the techniques are" and how "you can really feel that punch whacking all the way into you! Bam!" For the men, more important than the particular cultural origins of martial traditions is the way in which they effectively appropriate different bodily techniques. The effectiveness of bodily techniques is highly valued in this culture that prizes the experiential element above all. These discourses are thus reflective of the de-territorialization of cultural practices epitomized in Apparadurai's idea of "-scapes." They are also revealing of the processes of meaning making undertaken by the men in their dual role as fighters, and as the audience for others' performances in the ring.

MARTIALSCAPES AND COMMERCIALIZATION

Inevitably, individuals bemoan how commercialization has negatively impacted martial arts. Professional fighters or martial arts purists are concerned about the quality of education that is imparted by teachers of questionable credentials. Rage, 26, an American professional fighter, expressed his disgust at how commercialized the martial arts scene is in America, with individuals with little or no fighting experience attempting to make a "quick buck." The disdain displayed by the men toward individuals who have questionable bodily capital reaffirms their identity as knowledgeable fighters who have the ability to discern and confer legitimacy onto other bodies. This ability is the result of the time and effort the men invested in cultivating their own bodies. Rage elaborates:

> *Rage:* But finding a good instructor in America is very hard. You go to all those schools in America, it's like ten feet tall trophies. Everybody is a world champion. That is what turned me off when I was in high school. I wanted to learn Taekwondo, 'cause I did it when I was a kid. I walked in and asked how much it will cost me. This guy goes,

"We will put you in the black belt course. You will get your black belt in two years. You pay $2000 upfront."

Sigurd: Like those two-hour Taekwondo black belts! [Laughs]

L.L: What are those?

Sigurd: You know those videos? Where they guarantee that you will be a black belt after watching their two-hour video! Instant black belt! The only faster way is if you dye the belt black yourself! [Laughs]

Another recurrent theme is that commercialization has resulted in individuals not being socialized into learning values such as respect. The extract below suggests that this may be due to clashes between different cultural norms and values in an increasingly globalized martialscape.

Paul: I love Jiu-Jitsu but I saw a lot of things in Jiu-Jitsu I don't want my kids to experience. I think Jiu-Jitsu is a bit too cavalier? At least in America.

L.L: Cavalier as in?

Paul: Guys used to bring girls home or to the gym and do them on the mats. They thought it was funny. I never thought it was funny. You would never find these characters in judo club!

L.L.: That's rather disrespectful...

Paul: Like I said, it is because Brazilians have a different culture and when they came to America, they brought those habits to America. Maybe it is okay in Brazil...When the Brazilians brought BJJ to America, they weren't so much about martial arts as fighting. Some of these other clubs, it is about fighting, about fighting.

The men often evoke a nostalgic martialscape, one that is untainted by commercial interests, to justify their discontent with the pedagogy of contemporary martial arts. Nostalgia, the selective reconstruction of an imagined utopian past (Chua 1995), becomes the yardstick the men use to critique contemporary martial arts. Within this martialscape, the men appear to be on a quest for "authenticity." In his conceptualization of "-scapes," Apparadurai argues that imagination is fundamental to "all forms of agency, is itself a social fact, and is the key component of the new global order" (1996, 31), resulting in individuals living in "imagined worlds" (1996, 222). In this fluid and disjunctive present, authenticity is revealed to be an impossibly contradictory idea that conflates and interweaves conventional social dimensions such as class or geography with people's dreams and imaginations (Beck 2000). When the men engage in meaning and sense making as they mix and match, not only is the "truly authentic" lost, but the notion of authenticity is also rendered marginal. Due to the conflation of two different types of authenticity—the quest for the monastic Spartan fighter's lifestyle and learning the "true" martial arts—operating at the gym, this quest for the authentic is extremely complicated. In choosing Kwaan-saa-maat Gym, a gym located in the provinces, the men reaffirm their quest to experience the monastic lifestyle of a fighter by subjecting their bodies to the Spartan discipline of "traditional fighters." This quest to experience the authentic lifestyle of a fighter is something that the men crave. However, I previously illustrated how the authenticity of cultural techniques is not as important as their effectiveness in inflicting pain on their opponents. At the gym, authority is indexed against one's prowess as a fighter. The latter illustrates how contestations over authenticity are the "province of authority" (Fees 1996, 122), that authenticity is an ascribed quality and that what is recognized as "authenticity" is fluid (see Bruner 1994; 2008; Fees 1996). Friedman (1992) also critically deconstructs the notion of authenticity by questioning the validity of an objective past. Through the men's narratives I have demonstrated how the men may buy into particular constructions of authenticity and construct a particular identity as fighters around it.

Unsurprisingly, the assumption that the transmission of martial arts was always coupled with the inculcation of particular values fails to consider how these current discourses may not be historically valid and that the past is discursively constructed (see Donohue 1994). Furthermore, the irony is that without the globalization of sport, it is unlikely that these individuals would have initially taken up a non-native fighting system, or positioned themselves as stakeholders in the evolution of contemporary martial arts. This is a point that David implicitly acknowledges. Although he is aware of the negative ramifications that commercialization could potentially have for martial arts, David recognizes that his ability to "put bread on the table" is the product of commercialization, since "MMA is where the money is. You know more money is coming that way, it's growing and overtaking MT and it's in the ring." This statement reflects how the commercialization of sports allows individuals to take up fighting as a professional career and is responsible for the current widespread popularity of martial arts.

CONCLUSION

In conclusion, I illustrated how the rise of the contemporary martials-cape, embedded within global flows, is due to various factors, such as structural isomorphism and capitalism. In this global martial circuit, as fighters strive for supremacy, there has been a diffusion and adaptation of bodily techniques across different cultures. One caveat is that this mixing and matching is not a *laissez-faire* process because of the rules and regulations that characterize the sportization process. As capitalist institutions heavily influence this martialscape, I elucidate the tensions arising between the opportunism that commercialization of the sport promotes and ideas of authenticity and suggest that these struggles are reflective of attempts by individuals to be recognized as having the necessary and legitimate bodily capital to be a fighter. The men's presence at the gym reflects how globalization and commercialization have resulted in the deterritorialization of global sports and the "mixing and matching" of various disciplines as they attempt to find the most efficient and effective combination. These men value practicality and efficacy over other considerations such as martial traditions. However, they also comment about how martial arts have taught them discipline and focus. Given that these men are embedded within global flows, I shall now briefly discuss what the men do with the bodily capital that they gained in exchange for monetary capital upon returning home.

As the men continue to travel across different martialscapes to learn, teach, or compete, these somatic experiences come to be constituted within larger transnational flows of bodily dispositions and knowledge. For some, their quest to be fighters stops when they leave the gym. However, their immersion in this somatic, masculine culture has transformed their outlook on life and their bodily dispositions. In general, the men become more confident. For example, Kelvin says,

> I wouldn't go around trying to get into a fight now, but I know that if anything happens, I can defend myself. There is this confidence that I can do it.

Some men also comment on how the transformation of their physique, coupled with the knowledge that is embodied within them, results in their carrying themselves better, having a better posture, and a keener ability to discern changes in their immediate surroundings. After leaving the field, I continue to interact with the men through Facebook. Many still express their desire to return to the gym, nostalgically remembered as a period where "life is good. No need to worry about work, bringing home the bacon. You just wake up, train, and sleep. You can be focused on just training" (Rage). They talk about saving money for another trip back to the gym. This extract highlights how despite the gym being constructed by the men as a liminal space, divorced from the rhythms of everyday capitalism, monetary consider-ations will always intrude upon this martial space. This alludes to the transformative aspect that globalization and commercialization have on the transmission of martial disciplines. The men's quests across the globe to learn different martial techniques are thus reflective of transnational flows. Different martial disciplines and cultures come to be embodied in the men. As the men then transmit their bodily know-how and techniques to other neophytes, the circulation of knowledge within these martialscapes continues.

NOTE

1. Bourdieu uses the concept of "field" to describe the "rules of the game" (Bourdieu and Wacquant, 1992). The field is a social arena differentiated by power relations, a site of contestation where relations, networks, and struggles over resources occur. This power struggle or the quest for capital only has meaning in a particular field (Bourdieu 1977; 1984; 1986). In the context of the gym, the men vie to demonstrate their body capital, such as possessing hard lean bodies and powerful punches. This bodily capital has currency only within the context of the pugilistic world.

2

WEST INDIAN IMMIGRANT WOMEN, BODY POLITICS, AND CULTURAL CITIZENSHIP*

Kamille Gentles-Peart

As a woman from the English-speaking Caribbean, now residing in the United States, I can attest to the fact that surveillance and regulation of women's bodies occurs in the West Indies as in the global North. West Indian women thus come to the United States already habituated to monitoring their bodies, and being surveyed by men and women in their communities, a practice that persists in the diaspora. In addition, migration places them in dialogue with the Western beauty ideals of the United States, and necessitates engagement with beauty discourses cultivated outside of their cultural and political spheres. In this chapter, I examine how West Indian women negotiate and contend with the beauty ideologies from both their homelands and the United States. I explore the racial and sociocultural discourses that shape the body politics that they embrace, and the extent to which the women claim cultural citizenship (discussed later in this chapter) through these processes. Using black West Indian immigrant women as its subject, this chapter addresses the little discussed body discourses of a black diasporic population in the United States, and thus explores the intersection of race, ethnicity, body image, and diaspora.

RACE, NATION, AND BODY IMAGE

Women's bodies are sites that are most vividly policed by cultural norms and ideologies. As such, women have to continuously negotiate the practices and policies through which powers of society endeavor to regulate not only the capacities and activities, but also the appearance, of their bodies. These dominant beauty ideals standardize and normalize certain body shapes and sizes, and uphold them as the central criteria of femininity. These discourses are shaped by the specific cultural and historical settings within which they are produced, and are thus expressions of cultural identity.

Given this relationship between discourses of the body and cultural identity, diasporic women, who emigrate with a particular cultural subjectivity, enter their new homes with the body politics cultivated in their homelands. These women also enter a cultural space that fosters its own beauty ideologies, and thus, in addition to contending with the body politics of their homelands, immigrant women necessarily have to interact with the beauty expectations of their new homes as well. This interaction is particularly pronounced among black women from developing nations migrating to the global North, where the dominant Caucasian-European beauty ideologies largely exclude women of their racial and cultural heritage.

Existing research on beauty ideals and body image indicates that black women in the United States do not ascribe to the thin ideal of Anglo cultures (Flynn and Fitzgibbon 1996; Lovejoy 2001; Thompson and Corwin 1997), and subsequently are relatively resistant to the dominant standards of thinness, and develop a healthier body image than their white peers (Beasley 2000; Botta 2000; Schooler et al. 2004). However, these findings are problematic. First, by asserting that black women holistically reject the thin aesthetic, they simplify black women's relationship to the dominant ideals of beauty in the United States, masking the complicated ways in which they engage and contend with mainstream body discourses. Furthermore, the idea that black women are resistant to thin-promoting ideologies reinforces the "strong black woman" rhetoric that has been rehearsed and venerated in black communities, to the detriment of the vast majority of real black women who strive to live up to this invulnerability (Beauboeuf-Lafontant 2009; Harris-Lacewell 2001; Lau 2011). Through this "strong black woman" trope, black women are reified as indomitable and undaunted by oppressive systems, but simultaneously indelicate, unfeminine, and ultimately "other." Concluding that black women are not affected by thin ideologies suggests that they do not experience the anxieties of their white counterparts, making them stronger and therefore less "woman" than white women.

Second, these studies examine the occurrence of anxieties associated with the dominant thin body type, which excludes discourses that are related to other forms of beauty norms in the United States.

By highlighting anxieties as solely the result of the pursuit of thinness, the studies uphold the thin aesthetic as the standard. Moreover, they imply that black aesthetics[1] (both in and outside of the United States) are harmless and even empowering for their adherents, and obscure the struggles that black women may face as they have to mold and sculpt their bodies to fit the ideals expected of them within their communities. In other words, body dissatisfaction among black women in general often goes unnoticed because it does not reflect the dominant obsession with a thin ideal body type. To accurately assess the body image disturbances of non-white populations in the United States then, it is important to examine the cultural and ethnic contexts in which they are produced, as well as the strategies these contexts provide to negotiate dominant expectations of the body.

NegotiatedB odyPoli tics

In recent years, body image research has supported the dialogic approach to understanding beauty. For example, J. Robyn Goodman (2002) used small focus groups to assess Anglo women's and Latinas' readings of the mediated ideal of thinness and found that, rather than size and weight, both groups of women thought the toned, flab-free body of the dominant culture was ideal. In addition, both groups interpreted mediated images as unrealistic and "touched-up," views that helped them to resist the thinness ideal. However, she also found that media's depiction of thinness as guaranteeing social rewards (such as attention from men) made thin bodies desirable to her participants, and led to weight-controlling practices (Goodman 2002).

Goodman (2002) argued that the Anglo women in her study felt that mediated images affected their self-worth/self-esteem, and some had incorporated the thinness ideal into their everyday lives without realizing it. Her Latina participants saw the dominant ideal, which discouraged curves, as lacking femininity, a critique on a standard of beauty that excluded them. On the other hand, she found that, while these respondents justified a more voluptuous figure by saying that food was more central in their culture, and that men were attracted to bigger women, they simultaneously held the dominant ideal of thinness, citing health reasons for dieting and weight control (Goodman 2002).

Similarly, J. Robyn Goodman and Kim Walsh-Childers (2004) found that the white college women who participated in their three focus groups engaged in both dominant and negotiated or oppositional readings of mediated bodies, particularly as related to breast size. The authors reported that the women knew what the ideal breast and body looked like (c-cup and thin, respectively) even as they admitted that the perfect breast size depended on the context in which the women were viewed (for pornographic pleasure or on the street, for example) and on body size. In addition, they found that, though their participants desired "perky" breasts that were proportionate to their bodies (resisting the dominant ideal of very big breasts prevalent in the media), their preference for thinner frames corresponded with the dominant ideal. Furthermore, their desire for "perky" breasts was indicative of the influence of media that associated "perky" breasts with power and desirability (Goodman and Walsh-Childers 2004). Their participants also said that the weight and size of one's stomach were more important than breast size, but considered flat-chested women unattractive; they felt the images in media were fake, based on their personal experiences and knowledge of enhancement tricks, yet they wanted to look like the models being portrayed (such as Tyra Banks); they also discussed images as illusions, yet many said they could attain the mediated ideal with enough time and money (Goodman and Walsh-Childers 2004). These contradictions signaled negotiations of personal experiences and mediated norms that moderated their desire for an ideal body.

TransnationalB odyPoli tics

Evidence of negotiation of competing body discourses may also be found among non-US, non-white women. Erynn de Casanova's (2004) study of Ecuadorian teenagers revealed that these young girls simultaneously held white (Western) and Latin ideals. They identified light skin, thin bodies, and light, long hair as the standard of beauty, but demonstrated attitudes and behaviors similar to those found among African Americans (i.e., they desired a voluptuous figure and focused on self-presentation) in their everyday lives. Casanova (2004) argued that their inclusion of dress and personality in the definition of beauty mitigated the effect of the thin ideology disseminated by North American media, but their esteem of white prototypes simultaneously validated the thin, white ideal.

Analogously, Fabienne Darling-Wolf (2004) found that, even though the Japanese women in her study critiqued their local and Western media representations of beauty, these images informed their conception of attractiveness as young, thin, tall, light-skinned, and having bigger eyes. Her participants placed a premium on having good character, but concurrently spent a lot of time talking about and caring for their bodies, reinforcing the emphasis on physical beauty that they critiqued in the media and society in general (Darling-Wolf 2004). They also hybridized the beauty ideologies of Japanese and Western cultures by identifying Japanese media figures with Westernized features as the most attractive models (Darling-Wolf 2004).

As demonstrated in these studies, while women of any cultural, racial, and ethnic heritage have the power to embrace beauty ideals that differ from those promoted within dominant society, it should not be assumed that this choice occurs without struggle with the dominant ideals, or that the resulting ideal is always empowering. Women develop a negotiated, rather than oppositional, body ideal and politics, one that comprises some resistive aspects, but that also has evidence of conformity to the mainstream ideal.

Body Politics and Cultural Citizenship among Diasporic Women

Conspicuously absent from the literature is scholarship on the negotiations of diasporic women. While much has been written on how women engage with body politics that are imported into their cultural space, there is a dearth of literature on how women negotiate the mainstream beauty discourses of the spaces they enter as immigrants, or how they contend with the dominant body politics of their cultures when they reside outside of their homelands. Aihwa Ong (1996) contends that cultural citizenship results from interactions between the cultural norms of immigrants' homelands and new homes. She defines cultural citizenship as a negotiated process of self-making *and* being made in relation to the authorities that implement criteria of belonging and exclusion. Receiving cultures disenfranchise and outright exclude immigrants from citizenship based on their race, ethnicity, and nations of origin. However, immigrants wrestle with these subject-effacing processes in an effort to resist marginalization and claim social and cultural agency. In other words, cultural citizenship is enacted through the everyday cultural practices through which immigrants (and other subordinated groups) claim personhood and challenge erasure. Diasporic realities reflect this process of self-representation that struggles against, but does not fully evade, the ideologies of the country of residence. Given this, we can presume that diasporic beauty discourses do not occur on a simplistic assimilation-acculturation continuum, but rather entail complex negotiations between the body politics of immigrant women's homelands and their new homes that reproduce, in a modified form, dominant beauty ideologies (Dayal 1996).

Scholars of the West Indian diasporic community in the United States have implicitly explored embodied cultural citizenship by examining body politics in the West Indian diaspora, particularly the beauty ideologies that West Indian immigrant women encounter in their new home. For example, Oneka LaBennett (2011) explored the manner in which West Indian teenage girls and boys in Brooklyn, New York negotiated the dominant ideals of beauty being promoted on the reality show *America's Next Top Model.* However, West Indian women in the United States (and other diasporic women) do not only contend with the dominant body politics of the United States; they also have to simultaneously deal with the expectations placed on their bodies by their homelands and the diasporic community. Therefore, to get a holistic picture of how they construct their body politics and negotiate cultural citizenship, we necessarily have to explore West Indian women's engagement with all the dominant ideals of beauty that police their bodies.

This chapter thus advances the work of scholars such as LaBennett by exploring the body discourses mobilized by West Indian women in their everyday lives to concurrently negotiate the body politics of the United States and their cultural communities. It also examines the cultural contexts in which these discourses are produced, as well as the strategies these contexts provide to undermine dominant expectations of the body and encourage cultural citizenship in the face of exclusionarydis courses.

RESEARCH METHODS

The analysis that follows is based on information gathered from 15 first-generation West Indian immigrant women across three focus groups. Such group discussions are ideal for this project because of their generative nature and their ability to allow participants to have a relatively open discussion of the topic, which engenders other topics that may not have been included in my original purview (Morgan 1997). Having the women liberally discuss their cultural conception of body presentation and care also fosters more inductive, grounded analysis.

I recruited participants primarily from New York City, which houses one of the largest West Indian diasporic communities in the world. New York City, and particularly the boroughs of Brooklyn, Queens, and the Bronx, hosts the largest concentration of English-speaking Caribbean immigrants in the nation (New York City Department of City Planning 2012). With a population of more than half a million West Indians (US Census 2010), it is about five times the size of Grenada, and twice the size of Barbados.

The initial partipants were recruited through vouching figures (Weiss 1989)—that is, friends, relatives, and associates with access to a variety of West Indian women in New York City—who recommended and solicited their West Indian friends, associates, and business clients for the study. Subsequent participants were recruited through a "snowball sampling" technique, a chain-referral system that entails asking respondents to refer other participants for the research study, thus enabling access to diverse sections of the community. The women who participated were working- and middle-class women between the ages of 20 and 55. Most of the women had migrated from Jamaica— which is not surprising, since Jamaicans comprise the largest group of West Indians in the city (US Census 2010)—but there were also women from St. Thomas, Antigua, and Barbados. All of them identified as black West Indians.

Working in the qualitative tradition, my analysis of the information gathered entailed data coding and interpretation: during coding or data reduction, I organized the participants' responses into themes, and while in the interpretation stage, I looked for the relationships and incongruities that emerged among these themes. Finally, I sought to ascertain explanations that might account for, and create connections among, the subjects that surfaced, thus organizing all the information into a coherent account (Weiss 1989).

WEST INDIAN WOMEN AND NEGOTIATIONS OF BODY POLITICS

The focus groups reveal that the women are actively and simultaneously engaging with both the body discourses of the United States and the West Indies. The women strategically deploy discourses to contend with the pressure placed on their bodies by both cultures. Two major discourses emerge in their negotiation of the cultural ideals. Specifically, the women employ both racial differentiation and their individual positions in society to contend with the dominant ideals of the body politics of the West Indies and the United States. In this way, the women create a space for themselves in both West Indian and American beauty discourses, negotiating cultural citizenship.

Racialization of Beauty and the Thin Ideal

While being cognizant that thinness is the acceptable and desirable ideal for American women, the participants admit that they subscribe to a very different beauty culture, one that promotes a voluptuous, curvaceous figure.[2] More precisely, the women in the study hold that in West Indian communities (in New York City as well as their islands of origin), the so-called "Coca-Cola bottle" or "thick" shape is the optimum body ideal. As with the Coca-Cola glass bottle from which it derives its name, this silhouette is characterized by average sized top, small waist, and, most importantly, generous (but proportionate) hips and buttocks. One respondent says:

> Culturally [West Indians] have a standard of what a woman should look like, but it is different from the American standard. When I was skinny the Americans would say, "Oh you're so beautiful, you're so small", however, my West Indian family would say, "You need to eat, why aren't you eating?" It was a big contradiction.

Similarly, another participant explains:

> Any woman with [the thick shape] is considered to be more attractive than a skinny woman. I believe it is a West Indian thing. When I lived in St. Thomas, I was really skinny and I noticed the girls that got more attention in schools were the ones who were…thick or who had a heavy[big]be hind.

Several Jamaican participants concur, proffering the significance of the voluptuous body in their culture as the motivation for their choice. As one respondent shares:

> When I was in Jamaica you had to be thick; being thick was a sign of health. Being skinny was associated with poor health. I remember there was a girl who was the same age as I; she got all the attention. She had big boobs, big butt and everything.

A Barbadian participant highlights the compliments she received when she gained the weight necessary to approximate the curvaceous ideal. She says:

> When I went away to [college], I didn't put on the freshman 15; it was like the freshman 30. And when I came back for Christmas break, everybody was like, "You filled out! You put on size!"

In addition to the cultural dimensions of their definition of beauty, the focus groups also reveal a racial component to the women's body politics. First, the participants constantly refer to the dominant American beauty ideal (thin, no curves) as the "white shape," as the body image that white women pursue. Meanwhile, they call their preferred body the "black shape." Second, the women proffer black women in the media as examples of the ideal body type they espouse, further underscoring their belief that the "thick" body they desire is predominantly a black aesthetic. The list of celebrities mentioned includes actresses Lisa Raye and Tracy Ellis Ross, Nene Leakes of the *Real Housewives of Atlanta,* and singers Nicki Minaj and Beyoncé, all of whom fit the "thick, but proportionate, not too skinny" ideal.[3] Moreover, women in their community who do not have this body type are disparagingly referred to as "white" as a way to mark their difference, their deviation from the norm. As one respondent confesses:

I have nothing...my mother's family all have little breast, large hips and big butts. My father's family has large chest and small butts...I have no chest nor butt. I have to work with what I was born with...[My family] call me "white girl" because I have a straight shape...It doesn't bother me...I am just different.

The women in the study thus suggest that beauty is intricately related to race and racial identity. More specifically, they believe that the ideals of beauty are constructed within the discourses of race, and the pressures related to body type and size are determined by one's racial identification. The responses of the women also suggest that the idea of the curvaceous black woman was not limited to their community, but rather is prolific and accepted in mainstream society as well, as evidenced by comments made by white Americans. One respondent explains the perception of her white peer, saying:

If there were two girls standing side by side, both are size 12, one is white, one is black, she wouldn't see the black woman as overweight, but she'd see the white woman as overweight...she's like, "I don't really think I've seen any person of color that's overweight to me," because in her eyes, she just sees that as normal. But then when she sees a white woman that's a little bigger, it's like, "Wow, that's sloppy," which I thought was interesting because you can see two women the exact same size, but just their color [is different].

Another participant had a similar experience with her white friend:

> [White people] expect us to be a little bigger, thicker, so to them it's not fat...that's how we're made up...I have a friend of mine and [she] and I are pretty much the same size, and we would go working out together, go jogging, and I'm like, "I have to try to lose my thighs, and my butt; I have to lose weight," and she would say, "You don't have to lose weight, you're perfect the way you are. I don't even know why you're working out with me."

The participants' acknowledgment and recuperation of this intersection of racial identity and body image is not unique. Critics of the American beauty system have long argued that given that whiteness is the central component and prerequisite of beauty in the United States, black women could never claim beauty in this system (Craig 2002; Patton 2006; Shaw 2006). As Andrea Shaw (2006, 1) argues, the erasure of blackness is necessary in order to "render women viable entities by Western aesthetic standards." In other words, the mainstream American ideals of beauty have always been associated with the white body.

On the other hand, African diaspora cultures, including those of the Caribbean, have historically valued an ample female physique, and have associated the slender body with the violence of colonization, desexualization, and poverty (Shaw 2006). The exaltation of the big black woman in black culture, with its esteem of blackness and voluptuousness, has been read by many as a counter to the dominant white ideals of the West (Shaw 2006). Therefore, it is not surprising that the participants of the present study discuss their "thick" ideal as the imperative of the black body, their black bodies. However, more than reflecting extant discourse, embracing the black aesthetic allows the participants to invert practices of exclusion and belonging, and take an empowered stance in relation to the beauty discourses of the United States that deem them irrevocably unattractive: rather than being shut out of spaces of beauty by racist body politics, the women refuse the ideal of thinness; they are not left out (and thus acted upon), but rather they do not desire inclusion (and are thus active in their body politics). The racialization of body ideals therefore allows the women to become agents.

The intersection of the discourses of race and body ideals in the women's responses also helps to construct a space where white culture is not revered. Colonialism and neocolonialism have bred Eurocentrism and the supremacy of Caucasian cultural forms, including language, dress, and racial schemas (Morley and Robins 1995). The focus groups reveal that body image in the West Indian diaspora does not follow this trend, as the respondents do not value the "white aesthetic." Furthermore, unlike other spaces where occupying a black body is undesirable and dangerous, their racial identification as black is advantageous in this context, as it allows the women to foster beauty discourses outside of the dominant thin ideal, challenging the hegemony of whiteness in American body image. Because they self-identify as black, they have no desire to be thin, and they do not have to be. Therefore, espousing this racialized discourse of the body allows the women to liberate themselves from the pressures and strictures of the thin body type; it allows them to foster Dayal's (1996) interpretation of "double consciousness," to oppose the thin ideal, and envision other ways of being apart from the dominant norm.

Notwithstanding the power that the women achieve, their statements reflect and reinforce the bifurcation of racial politics in the United States. Racial discourse in the United States is excessively preoccupied with the relationship between black (specifically African American) and white Americans, to the exclusion of other racial groups in the nation. By discussing beauty standards along black and white lines, the women in the study rehearse and reinforce the black/white binary that characterizes racial politics in America. Furthermore, in this racial discourse, body shape (like skin color; Hunter 2005) becomes a defining feature of gendered racial identity. More precisely, the voluptuous body becomes a representation and criterion of black femininity, and thus fosters exclusionary practices. As illustrated in the preceding quote, women who identify as black but do not achieve this aesthetic are labeled "white," or not "black" enough.

The Voluptuous Body as Negative Physical Capital

While they are able to circumvent the thin-promoting ideals of mainstream America in their private lives and in the shelter and safety of their diasporic communities, the women still have to interact with the United States public in spaces that cater to and reward women who meet the thin ideal. This interaction is a source of angst for the women, who believe that their bodies put them at a disadvantage in their new home. According to one respondent, "In certain environments [in the United States] I feel fine; in others I feel like people are judging and looking." Another woman shares:

> I am heavy with a stomach and nappy hair. If I and a slim girl was walking down the street [in the US] and there is a man on the corner, no matter how nutty she is he would choose her over me. He would not seeme .

The women's feelings of exclusion and rejection are predominantly experienced in relation to clothing. One respondent states, "it's hard to find clothes that fit. Now I feel like I have to lose weight, because I want to fit in." Analogously, another participant says in exasperation:

> The way the clothes are designed, even if you purchase your size, the pants will fit snugger in the thigh area for women with thick thighs. The pants aren't necessarily made to accommodate this body type. Who are they using as templates to design these clothes? I don't understand the proportions! It is not made for my body type.

Another woman states, "[West Indians] look at me and they're like, 'Why you complaining; you're fine…' Yeah, but when I put my clothes on, I don't feel comfortable in my clothes." The limits that their deviant body shape puts on their clothing choices are felt most acutely in white-collar, white spaces. The women who work in corporate America candidly discuss the difficulty they face in finding professional clothing that suits and complements their body shape and size, and talk about the general self-consciousness they feel about their bodies in their offices. As one respondent shares:

> I try to get rid of my butt because I don't fit into my clothes. I work in corporate America so I buy the clothes that all the white people make, Calvin Klein, Tahari, and I don't fit into bottoms for anything. I always have to buy two sizes up and then get the top tailored, and it's so annoying…[my butt] is the one thing that does not fit into anything…There are no designers that cater to curvy women…The clothes don't fit with my body type; my body doesn't fit with the clothes, so I'm just trying to assimilate to be able to fit into my clothes to fit into [corporate America].

The women are also candid about the judgmental comments they receive from coworkers about their "big" hips and thighs, and the differential attention they receive for wearing the same type of clothing as their white female colleagues. The following exchange between two respondents is emblematic of the general feeling among the women:

> *Respondent 1:* I was told at work that my pants were tight, but they weren't, I just happen to have bigger thighs.

> *Respondent 2:* I have that same problem. I had a similar situation where I was told my pants are too tight. I commented that if you put a

Caucasian of similar size in the same pants the fit would be completely different. I tried to make light of the situation by saying, "Don't blame me because I have a really good figure." I tried to not makeita nis sue.

First, we see in these examples how the women's bodies are objects of surveillance in their workplaces, highlighting the reality of the women's difference and marginalization in these spaces. Second, the statements also reveal that the women's voluptuous ideal seems to undermine their social and cultural status rather than enhance it. In this sense then, their curvaceous bodies are negative physical capital. According to Pierre Bourdieu, physicality and appearance are symbolically valued in social fields, and are significant in the accumulation of other forms of capital or social power. The effective conversion of embodied capital is contingent on the subject's ability to develop his/her body in ways that are recognized as possessing value in the social field (Shilling 2004): the more one's body mirrors or successfully replicates the dominant body ideals of the social space, the more one is valued, and the more opportunities one has to convert this physical capital into social, cultural, and economic gain (Bourdieu 1986). Non-white women, owing to their gender and race being relatively undervalued in Anglocentric societies, accrue little physical capital, illustrating how the production of physical capital influences social inequality (Shilling 1991).

In the case of these West Indian women, their deviant bodies negate any cultural capital they may have accrued in the United States through linguistic competencies, manners, and performances, and adversely affect their full participation and mobility in American society. Moreover, the women feel that the negative physical capital created by their curvaceous bodies further complicates their positions as immigrants in the United States. The lack of conformity of their bodies to the thin ideal presents yet another obstacle to their prosperity in the United States as it unfavorably affects their ability to fully succeed as immigrants; their race, their accents, their culture, and now their body type impede participation in the most lucrative parts of American society, reinforcing Shilling's (1991) assertion that physical capital (or the lack thereof) contributes to reduced economic opportunities.

Body Dissatisfaction and the West Indian Ideal

The fact that the women do not pursue thinness does not make them exempt from body-related anxieties and body dissatisfaction. The women's endorsement of a more voluptuous aesthetic creates many of their physical insecurities, and, subsequently, fuels constant body-improvement projects. The bigger women in the groups speak about their desire to lose the weight that accumulated in the "wrong" areas, and make their bodies better approximate this curvaceous image; they strive for bigger or smaller breasts, smaller stomachs, and larger buttocks, as illustrated by the statements below:

> Before I could eat whatever I wanted, I didn't have to exercise, but now I have a [stomach] and I am depressed. I wonder how do I get rid of it!
>
> I definitely want to lose my [stomach], and keep my [larger] butt, because I never had a butt before.
>
> I have done so many things [to get this shape]. I have done the Beyoncé diet[4] with the cayenne pepper...I did the clear wrap with the Saran wrap, the green tea...

The thinner women are equally consumed with the "Coca Cola" bottle shape, and also engage in dieting behaviors designed to avoid degeneration into the undesirable "white" skinny body type, that is, the hip-less, butt-less thin silhouette of mainstream America. One such participant confesses, "I used to be very, very slim and I didn't get a positive response [from family and friends]. I started to eat in order to gain weight." These statements indicate that body dissatisfaction is not the exclusive domain of women who pursue the thin ideal. They remind us that all beauty standards, even those that seem to endorse larger, healthier aesthetics such as the "Coca Cola bottle" ideal, are normative paradigms that engender self-contempt in the vast majority of their proponents.

Though body ideals emerge as the most prominent signifier of attractiveness, the women also participated in colorism. Similar to what Margaret Hunter (2004) found in her study of African Americans and Mexican Americans, the women spoke of a distinctive ideal for skin color or complexion. Specifically, even though the women go to great lengths to emphasize that dark-skinned black women are attractive, they agree that lighter skin gives black women more currency in Western societies and thus relegates dark-skinned women to the margins of what is considered beautiful. For the dark-skinned participants, their skin is a constant source of contention for them, one that began in their homelands, and continues in the diaspora. One participant explains:

> You had the "browning"[5] and the blackie. I had friends who were not more attractive but they got the attention because I was not a

browning...After a while, I began to wish I was lighter with long hair...I got teased; I was called blackie, lippo because of my thick lips. It made me self-conscious about my looks.

Another respondent says:

In Jamaica, we don't have black and white; we don't have racism in that term, but I would have to work way harder than [a lighter-skinned girl] would...My first job was at a bank and I was only one of three dark-skinnedw omen.

Similarly, another participant states, "In Jamaica the only issue I had was people saying, 'You are so beautiful...but yuh black.'" To emphasize that this colorism continues in contemporary times, one woman comments, "It still happens; the lighter-skinned person gets the job."

Because of the value placed on light skin, bleaching (the process of applying chemicals to the skin to make it lighter in color) is very prevalent in their communities, and that topic came up several times during the focus groups. All but one of the darker women in the study criticize and condemn this practice, and refuse to go to such extremes to alter their complexion. Yet, they are all cognizant of the fact that their darker skin tone deems them less attractive than their lighter counterparts. Therefore, in addition to struggling with their bodies, these women also have to contend with what is considered diminished facial beauty.

Hair quality is also discussed extensively in the focus groups, as the women candidly express their struggles to achieve the ideal length and texture for their tresses. In general, long, loosely coiled hair (referred to as "pretty" hair) is the ideal, which most West Indian women of African heritage do not have. Much of the women's discussion thus related to their frustration with projects designed to force tightly curled, often coarse hair into the acceptable texture. This included using chemical processing, putting in straight or loosely curled hairpieces (weaves), and wearing wigs. Interestingly, while they denounce practices that alter the complexion, the women are less opposed to these hair projects. In fact, much like other works on the politics of hair in the African diaspora (see e.g., Banks 2000; Patton 2006; and the documentary *Good Hair* [Rock and Stilson 2009]), I find that the women accept hair styling and dressing as a part of black culture and beauty ideals, developing a system of criteria for "good perms" and "good weaves," and seamlessly moving between processed hair, hair extensions, and wigs.

A few of the women decided to forego conforming to the hair aesthetic (a choice referred to as "going natural"), but they also have to
deal with anxieties related to their choice, particularly in white-collar
workplaces. One woman speaks candidly about her struggle to remain
"natural" in this context:

> I worked in corporate America, so it was really difficult for me...I had
> clients that I worked with that I dealt with their money, so they're
> looking at me like, "I don't know if I want to talk to you about how to
> invest my money with your hair looking crazy."

This comment, representative of the sentiments of other women in the
study, illustrates the women's challenge in balancing personal preferences and societal pressures. They also further exemplify the negative physical capital attached to black aesthetics in American society
and expose the risk involved in pursuing and maintaining non-Anglo-
European aesthetics, which are purported to signify unintelligence
andinc ivility.

Social Position and the Negotiation of West Indian Ideals

As they do with the dominant thin ideal, the women develop strategies
to deal with the pressures of attaining the round aesthetic. While they
deploy their racial identification to negotiate the dominant thin ideal,
the women employ discourses related to their sociocultural positions
to aid in this venture, drawing on various facets of their identities to
assuage the pressures, disappointments, and anxieties that accompany
the quest for the "black" ideal. For example, the college-educated
women in the group believe that educated women do not need to
conform to beauty standards. In fact, one participant implies that
only uneducated women feel the need to adamantly pursue the ideal,
because their bodies are their only social currency. As one woman says,
"Being pretty do not get you anywhere; education get you everywhere." In this sense then, beauty is perceived as physical capital, but
it can be replaced by education, so that educated women do not need
to rely on their physiques. In other words, education neutralizes the
need for women to live up to the beauty standard. At the same time,
this rhetoric recuperates elitist, classist ideologies, and positions West
Indian women of lower socioeconomic status as intellectually useless.
Furthermore, like their lesser-educated counterparts, the college-educated women in the group admit to participating in body-enhancing
projects, demonstrating that in spite of their erudition they still pursue

the West Indian ideal. Nevertheless, using the rhetoric of education allows the college-educated participants to negotiate the expectations of their bodies.

In addition, many of the women agree that only unmarried women and women without children need to live up to the ideal. The idea is that women who already had significant others do not need to cultivate the ideal since they are already attached, and women who had borne children have a noble reason for their deviant shape, and are therefore excused. A mother in the study states:

> I have a tummy, but I have an excuse; I have two children…I don't have perky breast because I breastfed two children. Overall, I am happy with my body…There was a song a few years ago called *Tuk in yuh belly* ["Suck in your stomach"]…In essence, what these guys were saying, "If you have children, you do not need to make excuses for your stomach and your breast; you have gone through the childbearing process. We know what nine months can do to the body for a lifetime, so don't feelba d."

By suggesting that married (or unavailable) women and women with children (or undesirable women) do not have to align themselves with the dominant standards of beauty, the women reinforce the idea that women's bodies are primarily for the consumption of others, and function to attract men. Nevertheless, some of the women used this discourse to relieve the exigencies on their bodies.

Some participants also deploy rhetoric related to their diasporic realities to negotiate the expectation of well-proportioned, voluptuous bodies. Specifically, some respondents highlight their responsibility to care for their families in their homelands as the main reason why they could not and should not be expected to maintain desirable bodies. One such participant says:

> Our families on the island believe that because we are in America we are in a better position financially. We then have the additional stress of supporting our families back home on the island…we feel responsible for our families. We squeeze ourselves here, and sacrifice so that we can supportthe m.

She later shares that body image is one of the major sacrifices that immigrants make, a fact that is most obvious when they return to their homelands and find that their relatives and friends actually look better than they who left their islands to live a "better life." Another participant similarly highlights the West Indian immigrant experience as defense for her deviant body. She says, "We are stressed because we have two and three jobs...we are trying to maintain here and [back home]." These women thus imply that they could achieve the curvaceous ideal under different circumstances. However, their current immigrant lifestyle, preoccupied with working, does not allow them to give the requisite attention to body image. While this realization and admission make the women sad, the immigrant lifestyle is proffered as an acceptable excuse.

CONCLUSION

In this chapter, I argue that the first-generation black West Indian immigrant women in this study actively negotiated the ideologies about the body from their homelands and the United States, strategically appropriating and deploying often deleterious discourses to construct a space within which they could at least partially resist the pressures of both the West Indian and American beauty ideals. The women deployed all of these discourses concurrently, using them strategically in their everyday lives.

This research study is by no means exhaustive, and much more work needs to be done in order to adequately explore the complexities involved in West Indian women's negotiation of American and West Indian beauty ideologies. This study focuses on first-generation migrants from the West Indies. Given that "the relationship of the first-generation to the place of migration is different from that of subsequent generations" (Brah 2001), migratory generations develop different diasporic subjectivities, and thus different and varied ways of negotiating the beauty ideals of the receiving country. The patterns discussed in this chapter are therefore not applicable to all West Indian women, and need to be supplemented with similar explorations of West Indian women who came to the United States at an early age, or who are second-generation women born in the United States to West Indian parents.

NOTES

* This study was made possible by funding from the Foundation for the Promotion of Scholarship and Teaching at Roger Williams University (USA).

1. This refers to the beauty ideals predominantly ascribed to the black female body, which generally promote a bigger body size and a voluptuous figure.

2. Colorism and hair politics, which are also raised in the focus groups, are discussed later in the chapter.

3. Interestingly, all of the celebrities discussed were American black women, and not West Indian or diasporic black women. This is not surprising, given that few examples of black West Indians exist in American mainstream media.

4. This refers to the diet plan that singer Beyoncé Knowles allegedly used to lose weight for the movie *Dreamgirls*. It consists of eating nothing for two weeks, surviving instead on a detox drink made of lemon juice, water, and cayenne pepper. While widely believed to be true, Ms. Knowles's use of the diet plan is unconfirmed.

5. In the West Indian, specifically Jamaican, context, "browning" is a colloquial term for a light-skinned black woman. This term is prolific in Jamaican popular culture, particularly dancehall reggae (see, e.g., Hope 2011).

3

DON'T YOU SEE?

(PersonalRe flection)

Mónica G. Moreno Figueroa

* * *

O my body, make of me always a man who questions!
Fanon(1991[1967],232)

* * *

"I can see you're not from here. Where are you from?" This has been one of the key questions in my life. It has taken me a long time to understand it, although I have been hearing it since I was a child, and even more often since I arrived in the United Kingdom. It was 1999 and I was studying for my MA degree. I remember going to a black students conference in Southampton. I was very excited. I had never seen so many "black" people in one room in my life! I was truly fascinated, curious, observing, looking at every single one of them. There, I started talking with a group of people, and at some point the conversation turned to issues of identity and "race." I told them I was a little bit confused about identifying myself as black. I explained I had been born and raised in Mexico and that I basically consider myself Mexican. One young woman looked at me impatiently, and pulled my hand towards her own and compared our skin color. She said: "Look, you are black, what are you arguing about, don't you see?"

The question of seeing has then been the second key question in my life. Better said, the issue of visibility, of engaging with how I see and imagine myself and what others see, how we cannot escape the inquisitive gaze that is always a step ahead, defining *a priori* who we are. This young woman's reaction, her impatience toward a more complex story of identity, might be related to reading the obviousness of "race" off the body and engaging with histories of particular contexts where the struggle against racism has at least appeared to have won the battle for recognition, as for example in the United States or the United Kingdom. Here, you can "see" you are black, you have the right to acknowledge it, and it is now safer to say it out loud: it is okay. However, my surprise at her reaction had more to do with questioning that precise assumption and wondering about the limits of identification, when the "here" and the "there" meet. The tidiness of racial identity comes to a head when different racial projects collide; when people move around and what can be read doesn't match the variety of histories of racial formation. I might look black, but it is just not that simple. There's a point at which some experiences cannot be heard, because they are just too messy. As Michelle Paulse writes:

> The colour of my skin shows that the line was crossed. Someone fucked someone who should not have been fucked. When people ask what is my mixture, they are trying to find out who those persons were. My origins do not haunt me. Attitudes about my origins do. (1994, 49)

I am a Mexican woman with a Mexican mother and a Cuban father. My mother is Mestiza with an apparently Indigenous and Spanish background and my biological father has Cuban and Haitian parentage (and at the same time, maybe, Spanish, French, and African "roots"). I was brought up in a Mexican Mestizo context having no contact with Cuban culture. My Mexican stepfather, with whom I grew up from the time I was five, is Mestizo and has Indigenous and Spanish ancestry. So which "roots" do I have to address? The Mestizo, the Spanish, the Indigenous, the Cuban, the French, the Haitian, or the African? All of them? None of them? Oh, I grow desperate with so much culture/nation/"race" mélange! So arbitrary, too messy: "Look, you are black", she said.

The impatient young woman reminds me of a phrase of Foucault's: "People know what they do, they usually know why they do what they do, but what they don't know, is what what they do does" (quoted in Dreyfus and Rabinow 1982, 187). What do we do when we insist on assuming or knowing where someone is from? When we don't want to deal with the messiness, the deep complexity of our humanity?

Five years later, on a Thursday morning, I was with a dear friend, a "white" English fellow student, having a cup of tea and an intense conversation about all the relevant things when you are finishing a PhD in sociology: love, friendship, loyalty, and the like (Rooke and Moreno Figueroa 2006). While we were sitting outside our college café, a psychology MA student approached us and asked us if we could participate in a brief experiment he was carrying out for his dissertation. We agreed, seduced by the idea of wearing an electronic helmet with a mini camera that would be recording our left eyes' movements and reactions to faces on a computer screen. Once in the laboratory, we were shown a first series of faces. After a short break, we then had to look at another series of faces, this time without the helmet, and say whether we had seen that face before in the previous series.

Everything seemed to be running smoothly, when at the end of my test, I asked how I did. He said I had made very few mistakes. Of the 32 faces we were shown, 16 of black men and 16 of white men, I made 10 mistakes and no false positives (meaning I didn't say I saw somebody that he didn't show me). He then asked what ethnic group I consider myself to belong to. I remained quiet for some seconds thinking (again!) how much I disliked that question and how uncomfortable it made me feel to give the long explanation that I consider it deserves if I have to go there. So I said (again as well!) that I am basically Mexican, but forcing it to ethnic/racial terms I would have to say I'm "mixed": *mestiza* or *mulata* (depending, of course). He looked a bit concerned, or maybe more like disappointed. What is he going to do with this, I wondered.

When we finished the experiment, my friend and I got really interested in the whole process and asked the student researcher more about the experiment and his work. He explained his hypothesis and showed us how our data looked in the computer program he was using. As we suspected, the experiment was about measuring how people look and what they see. Now I found out there is a long tradition within psychology in exploring what they labeled as "cross-race recognition deficit" (Levin 2000). Specifically, he wanted to prove that white people would recognize white faces more easily and would have more difficulty differentiating between black faces, while black people would have developed a better ability to differentiate both black and white people's faces. This is when we realized why we were only shown faces of black and white people and why we were chosen. We first thought we were randomly selected, because we were some of the few people still around the college in the last days of the summer. But we realized he chose us because of his assumption of my friend's whiteness and my apparent blackness, thinking that we would fit his criteria of black and white participants perfectly.

Following his logic, my friend seemed clearly unable to differentiate many of the black faces because of her white body: most of her mistakes, also at about 10 out of 32, occurred with black faces (does this mean she is racist?) and my similar number of mistakes (I got six black faces and four white faces wrong) seemed to show my predisposition for recognizing both phenotypical categories (does this mean I have learned the rules of the racist normative oppressor?).

I told him about my upbringing and that I did not have an experience of having black and white people around when growing up (remember the black students conference?). I explained how in Mexico, most of the population fit a completely different racial criteria, a mestizo one. He doubted why then I was able to differentiate with more precision. I don't have any idea either...Do I just have a very good memory? Was it because I could physically fit in the black racial category? Or was it because I was more aware of racial differences, since I was, at the time, quite concerned about racist practices due to my PhD research? The student pronounced these reasons improbable, because according to his research, people usually have learned to differentiate racial physical variations by the age of seven, and after that it becomes more difficult for people to make these distinctions. Does this mean then that my friend saw and learned to differentiate mostly white people in her first seven years? But if I just saw Mexican/Mestizo people in my first seven years, where does my expertise in black differentiation come from?

We were left with many questions. The experiment made me think again about the constant struggle and tension with the visibility of the body and the urge to categorize in everyday life, where the need to answer the "what are you" question seems to dominate quotidian interactions. Because the answer not only allows for a certain peace of mind to be granted to the question's asker, but also because it is then possible to assume what this subject/object is allowed to think, say, be.

As these two experiences occurred in the United Kingdom, my first reaction was to associate them with this specific part of the world and its colonial obsessions; however, every time I go back to Mexico (and surely alongside my developing research on Mexican racism), other things happen to remind me that the body is not safe from scrutiny anywhere. So now the colonized obsessions come to the fore in a once-familiar location. On the first of July 2012, Mexicans voted in the presidential elections. I had to stand in a long queue outside the General Hospital in Mexico City to cast my ballot in a special voting booth, as I was away from my hometown. My neighbor in the line, a woman in her 50s, and I started talking, both complaining about the disorganization of the elections authorities, the long time standing, and the dark cloud approaching (which eventually left us soaked). She then suddenly turned and asked me, quite seriously, if I was Mexican. I stared at her and thought over my answer for a moment. I said yes and asked her if she was Mexican too. She looked at me perplexed, as if saying: "It is obvious I'm Mexican, how could you even ask that question?" Funny thing, as it didn't seem at all problematic for her to ask me if I was a national, even though only Mexicans can vote. Why else would I stand there for nine hours to be able to vote? Not a tourist attraction as far as I'm aware. Now I wish I had pushed her question. But I didn't. We changed the conversation, as sometimes I do not feel like making a research or an awareness exercise out of the many occasions when these kinds of things happen. However, at times, these exchanges are so infuriating that I would like people to just spell out the reasons for their questions, the underlying assumptions of their comments: just tell me what you see! Maybe I should next time...Nevertheless, the point was again this body of mine, which, as Fanon says, never lets me stop asking questions, but also, seems to constantly provoke questions in others: Why are you here? Who are you? I don't recognize you! I can see you.

4

New Femininity, Neoliberalism, and Young Women's Fashion Blogs in Singapore and Malaysia

Joel Gwynne

A number of scholars have theorized the feminist potential afforded by cyberspace. Commenting on the "growing presence of women leading the technological developments and debates within online culture," Sarah Neely cites feminist blogging communities such as *feministing.org* and the British feminist website *the f-word* as markers of direct female engagement in transforming societal gender regimes (2012, 110). Similarly, Rebekah Willett has charted the growth of the term "gURLs" to denote "connected young feminists" who resist lifestyles that are marketed to them and instead reappropriate and produce their own forms of culture and community (2008, 57–58). While these examples constitute feminist activism online, the liberating possibilities of the Internet have been addressed in less direct terms through debates concerning embodiment and disembodiment. In this research, the empowering possibilities of the Internet are predicated on the invisibility of the body in cyberspace, described by Mark Dery as "the upside of incorporeal interaction: a technologically enabled, postmulticultural vision of identity disengaged from gender, ethnicity, and other problematic constructions" (1994, 2–3). In this understanding of technological disembodiment, possibilities are deemed limitless, with the performances of gender "more fluid and less bound by the binary distinctions attached to everyday realities" (Neely 2012, 106). While Neely proceeds to illustrate the fallacies of this argument—bodies are never truly invisible and are demarcated online in a number of ways—critical consensus often affirms the processes by which identity can be constructed online in ways that circumvent the prescriptions and exigencies of corporeality. As Howard Rheingold suggests, cyberspatial interaction provides a form of unrestricted freedom of expression that allows Internet users to deviate from and subvert the hierarchal codes that structure real-world social organization (1994). Even though online expression practices inevitably operate within cultural systems that influence how individuals construct themselves, and even though real-world power relations may become reinscribed online in a number of ways, many young women have nevertheless found the Internet to be a liberating space (Mazzarella 2005).

Drawing on these utopian proclamations of agency and disembodiment, this chapter seeks to explore the manner in which young women's fashion blogs in Singapore and Malaysia present online bodily self-management as central to female agency. It will position these blogs as part of a wider globalized paradigm in which young women's agency is formed and mediated by neoliberal discourse, and in doing so reject the positioning of postfeminist and neoliberal culture as "white and middle-class by default" (Genz and Brabon 2009, 56), thereby presenting a long overdue examination of the negotiation of these globalized discourses in Southeast Asia. By analyzing the construction of "new femininity"[1] in Singaporean and Malaysian fashion blogs, this chapter will aim to determine the extent to which regional blogs validate Western-originated media discourses in which the visual presentation of the self is celebrated as a form of empowered existential assertion in its own right. Through analyzing young women's fashion blogs, this chapter aims to offer an understanding of how materialism and agency in Singapore and Malaysia can be positioned in relation to neoliberalism, and how these discourses arbitrate the presentation of the female body in online spaces. It will demonstrate how young women in Southeast Asia perceive fashion blogging as central to their identities, not merely in the creation and performance of both traditional and nontraditional feminine subjectivities, but also in terms of female friendship and kinship networks. Prior to doing so, however, it is important to first situate neoliberalism as both a global market strategy and a cultural sensibility, and to contextualize its operation within cyberspace discursively and Southeast Asia specifically.

NEOLIBERALISM, CYBERSPACE, AND SOUTHEAST ASIA

Any attempt to understand individual agency in the twenty-first century must be understood in relation to neoliberalism. Neoliberalism emerged in the late twentieth century as a form of Western liberal governance that erodes the welfare state and reconfigures relations with its citizens (Harvey 2005). Under neoliberalism, governments across the globe have withdrawn economic support for education, welfare, and health care, legitimized by a philosophical conviction that nation-states are not responsible for social welfare, but rather for protecting individual rights and the free market. In this cultural climate, individuals are ultimately responsible for their own financial and personal health, regardless of the social constraints that limit one's agency. As Nikolas Rose contends, no matter how "external and implacable may be the constraints, obstacles and limitations," each individual "must render his or her life meaningful, as if it were the outcome of individual choices made in the furtherance of a biographical project of self-realization" (1992, 12). Neoliberal discourses of selfhood are primarily expressed through transference of authority from "official" (government) sources to private experts in fields ranging from psychology (self-help) to fashion, weight loss, and career planning (Tudor 2011).

As the most economically and technologically developed nation in Southeast Asia, Singapore can be positioned as a case study of the strategies of neoliberalism in both governmental and cultural terms. David Harvey observes thus:

> [The case of Singapore] has combined neoliberalism in the marketplace with draconian coercive and authoritarian state power, while invoking moral solidarities based on the nationalist ideals of a beleaguered island state (after its ejection from the Malaysian federation), Confucian values and, most recently, a distinctive form of the cosmopolitan ethic suited to its current position in the world of international trade. (2005, 86)

Regulated by polices of free trade and noninterventionist free markets, the island state is regarded by many as a model for Asian neoliberalism, "lauded for its championing of capitalism, free economic growth, and near-miraculous economic success" (Ng 2011, 261). Globalization has been central to the success of this economic project, and Kenneth Tan has described how Singaporean culture amalgamates "Confucian" and "Western" values in ways that benefit the financial stability of the nation and its citizens. Interpreting this as a "pragmatic project," Tan describes how Singapore's ruling People's Action Party (PAP) "picks and chooses useful and harmful values for the nation-state's survival and prosperity," marks them off arbitrarily as "Asian" and "Western," and then "promotes and demotes them respectively under these labels" to foster a national culture "conducive to and supportive of Singapore's performance within the context of neo-liberal global capitalism" (2012, 80).

While globalization has not impacted neighboring Malaysia to a comparably dramatic extent, and while the nation's economic growth has not been as visibly meteoric as Singapore's, an infusion of foreign investment since the 1980s has seen the country transform from a producer of raw materials into an emerging multisector neoliberal economy (Ong 2006). Since recovering from the Asian financial crisis of 1997, Malaysia's GDP has, with the exception of 2010, grown progressively each year, reaching its highest figure in the nation's history in 2012.[2] Globalization has inevitably brought about these changes, for the decline of agricultural industries has in part been a result of the nation's New Economic Policy, implemented through four five-year plans from 1971 to 1990 with the aim of restructuring the nation's productivity toward global manufacturing and service-oriented industries (Watson Andaya and Andaya 2001). Given the rapid development that has occurred in Malaysia in recent years, it is, then, useful to situate the nation and its culture as a site for comparison to neighboring Singapore. Accordingly, this chapter is motivated by the conviction that a juxtaposition of fashion blogs from these two nations may speak to the manner in which globalization has interpolated neoliberal femininity as a subject position fractured between tradition and modernity.

Indeed, in Singapore during the last 40 years, the PAP government has attempted to valorize a contradictory form of female identity constituted, on the one hand, by traditional feminine domesticity and, on the other, by a modern liberated outlook emphasizing equal competition with men in the marketplace in order to sustain economic growth and productivity (Chew 2008). Reflecting on the condition of Singaporean women, Phyllis Chew proceeds to observe that "materialism has offered [them] powerful opportunities" (Chew 2008, 203) through state-supported childcare, tuition centers, and assistance from full-time domestic workers (from the Philippines, Indonesia, Sri Lanka, and Myanmar). Yet, while economic prosperity inarguably benefits local women, Michelle Lazar notes that years of claiming government-given rights and opportunities "makes mainstream Singapore fertile ground for the postfeminist distancing of feminism to take root so well" (2011, 39). Chew arrives at a similar conclusion, declaring:

> Singaporean women have progressively become so busy juggling work at the office and at home, preoccupied with the affordability of houses and cars, and immersed in ensuring a "high standard of living' that

they have very little time or need for 'non-material" issues such as "equal opportunities" or "human rights": In this respect, the government can be said to have positioned women where they wish them to be (2008, 202).

Thus feminist activism—like other forms of human rights activism in Singapore—is nullified by the government as irrelevant in a nation where personal success is promoted as principally dependent on responsible self-management (Gwynne 2013). Under these conditions, it is hardly surprising, then, that women in Singapore understand agency primarily in terms of consumer power. Yet, in neoliberal times it is important to examine how exactly younger generations of Southeast Asian women configure online embodiment in relation to discourses of consumption and agency. To do so, it is necessary to begin by explaining why young women, rather than older women, have been chosen as the subjects of analysis of this chapter, and why fashion blogs have been chosen as opposed to other forms of young women's online participation.

YOUNG WOMEN AND NEOLIBERALISM

This chapter's focus on young women is premised on the belief that they have a special role to play in neoliberal economies. Since the mid-1990s, popular culture and academic scholarship have testified to this through "an incredible proliferation of images, texts and discourses around girls and girlhood" (Aapola, Gonick and Harris 2005, 18), exploring not only the relationship between culture and gendered identities, but also the role of social institutions in the formation of femininities. As Angela McRobbie explains, the 1990s saw female youth—rather than "youth" in more general terms—positioned as a site of political investment and utilized as a metaphor for social change, with girls and young women "recognized as one of the stakes upon which the future depends" (2000, 200–201). This recognition of the importance of girls and young women has been further evidenced by what Anita Harris has described as a "global investment in them as new kinds of workers, consumers, and citizens" (2004, 16), with their relationship to the labor market, their patterns of consumption, and their sexual lives the subject of close attention by the state, the private sector, researchers, and the media. Declarations of the agency of young women have risen commensurately with the proliferation of postfeminist discourse, which is itself strongly imbricated with neoliberalism. Rosalind Gill declares that through the ethos of choice, the "autonomous, calculating, self-regulating subject of neo-liberalism bears a strong resemblance to the active, freely choosing, self-reinventing subject of postfeminism" (2007, 57). As such, under neoliberal and postfeminist cultural conditions, discourses of female success are often "overly celebratory of women's increased independence and levels of educational and workplace success" (Budgeon 2011a, 284), problematically situating young women as the most confident, resilient, and empowered of all the demographic groups affected by risk, including ethnic minorities and the disabled (Harris 2004). Simply put, while young women are positioned as vulnerable and on the margins of white, patriarchal society, they are simultaneously hailed as the most self-reliant and autonomous demographic among all of the minority groups.

Even though academic discourse has focused on the centrality of young women to neoliberalism, scarce critical attention has been paid to the intersections between the two in Southeast Asian contexts. Reflecting on this troubling trend, Griffin states that "some girls and young women have been more invisible than others" (2004, 30). Scholarship has historically emphasized Caucasian girlhood as a site of universal significance and disregarded the lived experiences of young women across divergent national contexts. This attention to a very specific form of young womanhood derives partly from the assumption that Western discourses have neither impact on, nor relevance to, non-Western national contexts, despite the global emergence of the "New Girl Order," conceptualized by Hilary Radner as "young women who marry later in life, or not at all, and who have become fundamental agents (as workers and consumers) in the global economic system at the end of the twentieth century and the beginning of the twenty-first century" (2011, 14). While some academics have noted that young women are able to resist ideologies disseminated by foreign media (e.g., Casanova 2004), it has also been acknowledged that globalization and the propagation of Western media discourses are nevertheless radically changing many young women's perception of their physical selves (Attwood 2011). There has, however, been little research conducted on how these discourses are negotiated and appropriated within Southeast Asian contexts, and for the purpose of representational equality and inclusivity it is important to rebalance this critical neglect. By drawing on scholarship concerning neoliberalism and young womanhood, and by focusing on fashion blogs in Southeast Asia, this chapter aims to explore the tension that underlines debates concerning youth culture and online agency, between "seeing young people acted upon by societal forces and seeing them as independent actors in their own right" (Willett 2008, 50).

Why Fashion Blogs?

Fashion blogs are websites oriented around the pleasures of fashion, adornment, cosmetics, and consumption. They are almost exclusively created by young women, and while they usually contain personal information and document significant events and experiences in the life of the fashion blogger, they primarily serve to entertain and educate the audience by offering reviews of the clothes and products displayed on the website. Fashion blogs represent an important medium for examining notions of agency and neoliberalism, simply because fashion remains one of the primary means through which young women construct their identity (Gleeson and Frith 2004). If style is a way in which human values, structures, and assumptions in a given society are aesthetically expressed and received (Ewen 1999), then the process of selecting how to fashion oneself becomes an important way to name oneself, mark oneself, disguise oneself, and engage in multiple and conflicting social discourses (Zaslow 2009). This process can be intensely liberating and agentic, and a view of identity in which gender is seen as a matter of performance rather than a fixed state of being allows us to view the consumer activity of buying clothes as, more specifically, part of the process of constructing one's gender identity. Yet, in the age of global neoliberalism, it is important to refrain from naive optimism regarding the empowering possibilities of fashion, for as Rebekah Willett observes, consumption is frequently framed by a positive requirement to better ourselves through our purchases, so much so that it is "difficult to choose not to consume at all" (2008, 51). Even though consumers may subjectively experience pleasure—and interpret this pleasure as a form of agency—when choosing and buying clothes, scholars such as Arjun Appadurai argue that images of agency "are increasingly distortions of a world of merchandising so subtle that the consumer is consistently helped to believe that he or she is an actor, where in fact he or she is at best a chooser" (1996, 42). Fashion blogs are practical locations to explore debates surrounding consumption and agency, for they appear to document dramatic and deliberate declarations of agency and self-expression through their construction of "commercial femininities," a term used by Angela McRobbie (2000) to describe feminine subjectivities that are produced in media culture.

Methodology

This chapter focuses on two fashion blogs: one authored by Singaporean Zoe Raymond (www.zoeraymond.com) and another by

Malaysian Audrey Ooi (www.fourfeetnine.com). Fashion blogging is a popular activity among young women in both nations and, as an educational practitioner in Singapore, I frequently witness female students browsing fashion blogs in between (and sometimes during!) classes. While no research data currently exist on the number of active fashion blogs in Singapore and Malaysia, these two blogs were chosen from a list I compiled of 42 Singaporean blogs and 15 Malaysian blogs over a period of 4 months in 2012.[3] The blogs of Audrey and Zoe were selected for analysis as they were the blogs most commonly cited by my students as their favorites among the local bloggers. As such, these blogs were chosen for analysis with the hope that they may have much to say about why fashion blogs resonate with contemporary young women. The remaining blogs on my list were discovered somewhat opportunistically, through my own visits to the blogs of Zoe and Audrey and by following the links that exist on them. Among this list of bloggers, the majority are not "professionals." A professional blogger could be defined as an individual whose blog content is dominated by the presence of advertorials—an advertisement in the form of a blog editorial—that serve to create revenue, as exemplified by the high-profile Singaporean bloggers Dawn Yang (http://clapbang-kiss.xanga.com) and Wendy Cheng (http://xiaxue.blogspot.com). In contrast, the blogs authored by Zoe Raymond and Audrey Ooi were chosen as they are women who are employed on a full-time basis in occupations not related to blogging and participate in blogging principally as a recreational activity, albeit one taken very seriously.

This is significant, for as Zoe and Audrey cannot be defined as "professional bloggers," the manner in which they construct "commercial femininities" can be interpreted as motivated by their passion for fashion rather than for monetary gain. In this sense, and more discursively, these nonprofessional blogs can be viewed as offering a more "authentic" engagement with consumer identity, as opposed to professional blogs that may be artificially driven by the imperatives of corporate sponsorship. Both blogs have been active for a relatively long period of time; Audrey's for eight years and Zoe's for six. They both identify similar motivations for creating their blogs as formed out of their personal interest in shopping and as ways of sustaining relationships and sharing hobbies and personal interests with female friends. While both blogs do advertise clothes and cosmetics, and while both bloggers receive benefits in the form of free clothes and beauty treatments, commercial advertisements do not dominate the blog space. Simply put, there is significantly more content that is nonsponsored than content that is sponsored.

Illustrating the similarities between these blogs, this chapter demonstrates how—despite being authored by women in different Southeast Asian nations—they reflect the global impact of neoliberal sensibility on the construction of femininities.

IDENTITY AND AGENCY

Mark Poster (1995) argues that cyberspace promotes the individual as possessing an unstable subjectivity, one bound within a continuous process of multiple identity formation during which the self is perpetually transformed and renewed. This is perhaps no truer anywhere than in the case of blogs, which not only draw from earlier forms of literary expression—most notably diaries, autobiographies, and personal letters—but also differ in their allowance for ongoing and alterable self-expression. Through blogs, identity is constructed in a manner that is self-consciously unending and incomplete, and subject to an ostensibly endless process of revision. The agentic potential of this medium rests upon an awareness that the identity one presents to the world through the screen is not finite but may constantly change, calling to mind Anthony Giddens's declaration that, under neoliberalism, "we are, not what we are, but what we make of ourselves" (1991, 75).

Even though the blogs of Zoe Raymond and Audrey Ooi certainly testify to the flexibility of online identity, it is important to first emphasize that both situate "blogger" as a fixed category of identity that embodies a very specific cultural currency in the contemporary historical moment. Confirming her status as a nonprofessional blogger, Audrey declares that she has always been "very reluctant to refer to [herself] as a blogger,"[4] as this "sounds gross." She states that such a statement is presumptuous, for it implies a certain level of notoriety and media visibility which "only people like Xiaxue [Wendy Cheng] and Cheesie [a popular Malaysian blogger]"[5] have attained. She continues to express the view that bloggers in Malaysia "get a bad rep," and are perceived in the wider culture as "*kiasu* [competitive], greedy, pampered and arrogant."[6] Conceding that many of these accusations are true, and that she herself is guilty of possessing such traits, Audrey thus corroborates and distances herself from the term "blogger" as representing an individual from the wealthier sections of society who has the time and financial freedom to dedicate a significant amount of his/her personal life to fashion blogging.

The stigma experienced in identifying as a fashion blogger can therefore be attributed to a wider perception of female bloggers as self-indulgent and narcissistic. The experience of reading a blog is visual as much as linguistic, and photographic self-portraits of the bloggers—colloquially known as "cam-whoring"—accompany almost every textual blog post.[7] The self-presentation of the body to be consumed by the public gaze is an integral part of the formal and aesthetic composition of the blogs; therefore it is hardly surprising that many members of the public arrive at negative conclusions concerning the self-indulgent motivations of fashion bloggers. Audrey negotiates these assumptions by circumnavigating the term "blogger": "If I had to, I'd say I blog, or I have a blog."[8] Perhaps aware that this could be received by the audience as little more than semantic wordplay, she proceeds to present to the world more altruistic motivations for blogging, one of which is to disseminate information and knowledge to the blogging community. For example, after becoming aware that her friends have begun using *Formspring*—a question-and-answer–based social networking site—Audrey decided to sign up to the website in order to report on its use and functionality as "any good blogger [would]."[9] In other instances, when she finds that her iPhone "couldn't take any nice pictures of food" while visiting a restaurant, she refers to herself as a "failblogger"[10] and announces her decision to buy a camera. On both occasions Audrey unconsciously adheres to the term she rejects, demonstrating that there are indeed components of the "blogger" identity that she *would* like to be associated with, namely, a sense of professionalism in serving the needs of the audience and the fashion blogging community. Her commitment to blogging is underscored in a number of posts, in which she declares that "blogging can be a full time job too," and "as a result in the past four years I don't really have a lot of free time, but I don't mind."[11] Indeed, reiterating one's altruistic intentions is a pattern that occurs in both blogs. Audrey comments that a "big reason" why she blogs is because she "like[s] making jokes"[12] and entertaining the viewer, while Zoe states that she "get[s] a sense of satisfaction when people thank [her]"[13] for sharing her experiences. This declaration is followed by a number of testimonials and responses from readers, which range from simply expressing praise ("U're a sweet gal!") to seeking various forms of advice regarding financial management ("Teach me how to be a big saver!"; "I admire how independent you are").[14] In a similar manner, my personal interviews with Audrey support the interpretation of her blog as a personal leisure space yet one that serves her audience. She comments that her blog has "become as much for my readers as it is for me," and declares that she "always thinks about [her] audience." In addition, she declares that her decision to highlight charitable causes on her blog "sets [her] apart" from other fashion bloggers.

The altruistic features of Audrey's and Zoe's blogs could be seen as ways of deflecting accusations of self-indulgence by accentuating not only the pleasure they experience from helping others, but more importantly, the positive impact of their blogs on the wider cyberspatial community. In addition, the blogs reject the stereotype of the "*kiasu* [competitive], greedy, pampered and arrogant" blogger in less explicit ways, even when employing the blog medium in a self-indulgent manner. Audrey's post, "Things I want to do when I'm free," is a case in point, for while the title prepares the reader for a litany of selfish desires, the items on the list, in actuality, point toward self-improvement as much as self-indulgence. Audrey's aspirations construct her as a distinctly neoliberal citizen-subject who hopes to manage her life in a more responsible manner, and her ambitions include traditionally female-gendered activities such as "taking up some form of regular exercise," "learn[ing] how to cook more dishes," and "be[ing] a neater person."[15] Posts like this function to inform the reader that Audrey is self-reflective, attentive to her weaknesses and character flaws, and this form of public self-assessment serves to foster intimacy between blogger and reader.

Indeed, in the blogs of both Audrey and Zoe, critical self-reflection tempers accusations of self-indulgence and narcissism by illustrating that while the blogs are intensely personal spaces, they are not necessarily gratuitous celebrations of the self. Critical reflection is often confessional in mode, and functions in a way similar to conventional diaries and journals, allowing the authors to validate their identity to themselves as much as to the public viewer. For Audrey, her blog forces self-reflection, and when interviewed she referred to an occasion when she wrote a letter to her 16-year-old self and posted it on the blog, thus allowing her to reflect on her own personal growth over the years. More interestingly, while self-reflection more commonly occurs as focalized around her interests of shopping and cosmetics, even these ostensibly superficial habits are understood as markers of potentially significant transformations in subjectivity. For example, when comparing the current contents of her handbag to the contents that she posted online several years earlier, she comments, "I actually thought I had more black than this. Now I scroll through this whole post and everything is pink. Nothing changed from 5 years ago actually. Older but not wiser wtf [what the fuck]."[16] In this context, the color pink is implicitly positioned by the author as a sign of immaturity, and she thus presents herself as actively employing the blog to register her disappointment in the manner in which her identity has remained static. In this context, self-indulgence appears more forgivable, as introspection becomes the means to enact further self-improvement. In a similar manner, Zoe's blog asserts her subjectivity through reflection and self-assessment in ways that further deflect the stereotype of the female blogger as "pampered." The author declares that she is financially independent and responsible, stating "I eventually stopped taking money from my parents when I am 19," "started doing events, photoshoots," and "every cent is in [her] bank" because "[her] mom taught [her] to fix deposit [deposit cash in the bank]."[17] Her interest in fashion is presented, then, not as the capricious pastime of an egocentric blogger, but rather the means to create financial capital.

What this evidence suggests is that fashion blogs, while ostensibly a recreational activity performed by financially comfortable and self-absorbed individuals, actually provide a context in which bloggers can resist this stereotype and enact agency through presenting a more authentic, yet distinctly neoliberal, self. This is achieved by presenting fashion blogging as a means of neoliberal empowerment—in which bloggers can assert a sense of individual responsibility in the management of the self—and the neoliberal turn toward self-critique is central to not only the deflection of critique from others, but in cultivating intimacy between the blogger and audience. Thus, neoliberal discourse can be situated as the *modus operandi* through which the bloggers elevate their blogs from mere sites of self-indulgent excess to mediums through which they can engage with the wider blogging community and, as we shall see, develop close friendships and networks of sisterhood. The next section of this chapter, then, seeks to explore the manner in which fashion blogs foster kinship networks, and examines the role of the bodily presentation and "new femininity" in augmenting neoliberal cultures of sisterhood and selfhood.

BLOGGING AND FRIENDSHIP

Despite the inwardly focused rewards that online authorship offers fashion bloggers, it is impossible to ignore the fact that personal websites are not introspective enterprises, for an awareness that others will encounter their online expression is, after all, the fundamental appeal of blogging (Stern 2008). Jill Walker Rettberg has illustrated the communal interactivity of blogs, most visible through links: "Many blogs have blogrolls that provide a list of other blogs the blogger frequents. If the blog allows comments, commentators will generally leave links to their own blogs" (2008, 58). She attributes the prolificacy of these links to the performative element that blogging shares with other forms of social networking, for "when we blog or use social networking sites, we not only present ourselves as individuals, we also publicly proclaim our relationships" (2008, 75). As scholars have remarked, cyberspace has facilitated a deep restructuring of society, contesting traditional notions of community (Guattari 1992). This is perhaps especially the case where fashion blogs are concerned, as "most fashion blogs link to other fashion blogs," simply because "these are blogs they read and because their readers are likely to be interested in them" (Walker Rettberg 2008, 60). Thus, through the links that connect fashion blogs, we are able to see "a map of a social network or community of interest" (Walker Rettberg 2008, 60), created not by shared physical space or family ties but by the sharing of information surrounding a mutual recreational activity.

On Zoe and Audrey's blogs, the proclamation and celebration of female friendship is as important as the discussion of fashion, and bodily self-presentation through photography occurs in groups as much as alone. Audrey's blog is especially revealing, showing the extent to which blogging generates online interaction with blogging peers, which then develops into real-world friendships. In a blog post titled "8 years and counting," in which she reflects on her many years blogging, Audrey reveals the circumstances of her first meetings with close friends Angela, Suet, Tze Ching, Jammie, Hui Wen, Cheesie, Wendy, and Bobo, soon-to-be bridesmaids in her forthcoming wedding to fellow blogger Timothy Teah. Among these eight friends, six were "met through blogging"[18] or at blogging social events such as the NAPBAS (Nuffnang Asia Pacific Blog Awards).[19] For Audrey, blogging becomes the primary means of developing friendships, even to the extent that she fabricates more socially acceptable backstories: "The fake story: We met through our ex-boyfriends. Real story: We met because the three of us (me, Suet and Tze) read each other's blogs and Tze at that time had the best permed hair out of anyone I know."[20] Here blogging and fashion converge to create a lasting friendship, and parts of Audrey's website are dedicated to those friends whom she did not meet through blogging. Referring to her childhood friend Angela, Audrey declares, "She even has her own category on my blog called AngieEntry."[21] Thus, fashion blogging becomes the means to not only create friendships, but also to sustain existing personal ties.

It is, of course, hardly surprising that fashion blogs are a primary way of forging communities and friendships, especially in the globalized metropolises of Southeast Asia. As Howard Rheingold (1994) has argued, computer-mediated communication represents the opportunity to recover the meaning and experience of community that is rapidly dissolving from urbanized locales under global capitalism. Much of our public space, and hence our social fabric, is disappearing, and the places where individuals used to meet are being reclaimed for other purposes. In locations such as Singapore and Kuala Lumpur, where the impersonal mall has replaced the intimate café as the primary recreational space of youth culture, the Internet constitutes a new location to form relationships based upon shared affinity rather than the coincidence of location. What is surprising, however, is the extent to which the presentation and self-objectification of the body serves to celebrate and augment these relationships, suggesting that while cyberspace has provided new means to forge disembodied social connections, embodiment remains essential to the maintenance of female social relationships. Indeed, Zoe's blog makes this clear, for seldom do affirmations and celebrations of friendship appear without reference to the body. There is an emphasis on the relationship between the performance of femininity and the emotional bonds of friendship, through comments such as, "You looked so gorgeous that morning, you stole my heart, girlfriend!"[22]

In a similar manner, the blogs of Audrey and Zoe affirm the centrality of female bodily management as the new, preeminent marker of friendship, apparent in the manner in which they subscribe to a pattern of stylized self-presentation described as "new femininity." In order to demonstrate how this sexualized aesthetic operates in their blogs, it is important to first contextualize and define new femininity, shrouded as it is in ambiguity and contrariness.

NEW FEMININITY

In *Reclaiming the F Word*, Catherine Redfern and Kristin Aune proclaim that "many cultures now assume that something is fundamentally wrong with the natural female body and that [we] are duty-bound to reshape ourselves" (2010, 24). In accordance with long-standing cultural narratives that inculcate the importance of female desirability, the global media in recent years has employed the makeover narrative to further entrench the notion that female desirability is a goal to be relentlessly pursued. As Hilary Radner has observed, this process of "becoming" feminine is framed by global postfeminist media culture as a form of liberation, inviting women to reject the notion of a "stable, untested and fixed" self and embrace female identity as "subject to a multiple and on-going process of revision, reform and choices" (Radner 2011, 6). New femininity can therefore be recognized as a form of empowerment enacted by the financially emancipated neoliberal consumer-citizen through self-regulation and self-presentation/objectification of the body, which ultimately serves to reconfigure traditional femininity. As Yael Sherman notes, if traditional femininity connotes sex object, then new femininity "connotes competent subject," and if "traditional femininity is associated with the sin of vanity," then neoliberal femininity "implies that one is actively self-responsible" (Sherman 2011, 82). Scholars have located new femininity at the center of the sexualization of Western cultures and the mainstreaming of the porn industry, with Feona Attwood declaring that "discourses of sexual agency have been seen as central to the development of new femininities, part of a broader shift in which 'older' markers of femininity, such as homemaking skills and maternal instincts, have been joined by those of image creation, body work and sexual desire" (2011, 203). New femininity can thus be understood as a subversive form of modern female identity in its ostensible rejection of the passivity and dependence associated with traditional femininity. Yet, it is also important to emphasize that this positioning ultimately represents modification rather than repudiation. Shelley Budgeon observes that even though women must be "assertive, autonomous, and self-determining" under neoliberalism, they must also "retain aspects of traditional femininity, including heterosexual desirability and emotional sensitivity to others" (2011b, 54) while presenting themselves for visual consumption.

In the blogs of Audrey and Zoe, the discourse of new femininity is perceptible in the rigorous management of the body. In a self-introduction post titled "Why am I so cute?" Audrey declares that she is "the most shameless and shallow person you'll ever meet,"[23] deflecting potential criticism through ironic self-critique. She confesses that her "self-esteem and mood rely heavily on [her] outfit, and state of hair and make-up,"[24] suggesting that successful management of the body is central to personal fulfillment. In a similar manner, Zoe's blog post "15 know-hows—Flawless Skin" employs the language of pseudo-scientific discourse to encourage the audience to perform "microdermabrasion" and to "[take] your body weight and [divide] that number in half to get the number of ounces of water you should be drinking each day."[25] The presence of a series of "know-how" posts on Zoe's blog—in which the author guides and informs the audience on how to achieve physical perfection across a number of body zones—is further evidence that body management and corporeal perfectibility are reliant upon the disciplined acquisition of a body of knowledge the reader can then employ to reshape oneself. The blogs thus follow the format of reality television programming such as

What Not to Wear (2001 to present) and *Ten Years Younger* (2004 to present), in which neoliberal discourse constructs the responsible citizen as one who acquiesces to the advice of an external expert. In this manner, Audrey's blog similarly centralizes her role as an expert on cosmetics, and a number of posts document her speaking on the subject of makeup in the workplace at invited talks at Monash University, KualaLumpur.[26]

While it is to be expected that young women's fashion blogs would employ neoliberal discourse when presenting advice to audiences, it is interesting to note the extent to which neoliberalism and new femininity in Southeast Asia pursues and appropriates a sexualized aesthetic that is Western in origin. In her research on young women's embodiment online, Sarah Neely comments that "technology does not erase the body but enhances it," contending that women are more able to control how their body is represented in ways that "might entail the choice of an empowering avatar, or even posting images that present a more sexualized self than would be presented in real life" (2012, 108). It is precisely this level of control over the body that makes blogs a fertile medium in which neoliberal new femininity can flourish, and the blogs of Audrey and Zoe demonstrate this level of control when constructing feminine identities that oscillate between traditional "Asian" and sexualized "Western" identities. Commenting on the fluidity of female identity in online spaces, Weber and Mitchell have observed a dominant trend that runs through the personal homepages of teenagers in America, whereby the "nostalgic inclusion of cuddly animals and images that are associated with younger children" proliferate alongside "the sexy poses and images more typical of teen magazines" (2008, 31). The blogs authored by Audrey and Zoe follow a similar aesthetic, and yet—due to the authors' national locations within Southeast Asia—draw upon the dominant markets of Western and Eastern consumer culture to construct both traditional and sexualized feminine identities. "Cultural proximity"—which can be defined as the notion that cultural similarities, including "shared identity, gestures and non-verbal communication; clothing styles; living patterns; climate influences and other relationships with the environment" (Straubhaar 1997, 291), are key elements in determining preference patterns of certain imported cultural forms over others—is evident in the blogs with close reference to Japanese consumer culture, deployed to emphasize traditional Asian femininity.

This occurs through the construction of *kawaii* personas. The *kawaii* girl in Japan has been described as attractive yet "lack[ing] libidinal agency" (Treat 1996, 281), and therefore constitutes a way of adopting a traditional, and therefore sexually subordinate, feminine subjectivity. The blogs of Audrey and Zoe perform this identity by adorning their posts with pink Hello Kitty products, and by emphasizing their "friendliness" and "sweetness" in visual displays of friendship and sisterhood. In Audrey's blog, Hello Kitty products appear more often than any other commercial product, and she proudly displays Hello Kitty iPhone covers, chocolates, hairdryers, and even Hello Kitty road tax disc covers on the inside of her car. Yet, the centralization of a *kawaii* aesthetic occurs most dramatically in Zoe's blog, in which a series of photographs titled "Girlfriends' shots" employ the presentation of the desirable feminine body as a means of celebrating friendship. In a distinctly neoliberal conceptualization of sisterhood and solidarity, bodily self-objectification performed as a group becomes the most effective way to commemorate the women's nine years of friendship. The first photograph, which aims to affect a "girly, sweet look,"[27] shows Zoe and her friends huddled together clutching multicolored balloons, wearing flowers in their hair and light-colored dresses. The impression given is one of youthful naivety and uniformity in style and demeanor, implying childlike feminine passivity and a lack of independence. Through her post photo-shoot reflection—"I thought we did so well, many commented we looked like one of those k-pop bands like SNSD! Heeee!"[28] —Zoe marks the "cultural proximity" of this identity by aligning the girls' performance with a *kawaii* all-girl pop group in South Korea. It is also important to note that the production value of the photographs is very high, allowing the young women to feel special and worthy of such financial investment and, on some level, feel like celebrities themselves.

It is through these "Girlfriends' shots" that we also witness the construction of a more sexualized new femininity, thus illustrating the double binds of neoliberal culture where the visibility of the exposed female body is simultaneously extolled as sexually desirable but rebuked as socially transgressive (Eicher 2001). As a consequence of this contradictory social reality—where young women are expected to invite seduction but are denied sexual assertion themselves—Zoe's blog demonstrates a fluctuation between modes of passive and assertive feminine display, in which the *kawaii* aesthetic is counterbalanced by a group of photographs that uncover "the darker side of us."[29] The girls describe this style as "street and cool,"[30] yet this is clearly a euphemism for the expression of a more overtly sexual fashion sensibility. The photographs in this set differ from the first in a number of ways. Instead of uniformity and symmetry, the "darker" photographs emphasize difference and individuality through the adoption of a number of contrasting hairstyles. In counterpoint to the *kawaii* photographs, this individuality consciously presented could be read as an expression of maturity and a stronger sense of self. The facial expressions support this, and suggest that the girls want to be taken seriously, conveying hard and nonchalant expressions rather than sweetness. Their postures are also more assertive, marked by gestures such as the placing of hands on hips and the raising of arms, while attire is also strikingly different: All of the girls wear tight shorts and knee length stockings, exposing their thighs and waists. These two sets of photographs, then, clearly display contrasting feminine subjectivities that are symptomatic of the manner in which agency is conceptualized through fashion under neoliberalism. The second set of photographs—most clearly in the adornment of thigh-length stockings commonly associated with pole dancing—could be employed as evidence of how the "performances of acceptable femininity within mainstream culture have become increasingly regulated by values and an aesthetic associated with the sex industry" (Neely 2012, 104). Such a deterministic critical viewpoint locates young women as "regulated" by the wider culture, as opposed to agents who are making conscious decisions regarding the identities they choose to perform. With this in mind, I would like to conclude this chapter by proposing what can be understood from these blogs about young women's empowerment and agency in online spaces.

SELF-EXPLOITATION OR SELF-EMPOWERMENT?

It is easy to critique and condemn the way young women use their bodies online, especially for critics attentive to the limited terms of neoliberal agency. Scholars such as Rosalind Gill have described the neoliberal feminine subject as an identity position that embraces, affirms, and reifies an insidious cultural shift whereby women no longer submit to the external male judging gaze but to a self-policing narcissistic gaze. Gill argues that this self-policing gaze represents "a higher form of exploitation than objectification" (2003, 103), yet fails to explain how an individual is able to "exploit" oneself. In a similar manner, Shelley Budgeon rejects the agentic possibilities of bodily presentation for, she contends, this form of agency is contingent upon "self-objectification and dependence upon the approving gaze of others" (1994, 66). In this model of social power, women are offered the promise of autonomy by voluntarily objectifying themselves and actively choosing to employ their capacities in the pursuit of a feminine appearance and a sexualized image. In counterpoint to these positions, I would like to suggest that critics often overlook the extent to which young women consciously perform identities, and instead (mis)understand the sexual presentation of the self as a fixed expression of finite, authentic selfhood. To place too much importance on the feminine identity presented in an image fails to respect the image as a shifting, temporal construct that, while shaped by real-world discourses, is not ultimately defined and fatalistically governed by those discourses. In the context of Zoe's blog, it would be a mistake to place the women as blindly manipulated by consumer culture, for there is evidence that these women are actively aware that subjectivity is never fixed and that the blog does not represent their "true" self. For example, the balloons and thigh-length stockings that characterize the "*kawaii*" and "sexual" photo sets are described on the blog as "props," suggesting a cognizant playing with identities. It is also necessary to recognize that the presentation of alternative identities to the gaze of the anonymous viewer in an online space holds far less serious implications compared to face-to-face interaction, and thus young women are able to experience agency by carefully constructing their personas in a medium that accentuates the temporal and provisional nature of these personas. To conclude that these subject positions signal subservience to a culture of commercial hypersexuality only serves further to disenfranchise young women by locating them as passive victims of the machinations of society, rather than active manipulators of online identities.

More significantly, by deliberately drawing attention to multiple forms of feminine subjectivity expressed through their corporeal selves, these bloggers raise important questions surrounding foundational feminist challenges to the objectification of women. While critics such as Budgeon echo this debate by criticizing new femininity as nothing more than self-objectification, they fail to explain why objectification is a problem when it occurs in contexts where visual engagement is the only possible means of interaction, and by doing so neglect the complexities of the conventions of viewing. The visual medium of fashion blogs surely complicates the issue of objectification, simply because blogs *are created for the primary purpose of visual consumption.* Objectification, voyeurism, viewing, and looking are central to the experience of reading a blog, and the audience is aware that what is presented on the screen is a self-conscious and deliberate construction and, most significantly, only *one* aspect of the women's identity. As Audrey herself declared when interviewed: "I wouldn't say that my blog is a true representation of me." Only the most naive audience would assume that as young women choose to sexualize themselves in one set of photographs, they are indeed nothing more than sexual objects and perceive themselves to be so. While it would clearly be problematic if young women's fashion blogs exclusively convey sexual selves, this is not the case, for the blogs discussed in this chapter demonstrate that sexual presentation is merely one mode of feminine display amid a plethora of other subject positions available to women in an increasingly globalized world.

There are many competing definitions of globalization, yet David Held usefully defines the term as pertaining to "a process (or set of processes) which embodies a transformation in the spatial organization of social relations and transactions, generating transcontinental or interregional flows and networks of activity, interaction and power" (1999, 16). Globalization is, therefore, best understood as a continuum of development rather than a finite state or fixed cultural condition that includes, but is not limited to, the exchange, flow, and migration of goods, ideologies, and people across borders, the development and expansion of communication technologies, and a concomitant worldwide market expansion and economic integration driven by free trade and foreign investment. Yet, importantly, the blogs of Zoe and Audrey demonstrate one of the effects of globalization not explicitly described by Held's definition, for whether performing modes of sexual display contingent with the increasing sexualization of Western cultures, or displaying their "cultural proximity" through the enactment of *kawaii* personas, the blogs position globalization as offering young women the freedom to construct their identities from a range of culturally competing subject performances. Understood in this manner, it is arguably reductive and unrewarding to attempt to position young women's fashion blogs as either empowering or disempowering. Rather, it is more reasonable to conclude that these blogs reflect the problems and possibilities of neoliberalism within the contemporary historical moment. Young women are free to choose, and under the cultural logic of neoliberalism and postfeminism, it is specifically the ability to choose, rather than the choices themselves, that should be understood as an act of empowerment in itsow nr ight.

APPENDIX

List of blogs studied, from which the two analyzed in this chapter were selected

Singaporean Fashion Bloggers

Agnes	http://herdeepestthoughts.wordpress.com/
Amandina	http://www.amandinaxx.com/#!blog/ckiy
Beatrice Tan	http://www.beatricetan.com/
Charlene	http://sunbathing-muffins.onsugar.com/
Cheng Yan Yan	http://xiaxue.blogspot.sg/
Christine	http://chrispytinetoo.blogspot.sg/
Clara	http://www.dblchin.com/
Crystal Shong	http://crystalshong.blogspot.sg/
Dawn Yang	http://www.dawnyang.com/
Esther	http://thankgodforpink.blogspot.sg/
Fidelis	http://theluckiestchick-.blogspot.sg/
Holly Jean Aroozoo	http://www.hollyjean.sg/
Jayne Tham	http://www.jjjayne.com/
Jessica	http://www.shiberty.com/
Jolene Ng	http://jongsy.blogspot.sg/
Joyce Ng	http://joy-aholic.blogspot.com/
Kay Kay	http://www.kaykay.sg/
Michelle Quek	http://michellequek.xanga.com/
Ms Glitzy	http://msglitzy.com/
Nadine Tay	http://thisisnadines.blogspot.sg/
Nadnut	http://www.nadnut.com/
Nichole Then	http://blog.nicolethen.com/
Nira Chan	http://www.nirachan.net/blog/
Peggy	http://www.sixpegs.com/
Peggy Heng	http://thy-dowager.blogspot.sg/
Pei Ling	http://peonykiss.com/
Qiu Qiu	http://bongqiuqiu.blogspot.sg/
Rana	http://www.bonjoursingapore.com/
Rebecca/Becks/Beck K.	http://camerafilmroll.blogg.se/
Shanice (Yi Ting) Koh	http://blog.shanicekoh.com/
Sheylara	http://sheylara.com/
Silver Ang	http://thatsilvergirl.blogspot.sg/
Sophie Willocq	http://sophiewillocq.blogspot.sg/
Stephanie Tan	http://theimpulsiveact.blogspot.sg/
Stephie	http://www.stephieshop.com/blog
Velda Tan	http://belluspuera.blogspot.sg/
Wong Su Ann	http://sweethotjustice.blogspot.sg/
X-Wen	http://www.fash-eccentric.com/
Xiaxue	http://xiaxue.blogspot.sg/
Yasu Lee	http://yasulee.blogspot.sg/
Yina Goh	http://yinagoh.blogspot.sg/
Zoe Raymond	http://www.zoeraymond.com/

MalaysianFa shionB loggers

Audrey Ooi	http://fourfeetnine.com/
Carrot	http://carrotoh.wordpress.com/
Ding Xuan	http://crunchycoconut.blogspot.com/
Dottie	http://dfordot.com/
Esther Xie	http://www.estherxie.com/
Felicia Neo	http://www.felicianeo.com/
Tan Hui Ling	http://cheeserland.com/
Cindy Tey	http://teycindy.com/
Iza	http://thepinkstilettos.com/
Jacelyn	http://www.daintyflair.net/
Melissa Celestine Koh	http://melissacelestinekoh.wordpress.com/
Qin	http://www.qinatthedisco.com/
Sheila Mandy Tham	http://www.sheilamandy.com/
Tammy Tay	http://ohsofickle.blogspot.com/
Vivy Yusof	http://www.proudduck.com/

NOTES

1. "New femininity" is not a term coined by a specific scholar, but more a discourse of recent scholarly interventions, dominated by the work of Rosalind Gill and Angela McRobbie, interrogating the way in which traditional femininity has been reclaimed and reconfigured under neoliberalism and postfeminist discourse. New femininity is understood as a subversive form of modern female identity in its ostensible rejection of the passivity and dependence associated with traditional femininity. See Rosalind Gill and Christina Scharff's *New Femininities: Postfeminism, Neoliberalism and Subjectivity* (Basingstoke: Palgrave Macmillan, 2011).

2. See http://www.tradingeconomics.com/malaysia/gdp [Accessed Feb 18, 2013].

3. See appendix for list of blogs.

4. "8 years and counting," Apr 20, 2012, http://www.fourfeetnine.com [Accessed May 13, 2012].

5. Ibid.

6. Ibid.

7. On the blogs of both Audrey and Zoe, posts appear inconsistently and with no clear pattern, sometimes appearing only once a week and sometimes several times in a single day with several days of silence in between. This is perhaps not surprising given that both are not professional bloggers and are therefore under no external pressure to post blog entries with any degree of regularity.

8. Ibid.

9. "The day I quit Formspring," May 1, 2012, http://www.fourfeetnine.com [Accessed May 15, 2012].

10. "What's in my bag 2012," Apr 24 2012, http://www.fourfeetnine.com [Accessed May 15, 2012].
11. "Cos I had a bad day," April 2, 2012, http://www.fourfeetnine.com [Accessed May 15, 2012].
12. "The day I quit Formspring."
13. "10 things about Zoe," February 18, 2010, http://www.zoeraymond.com/2010/02/10-things.html [Accessed May 15, 2012].
14. Ibid.
15. "Things I want to do when I'm free," May 7, 2012, http://www.fourfeetnine.com [Accessed 15 May 2012].
16. "What's in my bag 2012"
17. "10 things about Zoe."
18. "8 years and counting."
19. NAPBAS occurs biennially to celebrate to celebrate the "hard work and contribution to the blogosphere" made by bloggers based in the Asia-Pacific region. Awards range from "Best Food Blog" to "Most Influential Blog," and in total comprises 12 award categories.See http://blog.nuffnang.com.sg/2011/10/31/napbas-2011-new-award-categories-and-nomination-period-extension/
20. Ibid.
21. Ibid.
22. "Jing's Big Day!" Aug 31, 2012, http://www.zoeraymond.com/2012_08_01_archive.html.
23. "Why am I so cute?" No date, http://fourfeetnine.com/about-2/ [Accessed May 17, 2012].
24. Ibid.
25. "15 know-hows—Flawless Skin," May 5, 2012, http://www.zoeraymond.com/search?updated-max=2012–05–08T21:15:00%2B08:00&max-results=10&start=7&by-date=false [Accessed May 17, 2012].
26. "Runaway," Apr 11, 2012, http://fourfeetnine.com/page/2/ [Accessed May 15, 2012].
27. "Purink Photoshoot 2011," Mar 6, 2011 http://www.zoeraymond.com/2011/03/purink-photoshoot-2011.html [Accessed May 17, 2012].
28. Ibid.
29. Ibid.
30. Ibid.

5

FASHION OF FEAR: SECURING THE BODY IN AN UNEQUAL GLOBAL WORLD

Barbara Sutton

GLOBALIZATION, MILITARISM, AND SECURITY

* * *

With calculated precision, Colombian entrepreneur Miguel Caballero shoots someone with live ammunition at close range. The person targeted gives consent to this action, but the body language of laughter, closed eyes, and small talk betrays nervousness. The gun goes off and the bullet rapidly pounds into the target's trendy jacket. The person is still alive. Relief ensues.

* * *

This scene illustrates a standard demonstration for a line of fashionable armored clothing produced by Miguel Caballero (MC), a company founded by the eponymous Colombian businessman. According to Caballero, these outfits combine "discretion, comfort, and security in a single idea"[1] (Metropolis 2009). They are for people who fear for their lives "but don't want to dress like members of a SWAT team" (Owen 2011, 69). The company sells jackets, polo shirts, tunics, undershirts, and other garments that protect users from bullets while also preserving style. The clientele includes politicians, celebrities, corporate executives, royal family members, and wealthy individuals from around the world. The cost of the attire is steep—which limits the pool of customers—but Caballero speculates that bulletproof[2] fashion might be the way of the future: A time in which "everyone," and not just VIPs, will also want this protection (Journeyman Pictures 2008;

see also VICE 2007). This type of clothing is a remarkable example of what I call a "fashion of fear": a move to dress the body so as to achieve security. This particular security strategy does not happen in a vacuum. It is symptomatic of the economic inequalities of neoliberal globalization, the militarization of civilian life, and a pervasive logic of borders and fences in the quest for security.

The current era of globalization is not only one of increased international travel, cultural exchange, transnational commerce, and rapid communications, but one also marked by conflict, fear, and anxiety (Bauman 2006). The uncertainty and negative effects of economic crises have spread across borders.[3] Neoliberal economic policies served as breeding grounds for impoverished, malnourished, and sick bodies (Fort, Mercer and Gish 2004; Sutton 2010), yet wealthy individuals have continued to amass fortunes (Wade 2004), which affords them luxury items for the body and beyond. As the gap between the haves and have-nots increases in various parts of the world, and as states abdicate responsibilities for guaranteeing the welfare of their populations, social breakdown and political turmoil have followed, sometimes meeting with violent state repression.[4] Widening social inequalities under neoliberal globalization have also been associated with rising crime (Portes and Roberts 2005) and the surge of fundamentalisms (Shiva 2005), both including violent actions that target the body.

Governmental initiatives such as the global "war on terror" or the United States' "war on drugs" have exacerbated the problem of violence and human rights abuses in already embattled societies (Human Rights Watch 2011; Incite! 2006; Riley, Mohanty, and Pratt 2008; Stokes 2005). These efforts link countries through policies that affect many more people than those who are the intended targets. The toll of death and physical injury of innocent civilians are among the "collateral" embodied effects of war, militarized borders, and militarized security (e.g., Hyndman 2008). At the same time, people in positions of power can, to some extent, shield their bodies from harm by hiring security guards or driving armored vehicles; yet they still fear robbery, kidnappings, terrorist attacks, and other threats. In the context of deep inequalities, people differently situated in the social structure adapt to the times in various (embodied) ways, including through seemingly superficial devices such as clothing and fashion.

The fences that separate different groups of people from each other, wealth from poverty, and safety from danger, have become closer and closer to the body. The dream of safety in a sea of inequality is pursued through a variety of strategies, including the walled-off country, the gated neighborhood, the guarded mansion, the armored car, the bodyguard, and closer to the skin, bulletproof wear. We can think of these approaches as concentric circles with the body at the center. Among military and other security forces, the use of armored vests, riot gear, and other protective garments are part and parcel of the profession. Yet bulletproof fashion shows the creeping of militarized security tactics into civilian bodies. The fashion of fear is designed to control exposure to violent threats via the embodied practice of stylish dress. Bulletproof fashion aims to achieve security through the illusion of a "fortress body"[5] (but one that does not appear to be so)—the operating dynamics being fear, separation, and privilege.

The move to secure the body through fashionable clothing with hidden armor is shaped by pervasive power differences in an unequal global world. This chapter explores gender, class, ethnoracial, and transnational dimensions of the fashion of fear by focusing on Miguel Caballero's company. This company was selected given that it is a leader in the industry, has significant transnational connections and a long-term trajectory, and has attracted extensive international media coverage. Other companies are also joining the trend and competing for a share of the civilian market interested in stylish armored clothing.[6] The fashion of fear illuminates aspects of how bodily practices and representations are embedded in critical social processes of the day, namely militarization, globalization, and efforts to gain security.

SECURING THE BODY

Concerns around security abound in contemporary societies and are reflected in media, political, and scholarly discussions. In the last few decades, studies and concepts of security have flourished in academic, activist, and policy arenas. Notions of security have broadened, from a main focus on national (state-centered) security and the role of military force, to greater attention to the security of people, including not only "personal" safety but also "food," "health," "economic," "environmental," "political," and "community" security (UNDP 1994, 24–25).[7] This expanded view of security incorporates both "freedom from fear" (e.g., in relation to armed violence) and "freedom from want" (e.g., in relation to poverty) (UNDP 1994, 24). These distinctions implicitly underscore the inequalities that shape security concerns: for example, while affluent individuals may fear robbery of valuable property or kidnappings for ransom, for others insecurity may mean not only the threat of violence but the lack of health care or inability to make ends meet due to an exploitative job. As we shall see, the fashion of fear reflects security concerns related to personal safety and not to broader social welfare; it reproduces notions of privilege by largely centering on the bodies of individuals with relative social power. At the same time, the fashion of fear reinforces inequality by giving affluent individuals a certain sense of invulnerability in the face of collective social problems.

The fashion of fear draws our attention to the increased privatization of security (Abrahamsen and Williams 2007). In much of the security literature, the state appears as a principal actor framing security threats and implementing security measures, often involving various degrees of militarization (e.g. patrolled borders, military budgets, new weapons, and surveillance technologies). However, recent studies have also explored the role of nonstate actors as agents identifying and responding to insecurity, including private military companies, nongovernmental, charity, and media organizations, and international institutions (Barthwal-Datta 2012; Krahmann 2005). While some nonstate actors' interventions may be alternative or oppositional to hegemonic state policy approaches, others may complement and bolster state measures. The fashion of fear presents a solution to problems of insecurity that is consistent with militarized state approaches, but is part of a wide range of private security initiatives that rely on the logic of borders and fences and focus on the threat of armed force against particular institutions, spaces, and bodies (e.g., banks, affluent individuals).

In the political arena, talk about security has been dominated by concerns such as terrorism, drug cartels, gangs, and certain forms of violent crime, such as shootings. A number of state responses to these problems are illustrative of processes of "securitization" in contemporary societies. Buzan, Wæver, and De Wilde argue that a public issue is securitized when it "is presented as an existential threat, requiring emergency measures and justifying actions outside the normal bounds of political procedure" (1998, 23–24). The declaration of states of exception or emergency, invasive surveillance, and detentions that do not conform to regular procedures are examples of policies and practices that may be implemented in the name of security. We live in increasingly securitized spaces, but private individuals do not necessarily trust the state to protect them from real and perceived threats.

As states, institutions, organizations, and individuals take security measures to avert or neutralize identified or perceived security problems at the local, national, and international levels, it is important to ask: *What is the role of the body and embodied inequalities in such processes?* After all, "the physical body is very often the site of security/

insecurity... [and] bodies often function as nodal or connection points in networks of security that are global in their scale" (Peoples and Vaughan-Williams 2010, 131). In this vein, who might be more likely to be construed as a dangerous body and who is seen as part of the body politic whose safety is to be guarded? How are bodies protected, surveilled, armed, or disarmed as part of societal, governmental, and individual efforts to produce security?

Recent studies have explored the role of the body in connection to "securitization," particularly in the aftermath of the 9/11 terrorist attacks in the United States. Scholars write about how states are using biometrics, body scanning technologies, and gender and racial profiling as part of their security apparatus, for example, at airports and border-crossings (Adey 2009; Currah and Mulqueen 2011; Shapiro 2005). In these cases, the body becomes a source of information that enhances surveillance capabilities, that is used by authorities to identify potential threats, or that already marks certain populations as suspect. Aware of revamped security systems and the prospects of unpleasant or invasive scrutiny, individual passengers at airports have tried to dress in ways that do not trigger antiterrorist alert systems. Some clothing marketers, designers, and retailers have joined these efforts by developing clothing that would help travelers go through checkpoints swiftly.[8] Such initiatives implicitly illustrate the embodied contours of a political economy of fear and state control flourishing under the banner of national security. That is, fear, securitization, and business profits can go hand-in-hand as market sectors capitalize on a more expansive and sensitive security state apparatus—and in this case, by producing checkpoint-friendly bodily garments that individuals can adopt to avoid being wrongfully targeted by state authorities as terrorists or perceived as potential threats.

In this chapter, I link security concerns to the bodily practice of dress from a different angle. While I see the fashion of fear as embedded in prevalent state and private efforts to achieve security with regards to selected forms of violence, the focus here is not on bodies constructed as potentially dangerous (Shapiro 2005), but *on the bodies of individuals constructed as needing or being worthy of special protection*. That is, fashion of fear technologies are not designed to verify whether particular individuals constitute a threat, but to secure the body against such threats (e.g., from criminals, terrorists, insurgents). This is in line with the inequalities produced by neoliberalism, in which the bodies of poor and marginalized people are often perceived as particularly dangerous, while those with economic means, particularly if ethno-racially privileged, can eschew the label and in some cases shield themselves from danger.

The fashion of fear is a way of "forting up" the body (Blakely and Snyder 1997, 1; Dupuis and Thorns 2008, 145), rendering it strong and impenetrable. Insecurity is often dealt with through borders, fences, and protective barriers, and the body is the last frontier. Enclosing the body in this way, while maintaining a sense of autonomy, is consistent with other individualistic strategies prevalent in late capitalist societies, such as gated communities (Caldeira 2000). In her essay, "Safe House?: Body, Building, and the Question of Security," Samira Kawash (2000) raises the question about whether such walling up is violent in itself, and whether it can really ensure safety in a broader sense: "Does enclosure endanger body precisely to the extent that it forecloses and denies the very connections and interdependencies that make it possible for there to be any body at all?" (189). The fortress body reproduces the logic of separation and suspicion. It may protect individuals from a concrete attack, but armor also embodies a particular way of being in the world that may be detrimental to basic relationships among people. It is hard to imagine a sense of openness to the world, to the connections that are essential to our lives, if we relate to each other in armor. Furthermore, as discussed later, the fortress body is not gender, race, or class neutral but is built upon pervasive inequalities and prevailing militarized ideals.

The fashion of fear constitutes a "technology of power" (Foucault 1977) to the extent that it helps foster forms of embodiment that are compliant with a militarized social order (i.e., armored embodiment), even outside the confines of military institutions. Through the fashion of fear, the ways of the military percolate into individual civilian bodies, while also sustaining existing power relations. According to Kenneth T. MacLeish (2012, 49), the military use armor as well as other technologies and training to produce "subjects who, thanks to their insensitivity to pain and their immunity from danger, can reliably be sent to face bullets, bombs, and the other attendant threats of a war zone." More and more civilian spaces are experienced as dangerous zones—thus the armor imperative—yet individuals also recognize that this is not wholly the case, so other codes of dress are in order. The goal of the fashion of fear is to produce immunity to bullets, but while individuals are engaged in business other than war. Whereas military attire stands out, bulletproof fashion seeks to blend in with civilian society.

The securing of civilian bodies through bulletproof fashion cannot be separated from militarization and the presence of guns in civilian life. Feminists have examined how militarization permeates policies, budgets, education, culture, and international priorities, as well as intimate aspects of the embodied self, such as the clothing we wear (Enloe 2007; Sutton, Morgen, and Novkov 2008). The popularity of "camo" (camouflage) fashion items, and the ways they normalize war, is one mark of militarization and a legacy of international armed conflict reflected on civilian bodies (Enloe 2007; WCRC 2006). Bulletproof fashion goes a step further, but in contrast to camo, the *appearance* of the fashionably armored body does not evoke a battlefield through the use of military fabric patterns. Yet in actuality it is a body prepared to fend off real bullets in a civilian setting experienced as a conflict zone. Unlike camo, which displays an overt military aesthetic, bulletproof fashion is based on concealment. The body is militarized, but does not appear to be so, reinforcing the social "secret" of inequality. This move also reflects one aspect of how global wars and armed conflict are integrated into civilian life, while also obscuring the violence that often accompanies capital accumulation and the maintenance of social privilege.

Even in wars, someone profits, as illustrated by the business opportunities seized by private contractors and weapons manufacturers. In civilian milieus with a strong militarized culture, with security concerns, or that are violent even in "peace time," clothing companies can also carve out a market niche. Miguel Caballero found inspiration for his line of clothing in Colombia, a country long ridden by state, guerilla, and paramilitary violence (Amnesty International 2004). In a media interview, Caballero echoed the idea that "a product like this, can only be created in a country like this" (Metropolis 2009), referring to the violent history of Colombia. Around the time Miguel Caballero started his company in the early 1990s, for example, Human Rights Watch (1992) reported around 3,500 political killings in one year in Colombia, as well as hundreds of disappearances. This violent climate was ripe for the emergence of bulletproof fashion.

In the United States, as the number of people with permits to carry concealed guns has increased (from 5 million in 2008 to 7 million in 2011, according to *The New York Times*), clothing companies such as Woolrich have designed fashionable wear that can also hide guns (Richtel 2012). The majority of states have facilitated this trend by passing laws that "allow citizens to legally carry a concealed weapon" ("right-to-carry or shall-issue laws") (Hood and Neeley 2009, 73). Furthermore, gun ownership (not just concealed guns) is common among a sizable sector of the population.[9] Garment businesses accompany gun proliferation by providing clothing that conceals guns "stylishly" (Richtel 2012). Both concealed-gun clothing and bullet-proof fashion are indicative of social milieus experienced as threatening, where some people decide that militarizing is an apt way to secure body and property. At the same time, these developments underscore the value attached to bodies that conform to hegemonic notions of style and fashion. Among the differences between Miguel Caballero and Woolrich clothing are price and technology. While an MC armored garment reportedly ranges from several hundred dollars to over $10,000,[10] Woolrich chino pants for the "fashion-aware gun owner" cost $65 (Richtel 2012). The latter does not require the research on and investment in protective technology that is vital to MC wear. Both forms of clothing raise ethical questions on whether the protective clothing is just that, or may actually facilitate harming others.[11]

These different types of clothing illustrate how the body is integral to militarized security initiatives. Dressing in security-related garb is meant to avert dangerous threats to the body (in the case of bullet-proof fashion or concealed-gun garments) or to being perceived as a dangerous body (in the case of checkpoint-secure wear). All of these clothing variants, however, are suggestive of a world experienced as dangerous and ridden by fear and mistrust of the "Other." The body becomes the focal point from which to negotiate security concerns.

Fashion of Fear

ContentA nalysis

This chapter is primarily based on content analysis of Miguel Caballero's main website (http://www.miguelcaballero.com/), conducted during June 1 to July 15, 2012.[12] I supplemented this data with information from media reports. Primary and secondary sources help us to understand the evolution of the business and the characteristics of the clothing made. The website introduced Miguel Caballero's philosophy, history, products, international distributors, testimonials, certifications, press information, and contact information in Colombia (where the headquarters and industrial plant are located) and in Mexico (where MC has a store). The website did not offer an exhaustive presentation of all the products available, as media interviews sometimes referred to products that were not featured in the MC official homepage. Nevertheless, the website allowed for a systematic examination of how the company has conceived its products and marketed itself to the world through the Internet. Miguel

Caballero's main website was referred to in recent media reports for contact information and contained up-to-date products, including the 2012c ollections.[13] Thus I decided to focus on this source. In order to analyze the website, I read all of the sections of the English version of the site (which featured virtually the same sections, products, images, and information as the Spanish version). Yet even in the English site there were some links and information in Spanish, which I also read. I also viewed four short informational/promotional video clips about the company and/or its products. To analyze the text and images on the site, I created coding categories based on the following concepts: class, gender, race-ethnicity, transnationality, and the blurring of military and civilian realms. I inductively noted keywords as well as the emerging themes conveyed by the combination of written language and images. I analyzed the product collections in terms of their general features and targeted clientele, comparing words and pictures. The website also contained links to media reports (videos and news articles), which presumably help to bolster the message that the company wants to deliver. I accessed and noted the information covered in 21 video clips and 30 news articles linked through the website. I also read 40 news reports that I accessed through Lexis-Nexis, EBSCO, and Google searches.[14]

While the content analysis of the website yielded important data, as it is the public face of the company on the Internet, there are limitations to studies based on these kinds of representations, given that they do not allow for comparison with actual practices or talking directly with the different social actors involved. In the media reports I covered, I paid particular attention to reports in which Miguel Caballero or members of his staff speak directly or are quoted; and I sought to corroborate information by cross-checking different sources.

The Miguel Caballero Company

The Miguel Caballero company takes pride in providing "the highest protection standards" for its customers, and throughout its website one could learn about other characteristics of different products: fashionable and comfortable design, light weight, versatility, good-quality materials, thermo-regulating capacity, and innovative technology. The bulletproof fashion garments promoted in the website offered several levels of protection, such as shielding from pistols and submachine guns, among others. In media interviews, Caballero reported the need to keep up with the new armaments available and tailor protective wear accordingly. In addition to an inconspicuous appearance,

Caballero claimed that an advantage of this clothing over more traditional armor is its relative light weight, resulting from years of research andde velopment.[15]

To attest to the quality of his products, Miguel Caballero himself has shot scores of reporters dressed in jackets, as well as his own employees, lawyer, and relatives. He even has a souvenir T-shirt that reads, "I was shot by Miguel Caballero," handed out to visitors shot while wearing his garments (The Global Trip 2008). David Owen, a reporter for *The New Yorker*, visited the MC plant in Colombia and interviewed Caballero:

> Before shooting me, Caballero hollered across the main manufacturing area to warn the several dozen workers there—most of them women sitting at sewing machines—to put on ear protection. They complied without apparent curiosity. Carolina Ballesteros, who is the company's design director and Caballero's fiancée, told me that being shot by her boyfriend is "very normal": he has more than two hundred employees and has shot most of them (including Ballesteros) at least once, a practice that encourages team loyalty and close attention to quality control. (Owen2011,69)

In this passage, we start getting a glimpse of the inequalities that permeate MC armored fashion: as described later, while much of this production has been geared toward the protection of elite men's bodies in various parts of the world, the laboring bodies sewing such garments—as presented in several media reports, videos, and photos of the factory[16]—are commonly those of working-class women in Colombia. What does this arrangement—in which workers not only make but become the testing grounds for the protection of more privileged bodies—tell us about the power relations pervading high-security fashion for export? What are the global inequalities that "demand" that the quality of products manufactured in a developing country be assured by putting certain bodies on the line? Miguel Caballero suggested that this strategy emerged as way of instilling confidence in Colombian products in a market dominated by the United States, to demonstrate that even if a security product was not "made in the USA," it could still be of excellent quality (Dueñas Villamil 2011). In contrast, DuPont, a US-based producer of armored clothing, does not do similar tests on human beings (Owen 2011). While this may be due to caution or legal constraints, in an unequal field, business players based in the Global North may also benefit from cultural assumptions about the superiority of "First World" products.

Miguel Caballero has developed an international reputation, and
the live demos are an effective marketing practice. His unorthodox
methods exemplify corporate risk-taking and competitive masculinity,
hailed as a model of successful entrepreneurship in the age of globalization (Acker 2004). A number of media sources report on his success, telling variants of the company's origin story (e.g., AFP 2006;
Kubisch 2009; Owen 2011; Wyss 2012). This goes back to the time
when Caballero was a university student in Colombia and noticed the
cumbersome body armor that the security guards protecting elite or
prominent individuals were supposed to wear. He thought of creating a better alternative by providing garments for the latter, but by
designing attire that was not obviously militarized, different from the
heavy armor of security forces. He started the company on a relatively
small budget and on a local level. The company is now a multimillion
dollar venture with transnational connections (Wyss 2012). In addition to Caballeros's entrepreneurial skills and the quality work of his
employees, conditions of violence and insecurity combined with key
features of global capitalism constitute the backdrop of MC's business
development and success.

The World Is an Open Market; the World Is a Scary Place

Miguel Caballero started in Colombia in the early 1990s, and now
exports around 95 percent of its products (Owen 2011, Chagüendo
2011). The company has distributors in North America, Central
America and the Caribbean, South America, Western and Eastern
Europe, Asia, the Middle East, and North Africa. In order to market its products to diverse national contexts as well as hold the business to international standards, MC has also obtained certifications
from specialized institutions in a number of countries (e.g., the US
National Institute of Justice), including Argentina, Chile, Colombia,
France, Holland, and the United States, among others. Conditions
of economic and cultural globalization likely facilitate the expansion
of companies such as Miguel Caballero: from more rapid forms of
communications and the ability to market products online, to international media coverage, trade agreements between countries that
enable the flow of goods, and increased cultural exchange that permits
the "translation" of products and marketing strategies.

An indication of the transnational aspirations of the company could
be found as soon as one opened Miguel Caballero's website, which
was written in two major world languages: Spanish and English. The
website also contained links to international media coverage about

the company, including video sources from important news networks such as Telemundo, BBC, and CNN, as well as print articles from sources in different countries, including Mexico, Spain, the United States, the United Kingdom, Argentina, Venezuela, and Ecuador. The site also posted information about Miguel Caballero international distributors and "global certifications that support the quality of [the company's] products."

The transnational dimensions of the business are not limited to marketing and flow of products, but are reflected by the considerations that shape the production of garments themselves. MC is able to better place the products internationally by adapting to local contexts in at least two ways (Owen 2011): (1) the products are developed to be resistant to the forms of violence more prevalent in each country, from different types of ammunition to designs that are stab resistant (González Velázquez 2011), and (2) the style of the garments also follows the dress preferences and fashion in different cultures. Even though many of the products match Western trends, MC has also developed "ethnic" clothing. Caballero explains, "We now make bulletproof chilabas and saris to dress Asian entrepreneurs and leaders" (Assía 2010).[17] He also produces guayaberas, "shirts typical in various Latin American countries" to match preferences in this region (EFE 2010). Through these cross-cultural adaptations, MC products provide an embodied map of the violent world.

What vision of the world emerges if one focuses on the social forces that shaped the success and aspirations of MC? First, we learn from Caballero about the desirability of open markets to allow for the unobtrusive movement of products across national borders. For example, in an interview with CNN (2012), Caballero lamented certain protectionist policies of Brazil, designed to stimulate local jobs. Apparently, this was a hindrance to what Miguel Caballero described as the export of high-quality products (and presumably also to his business profits via access to a large and lucrative market). Miguel Caballero advocated for more free-trade agreements, and fewer barriers, a key to his successful international product placement. Critics of corporate-driven globalization, however, point out how free-trade policies have bred a myriad of social problems by trampling on workers' rights, fostering environmental degradation, and exacerbating economic and social inequalities (e.g., Nader et al. 1993, Shiva 2005). This is related to what Zygmunt Bauman (2006) calls *negative globalization:* "the highly selective globalization of trade and capital, surveillance and information, coercion and weapons, crime and terrorism, all now disdaining territorial sovereignty and respecting no state boundary"

(96). He argues that "the perverted 'openness' of societies enforced by negative globalization is itself the prime cause of injustice and so, obliquely, of conflict and violence" (97). This brings us to the second dimension of contemporary societies that matters to the business of armoring: violence.

The need for Miguel Caballero's products rests on the premise that the world is a scary place ridden by violence and crime—and some places are scarier than others, as evidenced by the different types of clothing produced. A key preventative response is armoring. We do not hear much about alternative or more holistic responses to insecurity such as attempts to reduce inequalities, governmental account-ability, less militarization, or policies that emphasize human rights. Instead, what makes a country more secure seems to be increased use of armor, from vehicles to the body. Though not exclusively, Miguel Caballero's business has thrived in places with severe violence problems, starting with his native Colombia.[18] The Colombian case illustrates how different social actors have grappled with the intersections of security concerns and the opportunities of globalization.

Caballero presented his bullet-resistant products as a needed response to the problem of violence and insecurity in Colombia. In some media reports, one can see an MC promotional poster with the yellow, blue, and red colors of the Colombian flag, which reads: "Colombia: The safest country in the world" (e.g., Metropolis 2009, The World 2011). What contributes to making Colombia safe? Bulletproof solutions. There is an interesting compatibility between the MC slogan and Colombia's government international tourism campaign's slogan in recent years: "Colombia: The only risk is wanting to stay." In both cases, playing with ideas about risk, fear, safety, and security is essential to international business development (armor in one case, tourism in the other). In the case of the tourism campaign, Colombia's cultural attractions and natural beauty are presented as the "risk," the irresistible magnets that might compel visitors to stay. However, the use of the word "risk" is not coincidental; it has a double meaning. The phrasing is also meant to defuse tourists' potential fears in relation to the possibility of violence in Colombia (Proexport Colombia 2012).

Perhaps not surprisingly, the tourism campaign emphasizes a very different kind of embodiment than that offered by Miguel Caballero's armored wear (even the most fashionable, thermo-regulating, and lightweight garments). The touristic campaign—while still resorting to tropes of exoticization and romanticization common in touristic advertisement—portrays a world of embodied openness, the reign of the senses, a bodily immersion in nature, and embodied connectedness with a friendly people. Among the representations in the campaign's video clips are those of scantily clothed people dancing, a woman in a bikini coming out of the ocean, a man in a swimming hole by a waterfall, the energetic cadence of salsa music, the relaxed enjoyment of delicious food or a cup of coffee, peaceful exploration of rainforests or mountains, the friendliness of diverse Colombians, smiles, kisses, and welcoming arms (see, e.g., Colombiatravel 2009).

A series of questions arise if one juxtaposes the sense of fear and violence necessary to promote MC armored fashion and the images of sensual embodied experiences prevalent in the touristic campaign: How is one to reconcile these different types of bodies as agents and objects of globalization? Can Colombia simultaneously be a country that needs more people in armor *and* the place of sensual, carefree, and friendly embodiment portrayed in the tourism-oriented clips? We can see in this paradox a hint of the "contradictory corporealities of globalization" (Sutton 2012, 112): complex forms of embodiment that are shaped by interests that at times merge with and bolster each other, but that also negate each other. After all, the militarized security trends that protect capital or give birth to particular business ventures are also signs of a world that not even the most privileged individuals may want to live in. As the saying goes, a golden cage is still a cage. The fashionably armored body is a fenced body; it is a militarized, hyper-vigilantbody.

The Collections: Where the Civilian and the Military Meet and Diverge

Miguel Caballero's website (as of June-July 2012) presented two main lines of products: private and governmental (see table 5.1 for summary descriptions of collections under each category). His products have diversified, including not only bulletproof fashion but a wider array of high security apparel, gadgets, and devices. All of these collections had safety-oriented components—they were presented as "personal protection solutions"—but they also fulfilled different functions and were aimed at different kinds of people.

The distinction between private and governmental lines is the boundary between civilian life and state security forces. However, between and within these two lines of clothing there is some blurring of such boundaries. Within the private collections, for example, one could find fashionable wear, but also garments used by private security companies, which are increasingly supplementing and sometimes replacing state security forces in their functions (Abrahamsen

Table 5.1   Miguel Caballero Website Collections

Governmental

Tactical: "Apparel and accesories [*sic*] made for all kind of specialized groups of intervention and tactic reaction."

Demined: "Focuses in solutions for detecting and neutralizing antipersonal [*sic*] mines, both for tactical and humanitarian implementation."

Special Projects: "Line of hard armor, designed for the development of goverment [*sic*] security projects and personal protection."

Private

Black : "Sophisticated, elegant, and with 'intelligent design'…offers discreet protection for people with top fashion and top comfort requirements."

Gold: "Developed for people looking for contemporary and avant-garde trends that demand multifunctional, comfortable, and simultaneously discreet garments."

Silver : "Offer[s] protection required by cash in transit companies, bank security, bodyguards and monitoring reaction companies."

Motorcycle: "For people that makes [*sic*] motorcycling a true experience of life…[for whom the motorcycle is the] main tool of work and whose professional performance involve [*sic*] high exigency in security."

Source: (http://www.miguelcaballero.com, as of July 2012).

and Williams 2007). The garments in the Silver collection (vests) were not only about protective armor, but some items also included pockets for guns, handcuffs, ammunition, badges, and pepper spray. In the Demined collection, there was also fluidity between the military and the humanitarian. For instance, the descriptions of the "humanitarian" and the "tactical" garments were practically the same: the main difference being that the humanitarian was for "special front protection for entities recognized in peacetime" and the tactical for "complete protection and defensiveness. For hosts and/or tactical teams in combat, operations and wartime." Yet both shared a similar aesthetic, with the colors and patterns available being green, black, gray, and camouflage. The Motorcycle collection seemed to be more conventionally civilian; none of the products mentioned antiballistic armor and only one item out of eighteen highlighted something related to guns (a "removable lining with pockets for mobile phone, documents and gun"). These products had a "high impact system" to protect elbows, shoulders and back.

Private or governmental, for security forces or civilians not in such occupations, the armored collections reveal how the body becomes militarized. The separation between these realms becomes more fluid as civilians adopt features of military dress, from "camo" and portable-gun attire to body armor. Cynthia Enloe (2007, 4) argues that to "become militarized is to adopt militaristic values (e.g., a belief in hierarchy, obedience, and the use of force) and priorities as one's own, to see military solutions as particularly effective, to see the world as a dangerous place best approached with militaristic attitudes." The ways in which dress is militarized, either visibly or in disguise, reinforce the expansion of military domains into more and more realms, including civilian bodies. However, as discussed later, we can see that even as some boundaries blur, others very much remain in place, as clothing representations are also distributed according to familiar tropes of inequality.

Stylish Bodies, Utilitarian Bodies

In an unequal global world, who can afford to be protected with bulletproof fashion? Miguel Caballero exhibits an exclusive clientele: from royalty and Hollywood celebrities, to several former and current presidents, and other elite individuals. According to media reports, among MC clients were actor Steven Seagal, Colombia's former president Álvaro Uribe, Venezuela's former president Hugo Chávez, King Abdullah II of Jordan, and the Prince of Asturias (Adams 2008, Lacey 2008, Owen 2011). Miguel Caballero's store in Mexico City is located in the posh Polanco neighborhood, "not far from Hugo Boss, Gucci, Porsche and a spotless body shop for bulletproofing vehicles. In Mexico, high-end shopping goes hand in hand with high-end security" (Villagran 2012). Miguel Caballero has also sold its products through Harrods in London, with lines of clothing that particularly attract "by appointment" type of customers, benefitting from personalized attention (CNN 2009).

The elite nature of some of these products was signified by the names and descriptions of the clothing collections. For instance, "Black" and "Gold" evoke status symbols by mimicking the function of such colors in elite credit cards. The Black collection could appeal to a cosmopolitan upper class, as the website read: "The lifestyles of world travel, professional gatherings, and social engagements are met with a casual sophistication." The Gold collection emphasized leisure by referring to people with "a lifestyle full of hobbies, sports and entertainment activities." Except for the "professional gatherings" indicated in the Black collection, work did not seem to be the defining feature of these lines of clothing. The exclusive character of different garments was reflected in the high price tags stated in the media. In addition to the clothing lines featured in the website, a media report mentioned "Caballero's maximum-security Platinum collection, custom-made for presidents and other dignitaries" (Pratt 2005, 100). In some cases, Caballero's products have reportedly also become status symbols (Lacey 2008), "not just a protection item, but a luxury fashion item" (Drost 2009). Clearly, these are not products for the masses.[19]

Social hierarchy demarcates the lines between different high-security items. Connections between bodies, class, and racialization were inscribed in the combination of words and images in Miguel Caballero's website.[20] The portrayals of who seems fit to wear which collections reproduced social boundaries through implicit messages about status, labor, leisure, and choice. While class has been a defining feature in terms of product accessibility, the images in the website also suggested how class is racialized. The world traveler, the elegant professional, or someone likely to emerge from a "Eurocopter"[21] (as portrayed in one of the images) is not just anybody. The mostly male models who were wearing the Gold and Black collections in the website fitted normative ideals of Western masculine beauty. Their bodies were slender and stylish, conveying class privilege through their sleek appearance. While the models included both men who were blond and light skinned and men with black hair and olive/darker skin hues, they exhibited phenotypes akin to those in Western fashion magazines. A light-skinned blond man with light-colored eyes was prominently featured in both collections. In one picture, he wore a fashionable tweed hat, a neck kerchief, and a leather jacket. In another one, he was relaxed, sitting at the table, apparently having a drink with a companion. The leisurely bodies in these elite collections differed from those in collections such as the Silver one, which was more utilitarian.

The Silver Collection (vests) presented men who tended to be more brown-skinned, stocky, and with seemingly *mestizo*[22] or perhaps indigenous features. The collection portrayed the bodies of workers employed by security companies. The racialized bodies in this collection were already coded as working class. No blond, light-skinned man was portrayed wearing the garments in this collection. Whereas the previous collections emphasized style and fashion in addition to bullet protection, the Silver collection emphasized functionality rather than appearance. The only frill mentioned was the opportunity to print or embroider a logo, that is, to inscribe the corporate or institutional branding that regulates the bodies at work. This suggests that the customers buying these clothes are not necessarily individuals with choices and hobbies, but companies. While the vests are designed to protect the users' bodies, these are bodies hired to protect others—property and/or people. Another indication of the utilitarian nature of the garment and class location of the wearer was a reference about the products in the collection being "home washable." Presumably, this kind of information would be irrelevant for elite individuals, less likely to do their own laundry. In reference to the fashionable line, an article in *Time* stated tongue-in-cheek that in the "élite circle of the secure and stylish, there is a hidden cost. In the unfortunate event of stains—blood or otherwise—the garments are dry-clean only" (Adams 2008).

Even though armor protects the bodies of customers of different social classes and ethno-racial backgrounds, the bodies who are presented as the most stylish and fashionable tend to be those with social privilege. Embodied class "habitus" (Bourdieu 1984) is reproduced through militarized clothing that enhances safety while unequally distributing markings of taste and distinction among different groups of people. This is done in part by the ability to hide the militarized component of the garment: armor.

Armored Men, Inconvenient Women

The audiovisual opening of Miguel Caballero's website insinuated the gendered dimensions of "high security fashion." To the beat of techno music starting with the firing of a gun, three bullets traveled toward the target: a generic masculine silhouette. A shield with Miguel Caballero's insignia intercepted the bullets. Miguel Caballero products saved the day. This clip immediately evoked the male body as the main intended user of bulletproof fashion. This was confirmed in an interview for *Cromos*, in which Miguel Caballero explained that his clients are "95% men and 5% women...it is more of a masculine than feminine matter" (Dueñas Villamil 2011).

The male-dominated character of MC armored fashion also became evident as one browsed through the collections, which only depicted a small minority of images of women. In the case of the Black collection, while both men and women were mentioned in words, men were more prominently featured through images (only one female model appeared in two boxes in a corner of the page). The Gold collection site also mentioned men and women, but only men were represented in images. The Silver collection portrayed no women whatsoever.[23]

Even though armored wear may be experienced in different ways by diverse people and in distinct circumstances, certain aspects of body armor have a long lineage of cultural meanings associated with masculinity in the Western world—from the use of armor by gladiators, to knights in medieval times, through its current use by the male-dominated state and private security and military forces. Body armor, fortressing the body, is consistent with hegemonic masculine ideals about strong male bodies, and the illusion of impenetrability—in this case from bullets, but also as a touted feature of heteronormative masculinity (Waldby 1995). Within hetero-patriarchal discourse, women are to have a male protector, not to turn their bodies into impenetrable shields.[24] In fact, such a development may interfere with feminine ideals. Still, bulletproof companies try to create designs that emphasize the female figure. In an MC fashion show featured in one of the company's videos,[25] the female models looked normatively feminine, but men predominated among the models.

According to a report in *The New Yorker*, only relatively recently had MC started to produce a bulletproof fashion line for women (Owen 2011). In some cases, "low demand" prompted MC to make "custom order only" women's clothing (Villagran 2012). Miguel Caballero stated: "We have made feminine products, but the rotation that we reach in the feminine product with the lifestyle, and the favorite color and all, is more complex" (Dueñas Villamil 2011). Apparently, for much of its two decades of existence, the company implicitly conceived the male body as the one most suited for armor. The *New Yorker* report explains, "Women pose a challenge for a designer of fashionable body armor, since their breasts are situated inconveniently, in terms of panel placement, and since women tend to be more fussy than men about things like thickened abdomens and visible panel lines—although men can be troublesome as well" (Owen 2011, 71). Thus, while the popularization of women's armor would certainly expand the market and profits, the combination of Western hegemonic ideas of what constitutes a beautiful woman's body (e.g., slim and shapely), women's seemingly fickle preferences, and aspects of female bodily form, such as breast location, become obstacles for certain armored fashion designs.

The feminine "challenge" is not intrinsically rooted in women's bodily attributes or innate preferences, but more in cultural ideas about what types of clothing help enhance or hinder feminine beauty. In Western contexts, armored clothing may diminish women's chances to fit normative femininity ideals by making women look thicker than desired. In contrast, armor may somewhat bolster masculine appearance. Expectations about muscular men may mean that a little extra bulk is not all that bad—but not so for women expected to be thin and sexy. In different cultural contexts, women's reportedly inconvenient bodily form does not seem to present a problem. Miguel Caballero has also manufactured "'kurtas,' a kind of tunic, generally white, that men and women in Middle Eastern states wear" (though the report [Rodríguez 2011] does not specify whether both men and women are equally likely to buy the products).

Regarding MC garments in Mexico, an EFE (2010) report explains: "Miguel Caballero does not neglect the feminine public either, despite the fact that 'almost 90 percent' of aggressions 'are toward men and those of women derive, normally, from aggression toward the man she accompanies,' detailed DiCarlo [MC sales manager in Mexico], who attributed this to the scarce numbers of women with high political positions in the country." Instead of foregrounding ideas about feminine bodily form, this explanation underscores social location (likelihood of holding high-status jobs or being companions of high-status people) as an indication of whose bodies especially need armoring. Yet this representation leaves out any reference to the high levels of violence against women in Mexico, which has drawn national and international condemnation—most notably because of rampant "feminicide" on the Mexico-US border, a region with export-processing zones (maquiladoras), environmental pollution, barrios without basic services, drug-related violence, state violence, and impunity— (Fregoso and Bejarano 2010, Gaspar de Alba with Guzmán 2010). These comments also raise questions about prevailing notions of security, and which bodies are protected and not protected by strategies of militarized security. [26]

In a context of pervasive violence against women, it is only under a very narrow construction of violence and insecurity that attacks against women can be framed as deriving mainly from those directed at the men they are with. If we think more broadly about violence targeting women's bodies, which includes but exceeds gun violence, it is also evident that militarized security (fashionable or not) would prove unable to protect women from the kind of violence they are disproportionately likely to experience. Armored fashion cannot protect women from rape and other forms of sexual violence and torture; cannot avert domestic violence (including possibly by the men they accompany); cannot prevent their bodies from being brutally murdered and their parts thrown in the desert (Portillo 2001). The violence in Mexican society, and other parts of the world, is experienced in gendered and sexualized ways, and it is also marked by class and ethno-racial marginalization. Armored fashion is not only inaccessible to many women targets of violence (e.g., working-class women), but is also seemingly useless to protect them from many of the aggressions they experience. This points to the different positioning of diverse bodies with respect to bodily vulnerability and how to deal with the problem of insecurity. What models of security would materialize if we started from the embodied experiences of marginalized women, rather than those of elite men?

EMBODIED VULNERABILITY AND THE ILLUSION OF THE FORTRESS BODY

Bulletproof fashion is implicitly presented as an antidote to the embodied "vulnerability of human beings," in this case, to violent attacks (Turner 2006, 25). This is not an equal-opportunity solution, but one ridden by pervasive inequalities within and across countries. It is a strategy aimed at producing safety through the illusion of a fortress body. As McLeish (2012, 63) points out in referring to military armor, "the rhetoric and the material logic of armor are of an impenetrable surface, a hermetic seal between inside and out." However, while bulletproof fashion is made of protective armor, it is also created to be fit for civilian life by concealing its militarized inner workings. As popular as "camo" has become, it is still not seen as appropriate wear for multiple social settings, and it cannot fend off bullets.

Even though bulletproof fashion can protect some (bodies), and even save lives, it is important to think about embodied vulnerability and security in broader terms. What are the political, psychological, and social implications of the fortress body? What would it do to social relations if the dystopian vision of the armored society, where most people use bulletproof clothing, came to fruition? How might the use of armored garments affect the way we perceive and interact with each other? Is democratizing access to bulletproof fashion—by lowering prices, by making it suitable for people of different backgrounds—the solution?

While the popularization of armor might seem compelling to some, it is questionable whether conditions of fear and insecurity can be effectively addressed through this means of protection (any more than by increasing citizens' access to guns). Rather, we need collective responses to harder questions about how to achieve a more peaceful society and secure embodiment—based on holistic rights to bodily integrity that are linked to social justice. Miguel Caballero acknowledged that body armor is not *the* solution, but he still remained firmly grounded in the realm of militarized security—armored vehicles, bodyguards, and good communication technologies to avert attacks (Gómora 2010). This perspective is understandable given that armor is his line of business. However, not everyone needs to embrace this path to security. Rather, we might consider forms of security that do not entrench the conditions of militarization, economic inequality, gender and racial discrimination, and human rights violations that make so many bodies especially vulnerable in the first place.

The processes of neoliberal globalization and militarization have created and exacerbated myriad inequalities and vulnerabilities. Bulletproof fashion emerges as a way of coping, for some people, with the sense of insecurity that is rampant in such contexts. At the same time, the transnational success of bulletproof fashion, as illustrated by MC's global ties, relies heavily on various dimensions of neoliberal globalization and on the continued prominence of a military logic as a response to social problems. Bulletproof fashion becomes globalized through the translatability of the language of fear, business flexibility to adapt to the aesthetic demands of different cultures, and entrepreneurial attention to specific violence threats in different locales. Other enabling factors include the lowering of trade barriers between countries, the dissemination of product information through global media, and the continuation of conditions of violence within and across countries. The fortress body that MC bulletproof fashion advances is enabled by the "materialities" of globalization as well as traveling "imaginaries" of security that find echo in different cultural contexts (Sassen 2007, 2).[27]

The ideal of the fortress body is predicated upon the notion that embodied vulnerability can be significantly decreased through militarized solutions. While this might be technically correct for certain types of threat, the type of embodiment promoted by the fashion of fear does not promote security in a broader sense, to the extent that it emerges from and reproduces the inequalities and social ills of a militarized and unequal global world. As much as the body in bulletproof fashion is celebrated as stylish, it is a body with a concealed fence, a protection that symbolically represents separation from and suspicion of the "Other." Meanwhile, embodied security remains elusive for the majority of people around the world. Ironically, even for the privileged bodies of globalization, the fashion of fear may be stylish, but still not fearless.

Notes

I am grateful for the helpful comments offered by Elizabeth Borland, Jennifer Burrell, Ron Friedman, Kate Paarlberg-Kvam, Erynn Masi de Casanova, and Afshan Jafar, as well as for the research assistance provided by Elmira Alihosseini.

1. This and all other quotes originally in Spanish are my translation.
2. Several media sources make the point that "bullet-resistant" is a more accurate descriptor of the garments as no bullet protection is completely infallible. Yet the term "bulletproof" is the more popular and widely used label for this type of clothing.
3. The latest spread of economic crises in the new millennium includes the European crisis and the US financial crisis, with devastating social effects (Foster and McChesney 2012). In the 1990s, the Asian crisis and the Mexican crisis showed the permeability of borders to economic woes in late capitalism (see e.g., Greider 1997, Muchhala 2007).
4. Recent examples of mobilizations featured in the media include the Arab uprisings, the protests in Greece against austerity measures, the movement of *Indignados* (outraged) in Spain, the protests of students in Chile and in Quebec, and the Occupy movement in the United States (for scholarly analyses of various of these movements, see e.g., the *Social Movement Studies* 2012 special issue on Occupy!). Another notable example is the case of Argentina, one decade earlier, in which widespread activism followed the 2001 collapse of the country's economy (Sitrin 2012, Sutton 2010).
5. Citing Emily Martin's work, Linda Birke (2000, 158) refers to the influence of militarization in Western culture in shaping people's ideas about how the biological body functions, including imagery of a "fortress body." Here I draw on this metaphor not in relation to biological processes, such as immune systems fighting disease (Martin 1994), but to stress how bulletproof fashion depends on a militarized notion of security, fostering a vision of an impenetrable body immune to the threat of violence.
6. Other brands that are also developing bullet-resistant clothing for civilians include Jack Ellis, Bulletblocker, Anxo Body Armor, and VIP Body Armor-Fortier & Co.
7. This approach has been promoted in the 1994 United Nations Human Development report, advancing the notion of "human security." In the academic arena, see for example, Booth (2005) for an expanded notion of security as articulated by the Critical Security Studies approach. Among activists, see Women for Genuine Security (http://www.genuinesecurity.org/index.html).
8. For instance, "Jockey International introduced a new bra...that uses Mylar under the cup rather than metal." A senior vice president of the company explained: "Internally, we would bring up how this bra 'won't set the detector off'" (Quintanilla 2003).
9. According to a Gallup poll in the United States, in 2011 "46% of all adult men vs. 23% of all women say they personally own a gun. Middle-aged adults—those 35 to 54 years of age—and adults with no college education are more likely than their counterparts to be gun owners." Political affiliation was also significant, as Republicans/Republican leaners were also more likely to personally own guns than Democrats/Democrat leaners (41 percent vs. 28 percent respectively) (Saad 2011).

10. Prices were not posted on the MC website, but the media reports indicated a variety of prices.

11. This may be less obvious in the case of MC clothing, since unlike guns, armor is not designed to harm. However, in the wrong hands, bulletproof wear can allow an armed person to shoot against others with greater impunity, and thus increase the amount of damage inflicted. Miguel Caballero aims to prevent this outcome by conducting background checks of customers (e.g., García 2010; Owen 2011).

12. I accessed the main sections of the website on June 1, 2012, and returned to the site multiple times during the June 1 to July 15, 2012 period to open and take notes on specific links (e.g., those containing detailed product descriptions), to view and take notes on posted videos, and to double check particular content. Given the rapidly changing nature of web-based information, it is essential to conduct the research within a relatively short period (McMillan 2000).

13. At the time of this research, other websites representing Miguel Caballero business branches were also available in various stages of construction, but had either more dated information and/or sections with incomplete information. For example, http://caballero.qlip.in/ was not as developed as the main website and seemed to be out of date. Additionally, a Miguel Caballero USA website with contact information in Florida (http://www.miguelcaballerousa.com/) specified that it was "under construction" and no year was indicated. The website presented a more limited range of products (only two collections). A website for a Miguel Caballero branch in Mexico (http://www.miguelcaballero.com.mx/) had various sections under construction, including the English site and several parts of the Spanish version. These websites featured some of the same information and images as the main site, with some variations, but seemed less reliable for a systematic content analysis.

14. A number of sources address similar issues: the novelty of combining armor and fashion, variants of the company's origin story, the gunshot demonstrations, the kinds of products included, the price of the clothing, the distinguished clientele, and discussion of contexts of violence that make such clothing relevant.

15. A common material for body armor is Kevlar, but MC has developed its own version of bulletproof fabric materials, its secret "Coca-Cola formula," as a company member explained (Owen 2011, 70; The World 2011).

16. See, for example, VICE 2007; CNN 2012; McColl 2009; The World 2011.

17. *Chilaba* means "djellaba" in English, a "loose hooded woollen robe or cloak of a kind traditionally worn by Arabs" and a sari is "a garment consisting of a length of cotton or silk elaborately draped around the body, traditionally worn by women from South Asia" (Oxford Dictionaries 2013).

18. Another example is Mexico, where Caballero opened a store in 2006. Mexico has been afflicted by drug-related violence, organized crime, political assassinations, and state violence, especially in the context of the government's "'war' on organized crime" during the last several years (Human Rights Watch 2011, 4).

19. However, in some interviews Miguel Caballero or company representatives have tried to make the case that the products are also for "normal" people afraid of violence, and not just the rich and famous (e.g., TVE 2010, VICE 2007).

20. Here it is worth noting that given that ethnoracial categories are socially constructed, and their meanings change from context to context, even the seemingly objective enterprise of describing depicted bodies is loaded and fraught with social assumptions and speculations. These descriptions are not simply transparent versions of reality, but reflect problematic modes of categorization, which are often used not just to describe difference but to reproduce inequality.

21. Eurocopter is a French-German company that makes helicopters. Miguel Caballero contracted with Eurocopter to armor such vehicles (*El Economista*201 2).

22. The term *mestizo* refers to people of mixed European and Indigenous descent in Latin America.

23. Regarding the government collections, aside from a slide that depicted a female police officer, no pictures clearly portrayed women in the featured collections (some of the pictures were especially ambiguous given the use of helmets and full body covering), perhaps reflecting the underrepresentation of women in military and other security forces that were the intended clientele for these collections. The motorcycle collection included two pictures of women out of eighteen pictures (the majority being images of men, and a few being more ambiguous, for example, showcasing only half bodies with pants).

24. At the very least, armor may place a woman outside the realm of normative femininity even if not turning her into a man. Citing a historical case, Thompson (2009, 5) argues that "Joan of Arc, for example, was unwomanly but not masculine in her armor." Yet her militarized role, in which armor was integral, was not typically feminine.

25. http://www.miguelcaballero.com/cms/flash/company_english.html (accessed during July 2012).

26. See Sutton, Morgen and Novkov (2008) for a critique.

27. See Casanova and Sutton (2013) on the roles of cross-border imaginaries, materialities, and social actors in the creation of "transnational body projects."

6

MY STRUGGLE WITH THE HEADSCARF

(PersonalRe flection)

Nahed Eltantawy

July 2005: My mom is visiting from Cairo, Egypt to help out with the delivery of my second child. I take advantage of a free day from graduate school and decide to treat my mom to a nice Italian lunch. So, we go to my favorite Italian restaurant. We walk in, are greeted by a nice waitress who proceeds to seat us close to a young couple. But as soon as the man and woman lay their eyes on my mom, they freeze. The man stops talking and the woman stops eating, and they both just stare at my mom for what seems like an eternity.

Why, you might think?

Because my mom wears a headscarf—the *hijab*.[1]

Immediately, my mom and I tell the waitress we want to sit in a different spot. I get so angry at the couple's reaction to my mom, who is a baby-faced woman with a cheerful smile that lights up her entire face.

Over ten years have passed since 9/11, and yet some people are still terrified of this piece of cloth on a Muslim woman's head. This piece of cloth, often vaguely referred to in the West as the veil,[2] is still seen as a symbol of Muslim women's oppression and as a threat.

I remember when my mom decided to wear a headscarf; it was in the late '80s. We had moved back to Egypt, after living in England for a little over five years. My mom, an artist, was teaching art at a private school. My dad didn't care either way; he made it clear that it was mom's decision. He neither encouraged my mom nor tried to talk her out of it. At the time, I didn't understand why mom decided to wear the hijab, especially since it was not very common back then. But she did, and she has stuck with it, despite the stifling heat and other practical challenges that women with headscarves face.

I don't wear the headscarf myself, but I have tremendous respect for Muslim women who choose to do so. Believe it or not, there are millions of Muslim women worldwide who decide to wear the hijab and are not forced to do so by restrictive cultures and oppressive regimes. My two cousins who live in Cairo, for instance, decided to wear a scarf when they were both in college. I could not believe it and, ironically, their parents were against it. I was convinced that my cousins would change their minds and take it off after a few months. But both girls have been wearing headscarves for years and they seem content.

To be honest, when I lived in Egypt, I didn't give the headscarf much thought. I knew many women and girls who wore it and went about their daily lives as usual. It did not change who they were or how others perceived them. Yet when I moved to the United States in 2000, things changed, especially after 9/11. This was the first time I examined veiling and headscarves more seriously. I wanted to find out if it was indeed mentioned in the Quran and whether or not God would punish me for not wearing it. I also wanted to understand the power that leads so many young and old women to wear it proudly. I began to investigate these questions because I was not happy with many of the Western media reports that focused on women who wear headscarves. Worse, I got mad when I saw newspaper cartoons caricaturing and ridiculing veiled women, or when I read opinion columns from prominent reporters who claimed to know it all, and referred to these women as "enslaved" or "ugly" or "ghostly" because of their headgear. I was mad because I knew it was not true. I knew that my mom and my cousins were certainly not slaves; they were definitely not ugly and there was nothing ghostly about them.

After reading verses from the Quran and hearing various religious *fatwas* (religious edicts/proclamations) by prominent male and female Islamic scholars, I am personally convinced that the hijab is required in Islam.[3] Even though Western media rarely mention this, hijab is just one element of conservative dress codes outlined by Islam for both men and women. Both sexes are expected to dress conservatively and treat one another with respect. Yet knowing what I know, I still don't think I'm ready for this step. I dress conservatively but, for many reasons, I still can't bring myself to cover my hair.

This is my struggle with the headscarf.

Sometimes I say to myself that it's important to work on becoming a better Muslim from the inside before worrying about my outside appearance. Then there are occasions when I think I would like to eventually wear the hijab. Deep down though, I feel torn between two cultures. On the one hand, I feel a strong need to follow other Muslim women and cover my hair, yet on the other hand, I want to blend in to the Western society that is my home. I also feel that, while I am convinced that hijab is mentioned in the Quran, it is not one of the five pillars of Islam.[4] So, if I don't cover my hair, that should not take away from my religiosity.

Additionally, while the hijab, at least theoretically, encourages men in Muslim societies to respect women by not staring at them,[5] I feel that wearing a hijab in a non-Muslim country defeats its purpose. I would be the odd one out, and I would definitely invite some stares from both men and women. I don't want to deal with that kind of attention. Plus, it is no secret that many Americans have very little information on Islam and veiling, and the little information they have is usually biased, leading to Islamophobia. So, not only would I be the object of stares, but possibly also a target for everything from sympathy to pity to hatred.

I see evidence of this Islamophobia everywhere. In my 12 years in the United States, I have often encountered people who know very little about the Muslim world and Muslim women. Sometimes, when I tell them that I am a Muslim Egyptian American, I get mixed reactions. Some people are surprised that Muslim women can be educated, dressed in colors other than black, and not always fully covered. Yet, others convince themselves that women like me—who choose not to cover their hair—are exceptions and that living in a Western country helped save me from some miserable destiny. The latter group usually relies on years of Western media stereotyping that paint a one-dimensional image of the Muslim woman as someone who is backward, oppressed, and invisible beneath her black *burqa*.

Traces of this Islamophobia can be identified within society in general. The incident with my mom in the restaurant is a case in point, but it is certainly not the only one. Earlier this year, a friend of mine told me that one of her acquaintances confessed to her that she would never board a plane should a woman with a headscarf be on it, because she fears this woman would blow up the plane. Even though it's not common, I have friends who wear headscarves and occasionally experience animosity or unfriendly treatment in stores, restaurants, and even in schools.

Bullying in schools is also not that uncommon. One of my best friends is an American-raised Muslim who wears a hijab. This past spring, her middle-school-aged daughter came home in tears and told her mom that kids at school have been calling her Bin Laden's daughter because she is a Muslim and her mom covers her hair. I also recall an incident that occurred to an American friend of mine who lives in Atlanta. This woman converted to Islam and decided to cover her hair. She was shopping in Wal-Mart one day, when a male cashier told her that Americans like her should not cover their hair.

I could go on and on with examples that demonstrate the widespread fear and contempt of the Muslim headscarf in the United States. The bottom line is such stories make me think twice before taking this big step. It's not because I'm a coward; I can probably put up with an occasional dirty look or a hostile cashier. But I hate to have to be in a position where I'm forced to be extra nice to people or I have to go out of my way to explain to each and every person who stares at me, that I'm not who they think I am. I don't want to be stared at, pitied, or viewed in Western societies as a voiceless, oppressed woman, just because of my hijab. I also fear for my children. What if they get bullied or forced to hear harsh, unfair words that could leave long-term scars because of my headscarf?

What puzzles me is this widespread hatred of the Muslim headscarf goes against American values and the idea of the United States being a "melting pot" that embraces diverse cultures. These are the values I fell in love with when I moved here in 2000, values that encourage us to respect each other's privacy and personal choices. But I guess we don't always live up to these values. This is especially true when, God forbid, we encounter a woman with a hijab.

What many Americans don't realize is that veiling is not a Muslim invention. The headscarf predates Islam, and many Christian and Jewish women covered their hair. I have not seen a single artistic depiction of the Virgin Mary that does not include a headscarf that hides most of her hair. Till this day, we see Christian nuns and Orthodox Jewish women who cover their hair. Many Catholic Christian women continue to cover their heads during mass. In fact, veiling by Catholic and even non-Catholic Christian women is encouraged by many conservatives today (Heath 2008). Yet, non-Muslim women who cover their hair do not receive the same negative reactions reserved for Muslim women. A Muslim woman's headscarf is the only type of veiling that is viewed as ugly, dangerous, and oppressive, despite the fact that many women adopt it by choice.

Muslim women decide on hijab for various reasons. Many choose hijab to express their strong Islamic faith and to strengthen their relationship with God. Others, however, wear the headscarf as a form of revolt against Western culture and values. This was the case for many Egyptian women in the 1970s, where hijab was part of a women's movement to promote the Islamic way of life and reject the West's extremely liberal lifestyle (Ahmed 2011). Some women wear the head-scarf because they want to be treated as equals to men. These women want men to pay attention to their brains and not their bodies. Others, however, believe there's nothing wrong with combining religion and beauty: they wear a hijab as an expression of religiosity and they still keep up with fashion and pay attention to their femininity. Here in the United States, many young Muslim Americans adopted the head-scarf right after 9/11 as a form of empowerment. For these women, hijab gave them strength to face negative portrayals and encouraged them to correct these stereotypes by engaging in dialogue with non-Muslims (Yazbeck Haddad 2007). Despite these diverse reasons for choosing the headscarf, it's fair to say that not all Muslim women have a choice. In Iran, for instance, women are required to wear long coats over their clothes and loose scarves around their heads. In Saudi Arabia, women must cover their hair and face and wear a loose-fitting black robe, or *abaya*.

It is obvious then that Muslim women are not one and the same; even those who wear the hijab, although they might look similar because of their headscarves, have varied reasons for adopting it in the first place. Sadly, though, many Western media lump all Muslim women into one monolithic group and assume that all veiling is oppressive. Just Google images of Muslim women, and I guarantee that you will see very few images of women with colored headscarves and even fewer of women who show their faces. Instead, you will get a sea of black head, face, and body covers.

It irritates me how Western media rarely bring attention to success-ful Muslim women who wear the hijab. Usually, if she's not a suicide bomber, then she's a helpless crying victim of some sort. It makes me mad that most media hardly invite women with hijab to talk about their choices and why they adopt the hijab. Instead, journalists either rely on unconventional Muslim women, who do not necessarily approve of the hijab altogether (or sometimes a former Muslim), to speak for all Muslim women. Or worse, the media choose to speak for these women, reinforcing images of the oppressed, covered-up woman.

And so my struggle with the headscarf continues.

I don't know when, if ever, I will take this bold step and don the hijab. It could be months from now, or maybe years. What I do know though, is that I will only adopt the hijab when I am 100 percent certain that it's what I want to do for the rest of my life. Because, when I make this decision, I want to feel confident and content, just like the millions of Muslim women worldwide who wear it by choice and wear it proudly.

Notes

1. I use the terms "hijab" and "headscarf" here interchangeably to refer to the scarf many Muslim women use to cover their hair.
2. The term "veil" is vague and confusing as it is often used in the West to refer to different Muslim practices. These practices range from wearing a hijab to wearing a full-face cover, otherwise known as a *burqa* (worn by some Muslim women in countries such as Saudi Arabia, Pakistan, and Afghanistan).
3. There are various interpretations by different scholars on the modesty requirements mentioned in the Quran. Some scholars believe the Quran specifically mentions a headscarf, while others say the Quran requires women to cover their chest and not necessarily their hair.
4. These five pillars define a Muslim. They are: faith in God and the Prophet Mohammed (peace be upon him); prayer; fasting in Ramadan; *Zakat* (giving a portion of our savings to those in need); and *Hajj* (pilgrimage to Mecca).
5. Muslim women who wear a headscarf are still subjected to sexual harassment in many countries, such as Egypt, where sexual harassment is prevalent. According to a 2008 survey by the Egyptian Center for Women's Rights, 83 percent of Egyptian women say they have experienced sexual harassment on the street at least once in their lifetime.

7

THE FACE IS THE MASK: GLOBAL MODIFICATIONS OF THE BODY AND SOUL

(PersonalRe flection)

ThomasJ.D . Armbrecht

I am a professor of French who has been a devoted body modification artist[1] for more than 20 years. I am halfway through a full Japanese-style bodysuit tattoo, am pierced, have silicone injected in my body, remove the hair from my head, and grow a long beard. I have collected these changes all over the world: my Prince Albert was done in Boston, my tattoos in the United States and Switzerland, and my body reshaping in Mexico. By participating in the global practice of body modification, I have brought my body into the world and the world into me. Although inhabited only by me, my body is a nexus of the identities, cultures, and genders I choose or am obliged to perform; it is an expression of both the world in which I exist and of my self.

French polymath Jean Cocteau wrote, "Style is the soul, and the soul affects, alas, the body's form" (1983, 174).[2] I, too, consider my body an expression of my soul, by which I understand the uniqueness of my being in the world. My style is the external representation of my singularity incarnated by my physical self. Cocteau's dismay at his body/soul relation is unknown to me; I enjoy expressing myself through stylistic changes to my body and also try to accept changes to my body as they affect my style. Altering my appearance is a way to enjoy the material part of myself and to show how the world changes me.

My motivation for modification is internal and hard to describe; it comprises many feelings and ideas. Some are constant; others pertain to particular periods in my life. Body modification is, for me, the most personal way to collect art and live artistically. It is also fun, involving imagination, risk-taking, travel, friendship, and creativity. My habit of changing the way I look *is* my style. If Shakespeare's adage is true, and "all the world's a stage,"[3] then I want to have a say in the costumes I wear and the roles that I play (with no illusions about directing the show).

Because my body is my avatar in reality, I use my appearance to make public statements, as we all do with varying degrees of consciousness and intention. My current body project seeks to cultivate secondary male sex characteristics performatively to make people engage with the *idea* of male gender. In other words, I wear my maleness like a costume by enhancing it and calling attention to the signs of virility I willfully exhibit. This performance reveals that gender is both innate and acquired and does not have a stable meaning. Even though I have always thought of myself as male and been identified as such, my gender is fluid and dynamic. Its expression has changed periodically with regard to my age, health and access to body-changing technologies.

Unlike clothing, which a person can take off, I wear my modified self all the time. The changes I have chosen reflect and allow me to participate in various communities, including Midwestern city life, academia, and gay male culture. Unable and unwilling to separate my job as a professor from the rest of my life, I integrate my ideas about the body into my teaching and research by exploring through literature the relationship of being and body. I try to accept mainstream cultures' attitudes about my body, which are not always positive, while remaining true to my own style. As personal as my modifications are, they are not meant to be private, but rather part of my public self. In changing my physiology, I have sought to give my body more contact and community to enhance my physical existence.

Telling the story of your body is to tell the story of yourself, since the body's function is to pass the self through time and space. I grew up in a very small town in Maine with little diversity. Even then I was attracted to unfamiliar people and things. The homogeneity of my surroundings made me feel different, which was probably linked to my homosexuality, but also to my health; I was clubfooted when born and had my feet and legs straightened with a Denis-Browne splint.[4] Thinking of this correction as a form of body modification means I was taught from the beginning that it is acceptable to change the body to improve it. This lesson was reinforced by the orthodontia I wore in junior high, after moving to a slightly larger town. I was fitted with a bionator, which enlarged my palate and lower jaw by using tension to encourage bone growth. The dentist's stated objective was not only to correct the occlusion of my teeth, but also to make me look more virile by giving me a more prominent chin and stronger jaw line. My parents reshaped my body to make it more functional and conventionally attractive. Although they lived in a fairly isolated place, they had foresight, means, and access to technology that came far from where they lived. (The Denis Browne splint was invented in England, the bionator, in Germany.) Their vision of and connections to the larger world mean that I have experienced permanent bodily change since I came into it.

Tattooing and piercing are activities as old as humanity itself and practiced all over the planet. Although local culture determines the meaning of ornamenting one's body, the impulse to do so is fundamental. I received my first tattoo when I graduated from college in Vermont, to mark the occasion. Like the diploma that I obtained, the *ouroboros* (a snake swallowing its tail) that I had drawn on my bicep was a symbol not so much of what I had achieved, but of differentiation and change; I wanted to distinguish myself from my peers and context by doing something that was typical of neither as I began a new part of my life. I traveled two hours from where I lived to get the tattoo, but was beginning a much longer journey that I am still undertaking. Associated with ideas of renewal and cyclicality since the Ancient Egyptians, my ouroboros marked a departure from the straight and narrow. The fact that I got a tattoo without my parents' consent transgressed the white, middle-class, Northeastern culture I knew, even as I pursued its ideas of acceptability. It was also a development in the way I thought of my body: for the first time, I chose to mark myself as different instead of trying to look the same. Many people view tattoos as unproductive or even self-destructive. Marking one's skin is, however, a visible, indelible statement of the self; I consider it a form of self-invention, as well as a representation of my temporal and physical past. My modifications map my body's trajectory through life; each change is associated with the time and place in which it occurred. Even as my tattoos blur and fade with time, they will remain a legible record of who and where I was—and am.

I began to get pierced in the 1990s and have since had more than 20 piercings in various parts of my body. Unlike tattoos, piercings can be removed; like tattoos, they leave evidence in the form of scars and are, therefore, souvenirs of the act. Piercings fall into two overlapping categories: embellishment and enhancement, since they both decorate the body and, if done to the genitals or nipples, stimulate it. Either way, piercings are an invasion of the body by a practitioner who places foreign objects in it (as does the tattooist who injects ink into the body). Transcending the physical envelope of the self is a common, but still universally symbolic act. It can also be the source of pain and horror if done violently. Creating fistulae in the body is, however, a way of making contact between the physical self and its exterior. The punch of a needle or the pull of a ring through flesh brings the world into the body. Wearing a piercing sensitizes the body to its exterior, and draws the exterior to the body both visually and materially. Getting pierced makes me feel alive because of a momentary painful intrusion that is neither unwanted nor destructive. Wearing piercings is my way of signaling my attitude about my body and creating physical and visual pleasure.

Having spent my life studying a foreign culture and language has made me aware of the cultural and temporal subjectivity of attitudes and conventions concerning the body. One only need compare ideas of beauty, health, and cleanliness in seventeenth-century France and twenty-first-century Karachi (or almost any other time and place) to be aware of this. I have realized that the culturally informed, goal-driven path I have followed gives me the means to practice and teach my ideas of self-conception, including the socially determined aspects of gender and sexuality. These insights enable me to link my job to my life through my art. Reconciling parts of my interior self to my exterior reality has encouraged me to undertake a larger transformation. I am changing my outside to create harmony within myself and to look as I am. I do not mean to imply that bodily changes "capture" my soul and display it, but rather that the act of transformation is part of my soul.

My body is more than just my self; it is part of when and where I live and of that global no-place of ideas that is the Internet. Thanks to information from sources all over the world, I have been able to change physically in ways I thought were only fantasies. The shared knowledge of online communities has helped me to conceive of my projects and shown me what is possible and where in the world I can do it. Many forms of corporeal modification would have been unknown to me before the advent of electronic media. The first piercing I ever saw, for example, was a Prince Albert featured in the erotic film "Ring of Fire" from Colt Studios (1986). I watched this American movie in France, at a friend's house, thereby encountering a foreign aspect of "my own" culture thanks to the exportation of both American erotica and Northeastern college students. Leaving the confines of the world in which I was living allowed me to see unfamiliar parts of it and, by extension, to imagine myself in a new way.

My bodysuit is the most visible representation of the global world in which I live: I began tattooing my back in Wisconsin, but had my arm tattooed in California and my legs done in Switzerland. I hope someday to be tattooed in Japan, even though I do not think my tattoos are Japanese except in inspiration. Before beginning the suit, I asked myself what right I had to wear Japanese iconography, and what sense it made for a professor to make his body resemble that of a yakuza, the gangsters who traditionally decorate their bodies with images from Ukiyo-e woodblock prints. Talking with tattoo artists and Japanese friends made me realize that although I might appropriate images and practices from Japanese art and culture, neither my tattoos nor I would be Japanese. Their "meaning" would therefore not be determined by Japan so much as by my own culture, and more importantly, by why and where I wore them. On the other hand, the tattoos' context would not erase their origins, which makes my skin a cultural palimpsest.

The overt enhancement of secondary male sex characteristics is an aspect of my style that I consider very American; I am attracted to men who fit Western gay physical ideals and strive to emulate some of them. I recognize the societal benefits of conforming to stereotypical conceptions of gender: being bald, having a large beard, being muscular, and having a large penis are all tropes associated with adult male power. Even though I readily admit (as part of my project) that I have depilated my pate and enlarged parts of my body, the illusion still works in my favor because it confirms assumptions about my gender more than it contradicts them. Many people do not understand or cannot believe what I have done to my body, even if they know that aspects of my appearance are the result of modification. With my bald head, long beard, and little glasses, I resemble what people imagine a male professor should look like (except perhaps for the nose ring and double industrial[5] in my ear). Even so, my appearance is unusual and draws attention, some of it negative.

Fortunately, I am not confined physically or mentally to the place in which I find myself; I can receive support, share ideas, and plan for future changes thanks to a worldwide community of body-modification practitioners and admirers through friendship, media, and travel. If the Internet has been an important tool in developing my modified, globalized body, it has also made my body part of another global phenomenon: consumerism. In today's world, access to information often means access to a commodity or service. Body modification is expensive and frequently involves travel since the people who practice it are a specialized few. By patronizing faraway artists, I have become a participant in the global economy and also a representation of it. I like to think of my body as a small international art gallery!

Physical existence in today's world raises lots of questions we all might do well to ask ourselves: Is it wrong to look the way we feel? Why not resemble those whom we find attractive, particularly if doing so creates diversity, not conformism? Why not enjoy our bodies and know them better by modifying them as they change on their own? Why should we think of our bodies as private, when they exist in the world to interact with it? What if they were a source of pleasure—or even a means of expression—for people other than ourselves? (Models' and athletes' bodies are such.) Given that culture determines bodily standards and acceptable modes of expression, could not the globalized body be a means of transcending these limitations? My modifications do not answer these questions, but they have made it possible for me to ask them. Although most of the changes are permanent, what they signify will change over time as I do. The only constant is my attitude about my physical self and how it reflects both the changing world and my ever-evolving style.

NOTES

1. I am the commissioner, canvas, collaborator, and curator, and creator all in one. Even if I have not been the artist to "install" some of my modifications, my participation in their creation and the way that I display them is mya rt.
2. Op cit. by Sontag (1983, 139), from which part of the title, "The Face Is the Mask" is also taken.
3. "As You Like It," act 2, scene 7 (Shakespeare 1942).
4. The first modification that I experienced was actually circumcision. It is the only change done to me that I would not have chosen myself.
5. An industrial is any two pierced holes connected with a single straight piece of jewelry, particularly the double perforation of the upper ear cartilage. I wear two of them in one ear.

8

IMAGES IN SKIN: TATTOOED
PERFORMERS IN GERMANY IN THE
TWENTIETH CENTURY AND TODAY

Verena Hutter

Anybody who visited a German fairground in the 1890s would have encountered a spectacular sight: the performer "La Belle Irene" not only displayed her fully tattooed body, but accompanied the exhibit with adventurous tales of violence, savages, and the colonies. Her audience was spellbound. Kiosks sold postcards of "La Belle Irene," and local newspapers circulated accounts of her show (and of shows by other performers). Irene even stirred scientific interest, as evidenced by hobby anthropologist, biologist, and medical doctor Rudolf Virchow's letters. In spite of the enormous popularity of these shows, however, there was no public outcry when the Bracht Ordinance outlawed performances by tattooed people in 1932. And nobody protested when these same performers vanished into concentration camps during the Third Reich. Thus we must ask ourselves: What had changed in such a short time?

Following New Historicist approaches (Foucault 1977; Greenblatt 1980; Orgel 2002), I draw on historic source material to trace discourses on tattooed bodies in Germany. I examine various discourses of the early twentieth century such as newspaper articles, postcards, and letters to gain insight into the existing attitudes of the time. Put against a sociopolitical background, I postulate that the tattooed body of the Other serves as an exemplary microcosm for the changes in body culture(s) in the early twentieth century in Germany. As Michel Foucault writes, the body is always "directly involved in a political field; power relations have an immediate hold upon it; they invest it, mark it, train it, torture it, force it to carry out tasks, to perform ceremonies, to emit signs. This political investment of the body is bound up, in accordance with complex reciprocal relations, with its economic use" (1977, 26). I therefore submit that the tattooed body always is a part of the culture it is in as well as a reflection of it (see also Atkinson 2003). At the same time, every tattoo signifies an encounter—if visible, it elicits reactions as well as communication. Tattooing is a global phenomenon, yet it cannot be universalized. The tattooed bodies of the early twentieth-century fairground performers, for example, wore a mix of South Pacific tattoos and tattoos anchored in a European tradition. Discourses about the tattooed body are intimately related to discourses about "Otherness" and body politics. Yet, the discourses around the performers were also specifically German, insofar as they were used to solidify a still fragile German identity by combining the performance of tattooed individuals with colonial fantasies. Moreover, the slow change in body ideal can be observed in the discourses on tattooed bodies. Tattooed performers can be read as indicators of societal acceptance of Otherness in early twentieth-century Germany. Seen in this light, "La Belle Irene" is the perverted mirror image of the healthy Aryan national body that became the ideology promoted by the state in the 1930s. Therefore it is safe to say that the tattooed fairground community was never fully integrated into German society, even though they enjoyed a certain celebrity status in the early twentieth century. In a second step, I examine post-unification (1990) and current discourses on tattoos to see how they echo the discourses of the early twentieth century.[1] In recent years, Germany has gained a leading role in the European Union, and has formed close political and economic ties with the United States and China. Together with the acceleration of media, travel, and communication technologies, the Other that was so conveniently relegated to faraway places in the early twentieth century is closer than ever. It is not only the right-wing jingoists who perceive the global community as a threat. In 2000, an outcry went through the German media— "Will Germans Go Extinct?" asked newsmagazine *Der Spiegel* in January 2000. The background of the story was rather unspectacular. Just like any industrialized nation, Germany's birth rate is low. From "Will Germans Go Extinct?" the headlines went to "Will the German Language Go Extinct?" (Degener 2010; Griebel 2001) to the ultimate question of whether German culture and identity will go extinct. From political talk shows on TV, to hateful books on how Germany "does away with itself" (Sarrazin 2010), underlying fears of getting lost in a globalized world are blown up and exploited by politicians and the media. The directly targeted victims of these discourses are generally immigrants, yet the conservative backlash emanating from these debates goes much further, to capture anything and anybody ostensibly different, such as the tattooed body. While Germans in the early twentieth century tried to position themselves among the leading imperial nations, it seems that contemporary German society now attempts to position itself among the industrialized nations, and does so with similar debates and discourses as in the early twentieth century. The tattooed body represents a microcosm in these discourses, yet is indicative of changes in attitudes toward the Other in society.

While globalization may seem a rather recent (twentieth- and twenty-first-century) phenomenon, it is important that we call to mind that the encounter with the Other is neither new nor unseen. Obviously, historical circumstances differ, yet the mechanisms of constructing national identities against the Other are eerily similar. I argue that contemporary Germans employ similar tropes of the seductive, yet evil tattooed temptress as they did in the early twentieth century, to establish their identity against a media frenzy that warns of a loss of culture, language, and identity.

The New Historicist focus on intertextuality and connectedness of discourses reveals that the discourses on tattoos within the contemporary German society are not "new" and do not exist in a vacuum, but are connected to the past. In fact, these discourses have not changed much since the early twentieth century. Examining contemporary media portraits of tattooed people, I claim that even though the practice has become more popular in recent years, discourses vilifying tattooing borrow heavily from early twentieth-century discourses. In order to move forward and become the progressive, tolerant, and globalized societies we would like to be, I believe that it is of utmost importance to not only pay attention to how bodies are used as projection sites for questions of identity, but also to how contemporary discourses resemble discourses on bodies in the past.

HISTORICAL BACKGROUND

The history of the tattoo in Europe is a history of cultural encounters. Recent research identifies two different traditions of tattooing in Europe. Contrary to popular belief, tattooing had been widely practiced in Europe before its reintroduction through explorers and seamen from the seventeenth to the nineteenth century. The earliest written sources refer to religious tattoos. The "Schottenmönche" (*Scottish monks*),[2] for example, tattooed Celtic figures on their skin (Schönefeld 1960, 46); the German mystic Heinrich Seuse (born 1295 or 1297, died 1366) tattooed himself with a JHS[3] around his heart (Huber 1910, 34–35; Oettermann 1975, 15; Schönfeld 1960, 46), and the crusaders chose Christian symbols to ensure that they would receive a Christian burial in the event of their death (Oettermann 1975, 15). However, there are only a few documents relating to these practices, and they are relatively neutral in tone. In contrast, when tattooing was (re)introduced through colonization and the exhibition of tattooed natives, it became noteworthy. Germany's European neighbors, England and France, imported not only "savages" such as the "Hottentot Venus" Sarah Baartman[4] from their colonies, but also tattooed curiosities such as John Rutherford, who earned a living as a live exhibit and very successfully sold his biography *The Great White Chief John Rutherford* (1830). Thus, the contemporary tattoo emerges from a mixed heritage comprising traditional religious European tattoos and the exhibition of exotic tattoos made possible by the colonial exploitation of other cultures.

Unlike England and France, Germany entered the quest for colonies as late as the 1850s (early phase, acquisition of territory) and the 1890s (colonial rule) (Dawe 2008, 135; Zantop 1997, 2), yet fervently and thoroughly, as evidenced in the propaganda of contemporary newspapers or the meticulous accounts of travelers. As Susanne Zantop's *Colonial Fantasies: Conquest, Family and Nation in Precolonial Germany, 1770–1870* has shown, even before the newly unified Germany (1871) had set out to find its "place in the sun" (a phrase attributed to German foreign secretary Bernhard von Bülow), an elaborate discourse containing "colonial fantasies" existed. Hence, when trade with the other imperial powers and the colonies flourished, and contact with so-called savages increased, the public imagination effortlessly wove fantasies of the Other into the construction of a national narrative. What changed after the unification of German territories in 1871? First and foremost, the self-perception of Germans. Instead of focusing on themselves as a confederation of several independent states and kingdoms, they now understood themselves as a strong, unified colonial empire. Therefore it is not too surprising that the German people "wanted to know everything possible about the people within and beyond their borders" (Rothfels 2002, 90). Since these "savages" hailed from faraway places and little actual knowledge (but many myths and fantasies) of their actual lives was available, they could easily be used as a screen for projection. Embodiments of the uncivilized world, the German spirit should heal them, as the popularized phrase of poet Emmanuel Geibel declared.[5] Zantop remarks: "By inscribing Germans into a colonial script, German writers were able

to define what was 'German' and what was 'un-German'" (1997, 7).
As European performers became aware of the great interest that the
public had in tattoos, they began to exploit it by copying the exhibitions of "savages" at fairgrounds, circuses, and freak shows. For the
most part, these displays were accompanied by "captivity narratives"[6]
of forced tattooing (to which female performers frequently added
explicit sexual undertones), designed to evoke feelings of empathy
from their "civilized" audience even as they appealed to their baser
instincts.

The discourse on tattooing in early twentieth-century Germany
therefore was complex: there was the culture of fairgrounds, circuses,
and sideshows, but there were also pseudoscientific and political discourses conducted by the bourgeoisie. At first glance, these discourses
are not blatantly intolerant or prejudiced. On the contrary, the performers enjoyed a great deal of popularity at first. Similarly, the scientists and researchers who wrote about them were ostensibly unbiased
and objective. In spite of this seeming integration, however, tattooed
performances slowly decreased in popularity toward the beginning of
the twentieth century. By the onset of the Third Reich in 1933, every
trace of their former popularity had disappeared, and performers were
persecuted, forced into exile, or transported to concentration camps.
This change happened within 25–30 years. Thus, we must ask when
and how the transition from seeming integration to open hostility and
cruelty took place.

HIDDEN DESIRES, OSTENSIBLE TOLERANCE: THE FAIRGROUNDS

According to historian Stephan Oettermann, the "tattoo-craze"
peaked between 1905 and 1910 (Oettermann 1975, 66). Walther
Schönfeld, a physician who conducted the first post–WWII research
on tattoos, believes that the "Tattoo Fashion" began to decrease in
1914 (Schönfeld 1960, 51).

Since Germany, unlike the United States, never had circuses with
sideshows, tattoos and other physical abnormalities were exhibited in
the fairground. In the United States, circuses commonly had sideshows, an exhibition attached to the circus, in which physical abnor-
mities were put on display. These "freakshows," as they were often
referred to, began to add "tattooed curiosities" in the late eighteenth
and early nineteenth century. While the circus is a space characterized
by mobility and temporariness, fairgrounds are more stable: usually
located in one spot on the city's periphery, fairgrounds were more

contained and regulated (i.e., a fair could happen only certain times of the year).

The history of the fairground in Europe is diverse and reaches back to the twelfth century with the establishment of the Bartholomew Fair in London. Hans Scheugl distinguishes two eras in which physical differences, or what he calls "menschliche Abnormitäten" (human abnormalities; Scheugl 1971, 12), attracted attention. In the early modern period, the gradual decline of the feudal system caused tremendous economic changes. The discovery of "colonies" promoted increased interest in the habits and appearance of the "travelling people." The exhibitions put on by the "travelling people" featured mainly physical deformities, with an emphasis on a monstrosity popular in the Middle Ages: giants. Secondly, performers also enjoyed immense popularity toward the end of the nineteenth century, the era of the rise of the bourgeoisie. Here, industrialization and the mechanization of labor had transformed everyday life. Germany, as a new European power, was eager to join the race for colonies and thus keenly interested in their inhabitants. Colonized territories were searched systematically for human exports for the very popular *Menschenschauen* (human exhibitions; Scheugl 1971, 158).

In Germany, the *Menschenschauen* are intrinsically connected with Carl Hagenbeck. Hagenbeck, who had made a name for himself as an animal importer, started exhibiting a group of Sami together with their reindeers in 1875 (Ames 2009, 70; Rothfels 2002, 82). After this initial success, Hagenbeck exhibited the natives of "Nubia"—for which he imported a group of people from today's Sudan. Hagenbeck himself considered his shows a "true copy of life" (quoted in Rothfels 2002, 88) and abhorred the comparison with regular fairground spectacles (Ames 2009, 70). Yet, the ethnographic exhibits were all carefully staged and the performers were taught certain activities, such as singing, dancing, and even hunting (Ames 2009, 74–75). And even though scientists such as Rudolf Virchow supported the *Menschenschauen* enthusiastically, the audience often came because the event appealed to the "most basic expectations" (Rothfels 2002, 126), and the narratives of the performers were crafted to appeal to audience's tastes. The *Menschenschau* was conceived as a semi-scientific event, oscillating between commercial fairground exhibits and serious experiments (Honold 2006, 170). Now, the focus was not only on physical deformities, even though those never fell out of favor, but also on ethnicities from the colonies, including their customs and tattoos.

At this point, European tattoos shared the stage with the tattoos imported from the colonies, but ethnic tattoos were more fanciful to the eye. At the time, European tattoos consisted mostly of disconnected images and resembled early modern emblems[7] in their rudimentary forms. They were also placed on random parts of the body, mostly the lower arm area (Schönfeld 1960, 83). In contrast, the tattoos of the exhibited "savages" were interconnected, formed strange symbols, and covered the entire body. The European performers soon developed a mixed style designed to bridge these differences: While they claimed to be European, they also purported to have encountered the uncivilized Other, and to have been tattooed forcefully on the entire body. Thus, the tattooed performers' shows were a hybrid form of the traditional circus spectacle (the display of an uncommon body) and the ethnographic exhibition, which aimed to educate people about others (the captivity tale). Of course, the images they chose belied their stories, since they were not interconnected patterns, as is common in Native American tattoos or tattoos from the South Pacific, but European and American motifs. For example, La Belle Irene's banner features the motto "Nothing without labor" in English (see figure 8.1). It would appear that these blatant imposters convinced no one but were tolerated only because they displayed their bodies at the fairground, "the true home of the European tattoo" (Oettermann in Caplan 2000, 193).

The world of the fairground has always been romanticized in German philosophy and literature (e.g., in the work of Ernst Bloch, Peter Rühmkopf). A carnivalesque place, located at the periphery of society, the fairground and its inhabitants are seen in a magical light, free from the constraints of bourgeois society. Calling the fairgrounds a "colorful, countrified fantasy," philosopher Ernst Bloch romanticizes the fairground as "a piece of borderland...for a very low price...with curious utopic meanings."[8] Referring to the allure of the fairground, he concludes: "It is a world that has not been examined for its specific areas of desire" (1959, 421). Tellingly, he calls it "a piece of borderland"— neglecting the fact that this borderland is daily life and hard labor for the performers who inhabit it. Certainly, it was not Bloch's intention to diminish the humanity of the performers, yet he too elides the fact that some of these performers had not joined the fairground by choice, but because there was no place in society for "freaks." This erasure is indicative of attitudes toward "Otherness" in the early twentieth century. And Bloch's prejudice is not any less harmful because it remains unrecognized. His text can be read as indicative of attitudes in the early twentieth century. The alleged openness toward the performers can again be explained by their otherness.

Figure 8.1 La Belle Irene. Courtesy of the Tattoo Archive, Winston-Salem, North Carolina.

To be sure, traveling people and tattooed performers could not easily be made to conform to social norms. To their bourgeois audience, they represented a threat as well as a curiosity. Whereas *Missgeburten*, that is, people who are born with deformities, could be classified as "naturally" different and could thus easily be relegated to a realm outside of society, tattooed performers are not an "absolute Other." Neither savage nor monster, the tattooed performer is as healthy and European as his or her spectators. The only thing that separates these performers from their audience is the mark on their skin. Thus, contemporary spectators must have wondered why a European, especially a German, whose nationality placed him at the pinnacle of civilization, would choose to undergo such a savage practice. I suggest that the invented captivity narratives were designed to respond to this concern. They averted the perceived threat a voluntarily tattooed body posed to the bourgeois taste and shielded the performers from aggression. La Belle Irene's tale is a prime example of this: according to her own rather unreliable account, she was born in 1870 and grew up "in the perilous jungle of Dallas, Texas" (Oettermann in Caplan 2000, 202; also Scheugl 1971, 148). Unlike many of the other performing damsels in distress who were forcibly tattooed, La Belle Irene declared that she was tattooed by her father in order to protect her from abduction and forced tattooing by the Sioux Indians. Clearly, a captivity tale such as that of La Belle Irene fulfilled two functions: it explains the presence of tattoos and bears witness to the victimization of the wearer, but it also caters to the desire for conformity among the bourgeoisie. The presence of tattoos on the body of a Westerner is logically explained, and spectators are free to revel in empathy toward the performer. Moreover, La Belle Irene's narrative plays into the German fascination with the Wild West during that time. As Eric Ames states, the Wild West was received in "many different and contradictory ways, but one aspect of the German reception stands out: the ardent embrace of fantasy" (2009, 105). Irene manipulated her audience by feeding into well-known tales à la Friedrich Gerstäcker,[9] while assuring her bourgeois followers of the validity of their own chosen way of life. Unsurprisingly, captivity tales were readily believed, as long as they were told within the confines of the fairground or the circus.

The interesting case of Annett Nerona, like that of La Belle Irene, attests to the performer's desire to reconcile her tattoos with bourgeois norms. Exhibiting her tattoos in the early 1900s, Nerona did not legitimize her tattoos through a captivity tale, but framed the exhibition of her body with the demonstration of several skills, including those of magician, snake charmer, and gymnast. Nerona made her own personal statement in the *Kulturkampf*[10] by sporting tattoos that featured famous German personalities, such as the poets Goethe and Schiller, the conservative politician Bismarck, Emperor Wilhelm II, and composer Richard Wagner (Mifflin 1997, 25; Oettermann

1975, 84; Scheugl 1975, 148). Ironically, the audience did not feel that such tattoos ridiculed bourgeois values, but rather felt confirmed in its worldview. If primitive practices were used to affirm bourgeois values, they were acceptable, especially in the realm of the fairground. We can only speculate whether Nerona's choice of tattoo was motivated by financial reasons or by a desire to please the bourgeois audience or both.

The tattooed body not only engaged the ambivalent interest of the bourgeois audience, but also captivated the artistic world. The poet Hugo Ball, for example, witnessed a performance of "Nandl, die fesche Tirolerin" (Nandl, the jaunty Tyrolean). He described his impressions as follows: "The blue velvety characters in the flesh are not unaesthetic and allow for a primitive amusement."[11] Ball's reaction is representative of that of the general population. As the choice of the adjectives "not unaesthetic" and "primitive" suggests, here too tattooed performers are relegated to the periphery of society. Again, this should not be misunderstood as a form of tolerance or even integration into society. The circus performers had no legal rights (Saltarino 1974[1895], 151) and were relegated to the fringes of society, the "borderland." At the same time, this form of intolerance is still far more accepting than the attitude that slowly gained momentum after WWI and eventually led to prohibitions, emigration, and even flaying. These cruelties would be realized through a confluence of several mutually reinforcing discourses. The most powerful among them was science.

THE TATTOO UNDER SCRUTINY: SCIENTIFIC DISCOURSES

Tattooed performers sparked the public imagination even as they inspired scientific research. In the late nineteenth century, the encounter with the marked body of the Other set off scientific inquiries that seem objective and logical at first glance, but, upon closer inspection, are characterized by the growing climate of intolerance.

The scientific reactions to tattoos can be divided into three different, yet overlapping schools of thought. The first is the discipline of anthropology. One of the earliest mentions of tattooed people occurs in Georg Forster's accounts from his travels with Captain Cook in 1780–1783 (Forster 1983[1782]). Forster's observations and conclusions are informed by earlier travel accounts of the Enlightenment. He describes tattooed people rationally and in great detail. Unlike Forster, who attempts to neither judge nor criticize, historian Heinrich Wuttke, writing a hundred years later in 1877, adopts a stance of moral superiority, although he also expresses a genuine interest in tattoos. Wuttke considers tattoos an important step in the development of signs into written language and literally attempts to read and categorize them. He sees tattoos as an early form of writing, what he calls *Urschrift*, and a marker of the development of the uncivilized masses. Convinced that "the dirty Bushman does not tattoo himself " (Wuttke 1877, 87), he concludes: "According to all of this [research], tattooing is irregularly distributed, yet very frequently present, in lower forms of life, during the initial stage of human development (96).[12] Although Wuttke is skeptical of tattoos and relegates them to a distant sphere both geographically and in terms of human evolution, his careful illustrations betray a scientific and personal fascination with the tattoo. Wuttke's blatantly racist language marks him as a true chauvinist child of his time, but he does not vilify the practice of tattooing itself.

Unlike Wuttke, natural scientist and traveler Wilhelm Joest approaches the subject of tattoos with calm discernment. Considering himself a pragmatic, he criticizes Wuttke's evolutionary explanation: "The author does not consider it right or necessary to resort to the Panthalassic Ocean,[13] primal mist and the primordial ooze, in order to explain the harrumphing, the spitting or the splotched fist of every savage" (1887, 18). Although Joest's text does not forward a plea for reason in the discussion of tattoos, he is highly critical of the criminalization of tattoos by Alexandre Lacassagne, a French criminologist, and others. Joest believes that the often stated link between criminal behavior and tattoos is a "frivolous utterance" (106), and warns purist apostles (such as Wuttke) that the popularity of the custom is more common than is assumed (104). Joest is an important dissenting voice among his fellow scientists who would like to situate tattoos in faraway lands. Yet even he maintains that tattoos are a vain practice common in underdeveloped societies: "Especially then we must consider the not tattooing as a cultural progress, as we have considered tattooing a progress from the earlier painting [of the body]" (28).

In sum, many scientists defined tattooing as a practice of faraway times, people, and places, and thus paved the ground for the criminalization and medicalization of tattoos. If tattooing is a practice of uncivilized societies, then Europeans who adorn themselves with tattoos must either be uncivilized (read: criminal) or have regressed in their developmental stage.

Paradoxically, these scientific discourses provided circus performers with socially acceptable plots for the aforementioned captivity tales. The fairground performers were supposedly not voluntarily tattooed, but were victims. Since they were white and "civilized" underneath their tattoos, they could be used to showcase indigenous peoples without forcing an encounter with the actual Other, the "savage." Much like television today, the confined space of the fairground or the circus allowed the respectable bourgeois middle class to indulge in their fascination and then walk away when they had reached a point of saturation.

The anthropological strand of scientific research soon morphed into medical and criminological theories about tattoos, with a focus on the European tattoo. A French doctor, Ernest Berchon, can be held responsible for the medicalization of the discourse on tattoos (Caplan 2009, 341). Berchon argued vehemently that tattoos endanger a person's health. Indeed, even today, horror stories of infected needles and tales of amputations link the tattoo to danger and antisocial behavior. Other medical practitioners and anthropologists, such as Dr. Rudolf Virchow and Dr. Johannes Ranke, were eager to defend circus performers and their tattoos, especially females. For example, Ranke refers to the tattoos of La Belle Irene as a garment and comments: "This pretty young woman's skin glows and has the feel of velvet. Her nakedness seems beside the point (quoted in Oettermann 2000, 82). His colleague, Dr. Virchow, stated a similar opinion in 1872 in his description of one of the displays. Instead of looking at a naked body (which would be frivolous), one " believes to see a person dressed in a tight-fitting shawl fabric. Looking at it, the sense of shame is not stirred." (Virchow and Rahnke, quoted in Arburg 2003, 415). From a modern perspective, the debate on nakedness may seem naïve, a threadbare ploy to deny the sexual titillation so obvious to the modern observer, but at the time, the display of the naked body required a justification. So-called *Sittlichkeitsvereine* (clubs to uphold moral authority) had embarked on a crusade to root out naked performances. Drawing on their medical authority, Virchow and Ranke were able to protect the performers (and satisfy their own voyeurism), at least for a while. One can only speculate about the motivations for such a vigorous defense. Possible reasons could range from a lurid enjoyment of the performances to a desire to protect objects of scientific interest.

While Virchow and Ranke defended the display of the naked body, Dr. Hugo-Ernest Luedecke developed a medical theory about "erotic tattoos": Deducing that if the strongest roosters have the most colorful feathers, most men who are tattooed will be "strong and sexually potent" (1907, 75). For Luedecke, the tattoo is a "sexual adornment" used by males to impress women. The fact that the most successful tattooed performers were women is also readily explained—they do it for a man: "In every real woman, a piece of masochism lies dormant, which is intinctively sensed by a man" (1907, 76). Luedecke's analysis of tattoos is embedded in a racial theory, and his interest in tattoos is truly global: that the untattooed individual is almost a rarity with "the libidinous East Asians, the Japanese, does not require any explanation" (78). Luedecke's theory was one of the first to link tattoos, race, and sexuality, but by no means the only one. In 1964, 53 years after Luedecke's rather absurd hypotheses, Walther Schönfeld declared that tattoos are a male phenomenon, while tattoos on females are found only on "eccentric, swanky women," prostitutes, or "respectable women" who have religious symbols engraved on their skin (1964, 66).

While Virchow's thoughts were inspired by tattooed performers, the criminologists Cesare Lombroso and Alexandre Lacassagne did not base their theories on observations at European fairgrounds. Cesare Lombroso's famous treatise *L'Uomo Delinquente* (Criminal Man) (published in 1876) is greatly indebted to the emerging field of physiognomy. He claims that his time as a young army doctor inspired his scientific endeavor. His professional practice convinced him that the only "characteristic that distinguished the honest soldier from his vicious comrade [was] the extent to which the latter was tattooed and the indecency of the designs that covered his body" (1876, xii). Lombroso argues that criminality is an atavism, a regression into primitivism, which the civilized European has overcome in his evolution. This moral defect is linked to phenotypical realizations, such as a narrow forehead, a mouth "horizontal like in apes" (66), and tattoos. Needless to say, his data were conducive to his purpose. Since Lombroso worked as a prison doctor, all the tattooed subjects he found were by definition criminal. When Lombroso's test group outside the prison also proved to have tattoos, but could not be considered criminal, Lombroso pointed out that these test subjects originated from a less civilized area in Italy where Celtic influences were still prevalent (Caplan 2009, 345).

The French school of Alexandre Lacassagne was less concerned with questions of hereditary criminals, but tried to systematize tattoos in criminals in order to develop a catalogue for the French police. Based on this classificatory system, the police would be able to draw conclusions about the criminal's "social condition or profession" (Caplan in Wetzell and Becker 2009, 342). An analysis of these discourses proves what modern readers may have suspected from the start. The voices of tattooed individuals are either completely absent or marginalized—the voice of the convicted murderer drowned out by that of the respected doctor. Upon closer inspection, ostensibly scientific findings are revealed to originate in discourses of criminalization and marginalization. Moreover, the discourse of "Otherness" in the sciences was in line with an increasing intolerance in German social and political life. The colonial project that had started out as identity-forming through encountering the other now turned into discourses of racial superiority. Even before WWI, circus people and fairground performers were suspect, but the perception of danger was also mixed with admiration and curiosity. In the post–WWI era, however, tattooed performers were increasingly considered to be a threat. This shift in perception can be explained if one looks at cultural, technological, and political changes in Germany.

THE WILD WEIMAR YEARS AND THE LURE OF LAW AND ORDER

Oettermann's thesis, that industrialization is the underlying topic of tattooing in the early twentieth century (1975, 72), has barely been challenged. Indeed, working in assembly lines and factories allowed for little individualism and self-expression. Yet, it is doubtful that there were enough tattooed workers to truly threaten what Oettermann calls the "discourse of the powerful." Industrialization and the resulting urbanization, however, did play a large role in discourses on the body. Due to a lack of political unity and infrastructure, Germany's industrial revolution was not to take off until the 1850s (Tilly 1993; Wehler 1995). Capitalism in the early twentieth century then was closely intertwined with colonial discourses, cultural transformations, and political upheavals in post–WWI Germany.

These changes were most visible on the body: from physical deformations due to factory work, malnourishment, and disease to fashion choices for a growing middle class and table manners, the human body is a reliable seismograph for changes in society. As Michel Foucault noted, culture is inscribed onto our bodies in various ways (1977, 26).

Needless to say, tattooed people were only one group that slowly but certainly became marginalized, discriminated against, and finally exterminated. One factor that informed changes in the perception of the body was political instability. During WWI and the Weimar Years (1918–1933), the experience of changing laws and norms was palpable. One of these changes was the Bracht Ordinance of 1932, which prohibited tattooed performers from exhibiting themselves. This law literally erased the public physical presence of performers. Moreover, the sense of insecurity and disorientation was enhanced by the growing economic misery of the postwar years. Historian Andrew Lees argues that the "rise of the Großstädte (large cities) exacerbated a moral crisis" (2009, 85), and this crisis was in turn met with activism, mostly from conservative forces. The fight against moral decay identified as its target the body. In the late nineteenth century, the idea of a healthy, clean body as an essential part of Germanness had begun to permeate society (Sax and Kuntz 1992, 6). The Turnverein[14] is one example of a movement with such an underlying philosophy. It was founded by Friedrich Ludwig "Turnvater" Jahn in 1811 and had become an established institution by the end of the century. Turnvater Jahn was a complex and morally ambiguous character with both democratic and anti-Semitic leanings, whose idea of physical prowess was abused by the Nazis. On the other end of the democratic spectrum was the socialist-leaning Wandervogel Youth. Responding to pauperism and fast urbanization, the Wandervogel Youth movement sought solace in nature through hiking, camping, and the joyful chanting of patriotic folk songs. In order to fight decadence and the decay of modern life, the temperance movement campaigned against alcohol and for a healthy family life in several industrial cities (Lees 2009, 97–100).

Urbanization and industrialization also motivated cultural changes. As early as 1908, Viennese architect Adolf Loos translated Lombroso's ideas of atavism into the realm of culture and specifically the arts. Loos was deeply concerned with the apparel of the modern man (women are likened to savages and children and therefore in a different category altogether). According to Loos, dress must reflect the process of civilization. His treatise "Ornament and Crime," written in 1908, became a foundational text for the modernist architecture movement in the early twentieth century. Here, Loos states, "Modern man considers an untattooed visage more beautiful than a tattooed one, even if the tattoo originated from Michelangelo himself. The same is true for the nightstand" (1908, 108). To Loos, tattoos are to the skin what ornaments are to buildings and furniture: superfluous and relics of a time past.

While Loos wanted clean and pure modern art and architecture, popular media promoted clean and pure bodies. The growing popularity of film, along with the emergence of early media tycoons, in particular, Alfred Hugenberg, German nationalist and later minister in Hitler's cabinet, also had an impact on the perception of bodies. The film industry was not only a factor in the decreasing popularity of fairgrounds and circuses; it was also a medium for the promulgation of nationalistic ideas and concepts of the body. In National Socialist films, such as Leni Riefenstahl's *Olympia* (1938), bodies were shown to be athletic, healthy, and strong, and with the exception of a few avant-garde and communist publishers and filmmakers who advanced their own agenda, these images and ideologies prevailed. The body became a metaphor for the German nation, and those who did not conform to the ideal were deemed "unhealthy" and undesirable members of the German community.

The Bracht Ordinance of 1932 was only the beginning of the end of tattooed performers in Germany. Their trade, now considered a "display of obscene human abnormalities" (8-Uhr Blatt [Berlin], quoted in Oettermann 1975, 56), was forbidden. Deprived of their livelihood, many saw themselves forced into exile or vanished into concentration camps. Survivors of the camps reported that some guards would flay prisoners. The Buchenwald camp survivor Edouard-Jose Laval, for example, described this gruesome practice:

> It is true that tattooed prisoners were murdered and their skin tanned. I myself saw this happen to 200 prisoners who at the very moment of their liberation, as they were about to board the evacuation trucks, were executed because of their tattoos. In order to preserve the freshness of their tattoos, the executioners made haste to remove the skin before the body turned cold. (quoted in Aroneanu 1996, 106)

The report of the Supreme Headquarters of the American Liberation Forces further documents that tattooed skins were turned into lampshades or wallets (Aroneanu, 1996, 107; Whitlock 2011). The tattooed skin of the non-Aryan enemy was treated like animal skin and turned into an everyday commodity. Body decorations, once a mark of individuality, became harbingers of the total destruction of the tattooed individual. A former marker of creativity and play had become a decorative accessory in the Nazi *Raritätenkabinett* (cabinet of rarities).

Of course, these changes relating to the body or body image and the transition from subconscious prejudice to open aggression did not happen overnight. Rather, these were long and uneven processes. *Sittlichkeitsvereine* (clubs to uphold morality) had protested the exhibition of the naked bodies of tattooed ladies for decades; chauvinist clubs had been virulently anti-Semitic for at least a century, and the political right had flirted with Germany's special role and its destined *Sonderweg*[15] for a long time. During the Weimar era, however, these extremist tendencies combined with political, technological, and economic changes gave rise to a general perception of danger that the Nazi regime appeased through conformity and the repression of any form of deviation from group norms.

THE TATTOO IN CONTEMPORARY GERMANY

Early twentieth-century discourses about the body did not simply disappear but rather inform contemporary discourses on tattoos in Germany. Whereas in America, tattoos soon became equated with patriotism and a positive can-do masculinity in the 1930s (Atkinson 2003, 37), the German discourse on tattoos never shed the association with criminality. Today's discourses not only echo the early twentieth-century discourses on criminality and tattoos, they are also combined with remnants of early twentieth-century discourses on healthy bodies. Finally, tattoos are connected to a fear of globalization. Instead of the savage from former colonies, today's tattooed body fulfills the function of a foil for fears of globalization and a potential loss of (German) identity. The tattooed body embodies the process of globalization: tattooing as a foreign, imported practice, the myth goes, takes over and eradicates the original, German-European culture. The current discourse on globalization therefore mirrors the discourse on modernity in the early twentieth century: the fear of social instability, and of loss of values and identity is certainly not a new phenomenon. This line of thought obviously fails to understand that tattooing is *not* a practice hailing from exotic faraway places, but has a long history in Europe and Germany; in short, it is as German as pretzel dough.

After WWII, the tattoo experienced a revival in diverse, often American-influenced subcultures, such as heavy-metal bikers or the punk scene. As those subcultures were often perceived as subversive elements, the same discourse on tattoos that had informed the early twentieth century was applied. As a result, the tattoo did not shed its association with criminality. For example, in the former GDR (1949–1990), tattooed individuals had to report to the authorities once a month, and were examined in order to prevent further tattoos (Feige 2003, 295).

During the 1990s, the public attitude toward tattoos began to change. Once more, alienation gave way to fascination. The fall of the Berlin Wall and the dissolution of the former GDR inspired many East Germans to adorn their bodies in order to celebrate their new freedom (Feige 2003, 295). While East Germans tattooed their bodies, the West experienced the rise of techno music, a subculture that celebrated dancing and corporeality. Techno culture was also accompanied by a growing interest in tattoos. The style of these tattoos, called "tribals,"[16] testifies to the apolitical self-understanding of the techno movement. The tribal tattoos are reminiscent of the tattoos of the Pacific islands, but, unlike the latter, they are devoid of any traditional meaning. Tribals "perfectly adapt their form to the body. Tribals are like music: in tune with the body" (Feige 2003, 314–315).

The use of tattoos in advertising also contributes to their renewed popularity in contemporary Germany. Many brands use tattoos to catch the eye, oftentimes relying on strategies familiar from early twentieth-century circuses and fairgrounds: the exploitation of sensational and sexual connotations. A prime example would be Volkswagen's 2010 advertisement of their SUV model, the VW Touareg.[17] VW, Teutonic in name and image, featured ads depicting a young man with a scorpion tattooed on his bicep and a young woman with a butterfly on her tailbone, both positioned against the backdrop of sublime African scenery and accompanied by the slogan "One with nature. Touareg." That a car manufacturer, known for its technical finesse, claims to be close to nature is ironic in and of itself. If we remember the early days of the company as a manufacturer for the National Socialists, who persecuted and brutally killed off tattooed people, the irony inherent in this ad becomes almost grotesque. VW presents itself as both worldly (their cars are everywhere in the world) and yet grounded (they are "one with nature," after all) even as it exploits exoticized images of the Other for commercial purposes.

German newspapers also rely on tattoos to lure young readers. The *Süddeutsche Zeitung*, one of Germany's oldest and most highly regarded newspapers, featured an ad with a tattooed, muscular fakir and his fire breath, underlined by the slogan: "Warme Worte gibts woanders" (Search for warm words elsewhere). In 2008, the news magazine *Focus* promoted its new online version of *Focus Campus* with a one-page advertisement showing a naked, heavily tattooed woman and the words "kostenlos. Sexy. Das pralle Studentenleben" (Free. Sexy. Student life to the fullest). Here the ambiguity of the message is especially pronounced: both the *Süddeutsche Zeitung* and *Focus* define themselves as authentic, reliable sources of news, but they seek to market their supposedly unbiased reporting by relying on images that for the last 60 years have been poster children of discourses of deviance, criminality, and subversion. All these ads are extremely gendered and sexualized, and they fulfill a function similar to that of the posters of the tattooed performers. As journalist Marcel Feige explains, tattoos in advertisement are not used to promote a more tolerant society.

"Tattoos...catch the eye, and attention is the paramount objective in advertising. Tattoos as eye-catcher are virtually predestined for use in advertising" (Feige 2003, 380). Again, it is not tolerance or the constantly propagated German *Weltoffenheit* (openness toward the world) and multiculturalism that create interest in tattoos, but their appeal of "Otherness" and exoticism.

During the 1990s and the early 2000s, the tattoo served as a site of projection for whatever product one needed to sell, or as a symbol of a newly discovered love of the body in the techno community. Now, instead of playing with hidden desires and the lure of exoticism, tattoos are again explicitly and unambiguously associated with marginalization. Gabriela Walde, a journalist for the conservative newspaper *Die Welt*, for example, declared in 2007: "The tattoo has returned to its origins: the lower class" (2007).[18] The ever-vigilant source of information, *Bild*—Germany's most sold yellow-press newspaper—even claimed that oxides found in tattoo colors can cause "Allergien, Entzündungen und sogar *Krebsgeschwüre*" (Allergies, inflammations and even cancerous growths) (Gast 2010). Ironically, the image that accompanies the article is that of a young woman, with a colorful tattoo, in a provocative pose. Whether this image expresses the acute medical danger *Bild* is trying to convey is doubtful. Tattoos, then, are once again medicalized, criminalized, and stigmatized.

In 2009, a quantitative study from the University of Leipzig attempted to establish a correlation between unemployment and tattoos. Indeed, among the age group of 24–34, 32 percent of the respondents were both unemployed and tattooed. Among the younger age group of 14–24, only 26 percent were unemployed and tattooed. It would however be unwise to come to the conclusion that young Germans find work easier and get tattooed less. As one needs parental permission to get tattooed until the individual turns 18, the prevalence of tattoos in this age group automatically will be lower. While it is common ethnographic practice to compare newly collected data with socioeconomic facts, one cannot help but wonder why employment would be such an important factor in the evaluation of the tattooed community. Moreover, the study did not differentiate between various forms of unemployment (short- term vs. long-term unemployment, unemployment caused by illness, and seasonal unemployment); it also neglected to mention that, with an unemployment rate of 7.7 percent in 2009 (OECD), the probability of finding unemployed people with tattoos would have been rather high. Hence, the study confirms the stereotype of the unemployed, lazy tattooed antisocial, who lives at the periphery of society.

In public discourse, from the news media to the entertainment industry, tattoos are also used to define and strengthen gender roles. For example, German party musician and "Kaiser von Mallorca" Mickie Krause declared tattooed women unattractive and uppity. In his popular song "Arschgeweih"—colloquial for a tattoo above the tailbone—he voices his antipathy against women with tattoos: "From 1000 Euro net on, they become presumptuous. They get a tattoo because they like it. I want a woman without a tramp stamp, without iso kay."[19]

Finally, the widely viewed German soap opera "Gute Zeiten—Schlechte Zeiten" featured a tattooed woman in a few episodes. Mary, a tattooist, who previously tattooed the character of John Bachmann, runs into John in a club and unambiguously indicates her wish for a sexual encounter. When he replies that he has a girlfriend, she smiles "Oh, I know. I am not jealous" (Episode 4318).[20] Mary embodies the stereotype of the morally depraved tattooed temptress; she has short, dyed hair, and dresses in a slightly masculine fashion. Her character contrasts with John's heavily pregnant girlfriend Caroline, who is blue-eyed, has long blond hair, and is looking forward to her role as housewife and mother. While all these examples may seem amusing, the response mechanisms of society to the tattoo are similar to those in the early twentieth century: the use of tattoos in advertisement is not indicative of increased tolerance, but rather the opposite. It marks the tattoo as different and fascinating, a sign of "Otherness." In TV shows and posters, as in the fairground, tattoos are on display, but they remain at a comfortable distance. One can look at the Other, but does not have to integrate it into one's own reality. Furthermore, the re-location of the tattoo into the "lower class" echoes the Lombrosian discourse of the early twentieth century. While the social connotations of tattoos have not changed, the response to tattooed women is arguably different. Ads still use nudity to sell products, just as the posters of La Belle Irene and her colleagues sold performances, but the vilification of tattooed women is a new form of culturally bequeathed sexism. In the past, a tattooed woman was either a prostitute or a dumb Dora who was tattooed for the love of a man. Now, tattooed women encounter open prejudice and intolerance. They are portrayed as full of "*Übermut* (presumptuousness)" as carefree home-wreckers, or cold-blooded killers as in Robert Schwendtke's movie *Tattoo* (2002). Women with tattoos are perceived as a threat. To be sure, these discourses are echoed in other countries as well and are globalized in many respects—the rhetoric of pure and unstained bodies, however, is specifically German and evokes the Nazi image of a pure, healthy German body.

All these different trends crystallized in 2010 when Christian Wulff became president of the state. The media paid more attention to his wife than his political career and aptitude for office. Not only did she have children from previous (unmarried) relationships, but she also had visible tattoos. While the aforementioned *Bild* decided to highlight her skills as loving mother and down-to-earth supportive wife, the *Frankfurter Allgemeine Sonntagszeitung* called her tattoos "a banner of asociality" (Wagner 2010).[21] Germany's self-appointed court jester, comedian Harald Schmidt, commented: "The Wulffs are our new glamour couple: They are a patchwork-family, she is tattooed. Many don't call them 'the Wulffs' anymore but 'the white-trash Guttenbergs'" ("Die Harald-Schmidt-Show" 2010).[22] It would appear that the bourgeois attitude has changed but little since the days of the circuses and sideshows. When confronted with nontraditional family models and the marked, "wild" body, the guardians of morality and values, the media, are quick to declare these phenomena symptoms of degeneracy and lower-class status.

CONCLUSION

This chapter traced the popularity of the tattoo in the early years of the twentieth century in Germany and its rapid fall from grace in the late 1920s to cruel intolerance during the National Socialist era and ambivalence today. While the tattoo was never part of the bourgeois strata of society, it was fascinating to scientists around the turn of the century. Initially descriptive and sometimes even admiring in tone, the articles of the various scientists progressively become more openly intolerant. I argue that the growing intolerance against the tattoo is part of a general sociopolitical movement toward intolerance and hostility. In the second part of the chapter, I have described the development of those discourses on bodies after WWII, in particular post-unification (1990).

Even though tattoos are now more common in Germany, they do not go unnoticed and, as this chapter has shown, they still incite a multitude of discourses about acceptable and unacceptable bodies. In many ways, current discourses mirror those of the early twentieth century. If one substitutes "globalization" for "modernity," the underlying fears of a loss of values, tradition, and identity are strikingly similar. As journalist and author Kurt Tucholsky wrote in 1928: "It is a great mistake to believe that problems of humankind are solved. They are left behind by bored humankind."[23] To be sure, tattoos are not problems and certainly not "problems of humankind," but the discourse on tattoos is. In the current (global) neoconservative backlash, we might do well to reevaluate discourses of tolerance and corporeality. Debates on what is German should not be influenced by skin color or religious affiliation, and mothering abilities should not be measured on the basis of whether one looks like a perfect poster mom. If Germany wishes to play a major role among the world's leading nations, it is time for Germans to open up to a plurality of opinions, family values, religious affiliations, and body types, tattooed or not.

Notes

1. I deliberately choose to not take the immediate post-WWII years into account, for several reasons: since the tattoo continued to be associated with anti-social behavior and criminality in West Germany and was relegated to the periphery of society, few documents exist. In the former GDR/East Germany (1949–1990), tattooing was considered a crime against the socialist community (as bodies were not supposed to be individualized). The GDR produced a large catalogue of tattooed individuals, but, unfortunately, it is almost impossible to view these records. Moreover, the discourses on tattooed performers in the early twentieth century and the discourses on the tattooed body as the threatening globalized Other become most similar after 1990.
2. The so-called Scottish Monks derive their name from the Latin *scoti*, and were British monks who came to Germany in the tenth century, the early MiddleAge s.
3. The monogram "JHS" or "IHS" for Jesus Christ derives from the Greek abbreviation of Jesus' name, denoting the first three letters of the Greek name of Jesus, *iota-eta-sigma*, or ΙΗΣ. Because the medieval transcription of the letter iota varies between "J" and "I," both monograms "IHS" and "JHS" can be found in medieval texts.
4. As she was born in the Afrikaans-speaking part of South Africa, often her name is also spelled as Saartje Bahram. Unfortunately, Sarah's birth name is not known. For further reading, see: Crais and Scully 2009; Holmes 2007; and Qureshi 2011.
5. *Macht und Freiheit, Recht und Sitte, // Klarer Geist und scharfer Hieb, // Zügeln dann aus starker Mitte // Jeder Selbstsucht wilden Trieb, // und es mag am deutschen Wesen // Einmal noch die Welt genesen.* In *Deutschlands Beruf,* 1861. (*Power and freedom, law and morals//clear spirit and sharp strokes// will discipline from the middle// the wild sprouts of egoism,//and the German spirit one day shall heal the world.*) These lines were written in 1861, but became wildly popular, mainly the last stanza. While Geibel's poetry is tinged with ideas of *Bildung* (education, broadly conceived), and was meant to edify Germans to adhere to the described ideals to be a mental role model to its European neighbors, his lines were interpreted by his contemporaries as a political battle cry for colonialism.

6. Captivity narratives have the common theme of abduction of a white, "civilized" person by the native population of a colonized country. Often the abducted person is tested in their faith and beliefs in the civilized world and experiences adversity (such as forced tattooing). The historical background for those tales is the struggle between Great Britain and France in the territories of the United States. The French colonists and their Native American allies would abduct settlers and vice versa. This sparked the genre of captivity narratives that became popular and was adapted to other colonized territories. Linda Colley (2004) and Pauline Turner Strong (1999) were the first to analyze constructions of self-identity and otherness through those captivity tales.

7. For more detailed information about the connection between emblems and modern tattoos, see Sabine Mödersheim's (1996) groundbreaking article.

8. Unless indicated otherwise, the translations from German are mine. Page numbers refer to the German edition of the work.

9. Friedrich Gerstäcker's (1816–1872) diaries and novels describing his travels through North America were wildly popular in Germany at the time. They certainly fostered the "colonial fantasies" I mentioned earlier and triggered an excitement for the American West in the German imagination.

10. "Kulturkampf" literally translates into "culture struggle." The term is used to describe the struggle between Bismarck and the Catholic Church between 1871 and 1878. Bismarck's original idea to subjugate what he perceived as "different culture," Catholicism, escalated into open conflict with the Vatican. Finally, a separation between church and state was achieved, and in an attempt to not lose all power, Germany's Catholics organized themselves into a political party. Nerona's tattoos seem to indicate where her loyalty was.

11. Quote in the original: "Die blauen Samtfiguren im Fleisch sind nicht unschönundge währene inp rimitivesV ergnügen"(64).

12. Quote in the original: "Es ist das Tatauiren nach alledem ungleich verbreitet, aber im niederen Lebenstande, auf den Anfangsstufen der Bildung, wenn auch nicht durchgängig, doch sehr häufig vorhanden."

13. The Panthalassic Ocean was the single global ocean surrounding the continent Pangaea, the supercontinent formed about 300 million years ago, before the continents began to drift apart. Weary of Wuttke's almost mystical explanations, Joest resorts to hyperbole and irony in his remarks.

14. A sports club to promote exercise and health as countermovement to urbanization.

15. *Sonderweg,* literally meaning "special path," is a theory that explains the unique path that a country took because of political, social, and economic reasons to reach a point in history. In the late nineteenth century and early twentieth century, German conservative and right wing forces considered Germany "special" (read: superior) due to its diverse history. Hence

Germany was to be a central European power between Russia on the East and France and England in Western Europe.

16. For examples of tribal tattoos, see http://pinterest.com/tattoostattoo/tribal-tattoos/.

17. The images discussed here may be found at online at: http://adsoftheworld.com/media/print/volkswagen_touareg_scorpion; http://adsoftheworld.com/media/print/volkswagen_touareg_butterfly; and http://autoadvert.tumblr.com/post/5763414261/vw-one-with-nature.

18. Quote in the original: "Das Tattoo ist wieder dort angekommen, wo es herkommt: In der Unterschicht."

19. Quote in the original: "So ab tausend Euro netto, überkommt sie Übermut. Frauen machen sich ein Tattoo, denn das finden sie gut. (...) Ich will ne Frau ohne Arschgeweih, ohne ist ok."

20. Quote in the original: "Das weiss ich doch. Ich bin nicht eifersüchtig."

21. Quote in the original: "Ehrenbanner der Asozialität."

22. Schmidt's comment compared the Wulff family to another member of Parliament, Theodor zu Guttenberg, and his wife, Stefania, who embodied the perfect conservative family (young, dynamic, but committed to tradition). Ironically, Guttenberg could not keep up his squeaky clean façade. Due to plagiarism in his dissertation he resigned in early 2011. In late 2011, Wulff also became the target of a scandal—he had borrowed large sums of money from friends and was forced to resign.

23. Quote in the original: "Es ist ein großer Irrtum, zu glauben, dass Menschheits-Probleme ›gelöst‹ werden. Sie werden von einer gelangweilten Menschheit liegen gelassen" (Tucholsky 1978 [1928], 133).

9

FRAGMENTS: STORIES OF AN-OTHER LIFE

(PersonalRe flection)

Anisha Gautam

If the body has a narrative, *is* a narrative, mine is fatally fragmented. This in itself is not significant, for none of us can escape those first fractures. What is significant, however, is my experience of living this body in this world. That is why I tell my story, because no two stories are the same, just as no two bodies are the same. Because stories— entangled in themselves, in each other—simply by being told and re-told open up more spaces for us to occupy, however briefly.

This is the story of my existence in my global world of middle-class, heterosexual privilege; one tempered, nonetheless, by the "problems" of my race and my gender. Morphology beyond my control tacitly used to enlist me into a war I neither started nor knew how to fight. As a result I've lived most of my life in intense competition with my own body in an attempt to wear it down once and for all, to force it to become lighter, easier, transcendent. Something and someone else.

It wasn't always this way. I can sense, if not remember, the way I was before: fat and happy in my grandmother's lap, running irreverent through the streets of Kathmandu. I have a memory. I am six years old and standing in front of my grandmother's mirror, resplendent in a frilly red dress, my curly hair defiantly framing my curious colored face. It's a new dress and I am proud. The world is right, certainty runs through me, through my legs, my bulging stomach, my plump fingers. I am beautiful and I am whole.

But that was a long time ago. The lingering arc of a different tra-jectory, trajectories unwinding just beyond my child's reach. Looking into the mirror that day I was unaware that my certainty wouldn't last. I was unaware either of the privileges that kept me from the other truths of the world, or of the burden of patriarchal colonial legacy I would soon bear, pulling me in all directions at once. I was unaware that I, my soft, gendered, colored body was already overdetermined by history.

We left Kathmandu less than a year later, bound for Australia. The Great Southern Land: just like that, father says it, like a proper name that attests to its own authority. And to this day, over and above all that has happened, I still think of this country—my home—as a mythical place of unimaginable, unfettered freedom.

Yet if I arrived in Australia so, in the blindness of innocence, it didn't take long for the awareness to set in that here things were different. I was different. And visibly so, as though the spaces I occupied had abruptly been flooded with light. It was a kind of ontological shock that drew me, finally, out of myself and into the world. And there I was reflected on the questioning faces of passersby, not as I thought I was, but as someone I didn't even know existed. Not able to understand just yet that what I was looking at was an image already refracted through specific histories of patriarchy and colonialism.

I imbibed difference without conscious awareness or choice, like a pure fluid action that arrested my agency. So I was not able then to articulate its social and political consequences. But I was wise enough to recognize it.

My body, my narratives, thereafter fragments, fragments of fragments. Each fragment both a part of me and wholly me at the same time.

* * *

I am at the beach, like innumerable, unremarkable times before, languid. Momentarily blinded by the crack of sunlight on water, I glance down at myself. And in that moment (or a moment just like it, I don't remember, it's not important) I can no longer see myself because I am no longer there, not entirely. I am flesh—unruly, abject flesh. Flesh that erupts wildly and willfully from where I think I am solely to mark me as different. I have never before noticed this perversity, nor my own burning consciousness of it. In that moment, though, my life is changed irrevocably, as is my relationship to the emerald shoreline I'd adored only months (weeks, days) before. From now on I will be caught by a hyper-awareness of being always in the gaze—both unforgiving and disinterested—of the beautiful bodies that lie burning in the sand, impossibly flat, thin and tanned. Even my earliest memories of artless days spent at the beach, I notice, are tainted by this future event; this excruciating pain I will come to feel at having to bare myself in front of others. The young girl in the red dress with her Medusa hair is gone and there, in her place, I stand.

* * *

I am at Girl Guides.[1] *It is a couple of months after I've arrived in Sydney and I want to make friends. Once a week for an entire year I persist, even after the first day when I am named, shamed, by the little girl who would never be my friend: "fat and shit colored." I can't see it right away, the way that my skin and my fat will work together against me. Or, rather, will be* made to work *together against me. All I can sense, instinctively, is that I am marked not once but many times over. And unlike some differences, mine are unavoidable, etched as they are into my skin.*

My skin, that which had once fit so well suddenly feels unnatural: too bright, too dark, too exposed. Raw. Tight as though it suddenly can't contain all that I have been made to become; unbound as though I have shrunk, become too small in this new world of differentiated, hierarchized color. I am haunted, haunting, caught bodily where I don't want to be.

* * *

Alone in the night I flick through smuggled copies of Cosmo *and* Cleo. *I haven't yet read* The Beauty Myth *or* Black Looks, *I don't yet know about ideology and discourse. I don't even really understand sexism and racism beyond the faint stirrings of a deep psychic dis-ease that is slowly vying for my attention. It will be years before I am that woman who is asked time and time again by men on the street, in the clubs, wanting to know how I like it and am I as wild as they think I am? And hey, why are you getting so angry, isn't that a compliment? Uppity bitch.*

*So on that night I buy it, the message with the magazine. I look to find myself there in images of the astounding amalgams of parts reconstructed to resemble women. I had two choices, it seemed. I could be the emaciated, asexual white woman held in servitude to the very commodities she's being paid to sell. Or the dark Other of fantasy, the sexual savage, the animal waiting,*w anting, *to be broken. One or the Other.*

No, not really One, only the Other. An imperative masquerading as a choice.

To this day, I think they are uncanny, these women. Both same, like each other, and different, unlike me. Both human, like me, and inanimate, like each other. An ambivalence that remains unresolved as long as

I don't look too closely, as long as we don't hear the rattling cages behind their pixelated faces. I sit and wonder where such women exist and how I can be, not like them, but they themselves.

* * *

I am standing in front of the fridge and a picture of myself taken at a school dance. I am, I think, unforgivably fat. I make a commitment to start exercising and eating "right." In a couple of months I've lost 22 lbs. But something is wrong. I'm still fat.

I can't mark the moment when that line was crossed, but it was, and there in place of self-care was self-obsession, an inability to stop. One more mile, two more miles. On a treadmill, on a bicycle, in the pool, blinded by shiny, plastic bodies (Madonna, Beyoncé, Jennifer, Jennifer, Jennifer— how many are there?). Bodies no longer whole but grotesquely dismembered: biceps, triceps, glutes, abs, backs, quads, and calves. Light-skinned pieces of bodies, fragments of bodies. Attainable, I am sure, through caffeine-fueled sessions of chin-ups, pull-ups, push-ups under flickering, gray fluorescent lights, in the early morning as the gym begins to stir and again later as it winds down for the night.

At home it continues. Kitchen scales, measuring cups, every morsel marked, cauterized, sterilized so that it no longer resembles food, but perfect portions of pain to be overcome so that I may, in turn, overcome myself. Later I stand at the sink wondering how it would feel to throw it back up. I'm not ill or weak like all those other girls, those with "real" problems, "real" disorders. I'm in control, under control, I can stop when I want. It's not the same. It's not the same.

The unbearable weight of idealized images a constant reminder of my deviance, an incessant call to turn against my dark fat, to binge and purge, in the mistaken belief that it was the food I consumed that needed expelling rather than the false idols of the beauty myth.

* * *

According to the dominant narrative, globalization is the unfurling of the world, the process of the local becoming the global, the production of possibilities unimagined. What they don't tell you is that such possibilities are not allocated equally. We may all, in some sense, circulate in the same global space-time, but the way we live our bodies, ourselves, depends on our individual and collective relationship to specific structures of power. Thus the privileges of globalization to the few, including myself, is the oppression of globalization to the many,

many others for whom it is an endless negotiation of the line between hunger and satiety, danger and safety.

In the very Western story I tell here, one in which globalization is strongly felt as an increasing commodity fetishism within mass culture, my body is both powerful and powerless. I have health, wealth, and education, but I am also gendered and raced in particular and peculiar ways. I am that person, that body used to delineate the boundaries of the system by safeguarding the place of the absolute Other. But I am also the forbidden Other who must give herself to be consumed so that the West can explore, in safety, all that it abjects. Thus, while it in itself did not lead to my self-dissolution, globalization did speed up and intensify the processes that recoded my sign as eroticized, exoticized flesh—and enacted my fragmentation—by speeding up and intensifying the movement of images and ideas across the globe. From where I stand, the diversification of such images does not feel like a true diversification, for there are no real options being offered. No, beneath the cold cleanliness and coherence of such image-bodies remains the pull of that same dirty war. Artfully altered, they travel the world to settle in our stomachs, undigested, attempting to make us someone else.

I had no choice but to resist. Because when you're marked as different, every movement of every sinew in your body, every decision transcends the personal to become an intensely political act. Ironically, it was the very process that made of my body a "problem" that in turn gave me both the weapons and the will to fight back. Living this body has allowed me to develop what Gloria Anzaldúa calls "*la facultad*": a sensitivity, a mode of being "excruciatingly alive to the world" developed by those who are marginalized (2007 [1997], 60). It is the capacity to understand the unsaid in hostile exchanges, curious questions, ubiquitous comments about origins and traditions. It is the ability to say the right words to alleviate anger and break through the fear of difference that binds people. It may be a sensitivity acquired through the loss of a certain perspective, a certain innocence, but that is a small price to pay for this gift, humbly accepted, of being able to call the world to account by simply *being*.

It took the words of the women who have come before me, like Anzaldúa—poets, writers, essayists, theorists—to allow me to finally understand intellectually something I'd always known instinctively: that power surges and gathers, unbidden; inscribes itself on bodies in precise and peculiar ways such that what is mine can never be yours. But I have also learnt that power is neither unidirectional nor static, but exists as ether, traces, and trajectories. And as Michel Foucault reminds us, power inheres in every being, every action, waiting to be realized. What we need to do individually together is reach for that potential; bend thought to the task of social transformation by consciously engaging with the dominant narratives that seek to colonize us. It is only then that we will be able to work toward the displacement of the interval that keeps us from ourselves and each other.

*   *   *

I am standing in a tattoo parlor in downtown Sydney, encased in the silent pain of seasoned "inkers" and the anxiety of new initiates. I hold in my hand a representation of the Celtic triple crescent: the virgin, the mother, and the crone. This will be my first step at re-engaging my body in a meaningful way, my first step in the fight to forge an embodied identity that defies the emptied-out images offered to women as legitimate choices. Because to mark your body permanently, whatever the method, is an act of alchemy, transforming the invisible flows of the discourses that surround us into visible, material symbols of enunciation. So I tattooed and I pierced, I wounded myself freely, to cover those that were inflicted on me unwillingly—each wounding a carefully articulated mark of who I wanted to be and what I wanted the world to see. That first act and those that came afterwards remain, even today, not a symbol of a final victory or revelation, but a symbol of my choice not to be co-opted wholesale into the machinery. Years later, again, I would stand in the same tattoo parlor with Medusa in my hands, to reclaim some sense of that six-year-old girl I used to be.

NOTE

1. Girl Guides, founded in the United Kingdom in the early twentieth century, is a parallel organization to the US-based Girl Scouts.

10

"*A Mover la Colita*": Zumba Dance-Fitness in Mexico and Beyond

DianaBr enscheidtge n. Jost

Introduction

During the last few years Zumba has become one of the main fitness programs promoted worldwide. Despite its relatively recent emergence in the 1990s, Zumba, together with Pilates and yoga, "is proving to be a mainstay program for fitness centers around the world" (Woods 2011, 41). *USA Today*, for example, includes it in the top-ten list of fitness trends in the United States for the year 2012, according to a poll by the American College of Sports Medicine (Lloyd 2011).

Living in northern Mexico, I encountered the Zumba craze in my own neighborhood, where motivated instructors offered classes every evening for just a few pesos. Female friends and neighbors already experienced in Zumba firmly supported my interest in taking part in the class and some of them told me that it would be a perfect opportunity for me, a European living in Mexico, to learn more about Latin American and Mexican music and, most importantly, to dance or move my body in a Latin American way. Although I thought myself to already have quite an understanding of Latin American dances, especially those danced among my friends and family at local *fiestas* (parties) or *bodas* (weddings), the prospect of enhancing my dancing or movement abilities together with training my body appealed to me.

But what was moving in a Latin American or a Mexican way supposed to mean? Was Zumba a Latin American or Mexican fitness routine Mexicans could identify with? And how was it possible that my neighbors in Mexico and fitness enthusiasts all over the world, including friends and family back in Germany, similarly enjoyed participating in Zumba classes at the same time? How do the Latin American aspect of Zumba, its body and movement ideal, and the global appeal of Zumba fit together?

This article is based on my experience as a participant in Zumba classes organized in the neighborhood I'm currently living in, in Hermosillo, Mexico, as well as regular observation for about a year of classes taking place in two public parks in the same city. Examining the link between Zumba's global and local appeal, its international Latin American image and regional success in Mexico, my work strongly builds on the analysis of international media sources (mainly from the United States, Britain, and Mexico) including Zumba Fitness's own homepage. Regarding the situation in Mexico, I further include information obtained while interviewing two Zumba instructors in Hermosillo. In the broader context of the discussion on globalization, transnationalism, and culture held at least since the 1990s (Appadurai 1996; Barber 1996; Hannerz 1996), including that linked with Latin American culture (García Canclini 2001), I've decided to focus on the concept of "glocalization" as analytical lens. Coined by Roland Robertson (1995) drawing on Japanese business theory, the reference to processes of glocalization will help to describe the simultaneous appearance of globalizing and localizing aspects in the current worldwide spread of Zumba.

A Short History of Zumba

In trying to understand more about Zumba's success, I first had to investigate what it actually was and how and where it originated, a task that turned out to be quite easy due to the widespread repetition of what one might call the "origin myth" of Zumba. Thus investigating Zumba's history, one immediately comes across the name of Alberto or "Beto" Pérez, the Colombian fitness instructor who is known to have developed this practice more or less by chance. As the official Zumba website tells interested readers, facts that are also regularly repeated in articles or written descriptions at various fitness clubs offering Zumba:

> Beto's life took an unexpected turn one fateful day in the mid-'90s when he darted off to teach an aerobics class and forgot his traditional aerobics music. He improvised using his own mix of music from tapes he had in his backpack (salsa and merengue music he grew up with). Spontaneously he created a new kind of dance-fitness, one that focused

on letting the music move you (instead of counting reps over the music). Energy electrified the room; people couldn't stop smiling. His class loved it! And on that day, a revolutionary new fitness concept was born—the Zumba® Fitness-Party. (Zumba Fitness 2012).

In 2001 Beto Pérez came to the United States and started to teach his new dance-fitness style in Miami, Florida. Here he came into contact with two other Colombians, entrepreneurs Alberto Perlman and Alberto Aghioni. Together, they decided to start a business called Zumba Fitness and the word Zumba itself became a registered trademark licensed by the Ohio-based company Fitness Quest (see Lapowsky 2010). Starting off with DVDs and various classes, by 2005 the company was so successful that it spawned a Zumba academy licensing instructors. Shortly after, they started selling Zumbawear apparel and accessories and accompanying music CDs. By 2010 there were even Zumba video games for the three major gaming platforms: Wii, Xbox, and PlayStation3 (Zumba Fitness 2012).

In the years since its emergence, Zumba has started an international showcase career. In 2008 Alberto Perlman was quoted in *The Washington Post* claiming that "about 4 million people in forty countries are taking the class, and 20,000 instructors have been trained to teach it" (Parcher 2008). In May 2010 the journal *Inc.* reported that "classes are taught in 105 countries across 60,000 locations with 7.5 million attendees" (Lapowsky 2010). Recently, in 2012, Zumba Fitness itself announced on its website that "the Zumba program has grown to become the world's largest—and most successful—dance-fitness program with more than 12 million people of all shapes, sizes, and ages taking weekly Zumba classes in over 110,000 locations across more than 125 countries" (Zumba Fitness 2012). Zumba's success story is further confirmed by the numbers published on the latest modified version of Zumba Fitness's website, where the company states that classes are taught across 140,000 locations, reaching about 14 million people in 151 countries (Zumba Fitness 2013).

In accordance with its Colombian origin, the name Zumba can be traced back to a Spanish root word, namely the verb *zumbar*, meaning "to buzz, to whir, to hum," obviously referring to the constant fast movements practiced. According to an article in the British newspaper *The Independent*, Zumba "is Spanish slang for 'buzz like a bee'" ("The secret to fitness craze Zumba's success?" 2011). Amber Parcher in the *Washington Post* translates it more freely, writing that Zumba is a Spanish expression for "to move fast and have fun," hereby hinting at its new successful role as fun-fitness routine in an international fitness world (Parcher 2008). Zumba Fitness, however, claims that the name itself doesn't have any particular meaning and "is an arbitrary or fanciful word...selected as the original brand name" (Zumba Fitness 2012).

According to the official website, there are currently eight different types of Zumba classes provided in various locations all over the world. Starting with the original Zumba Fitness, there is also Zumba Gold (directed at an older target group or those who don't have experience with working out), Zumba Toning (incorporating a wide range of body sculpting exercises), Aqua Zumba (a water fitness routine), Zumbatomic (for kids four to twelve years), Zumba in the Circuit (a 30-minute program combining Zumba with circuit training), Zumba Gold Toning (offering body sculpting exercises for older participants and fitness beginners), as well as the recently introduced Zumba Sentao, being a workout mainly based on choreographies using a chair. Zumba thus intends to address all kinds of target groups offering programs that serve their different demands.

In order to be able to reach fitness enthusiasts all over the world, Zumba Fitness makes use of a global licensing system. Thus everyone who seeks to become a Zumba instructor has to attend a training course, which provides participants with a one-year license that has to be kept current by attending other future courses. The instructor training is usually offered in a one-day or sometimes a two-day course and is available in major cities in about 50 countries around the world: from the United States to European countries including Turkey, Russia, and the Ukraine, Asia (e.g., India, Malaysia, Vietnam, Taiwan, Singapore), the Middle East (United Arab Emirates, Kuwait, Lebanon, Oman), Africa (Cote D'Ivoire, South Africa), various Latin American countries from Mexico to Costa Rica, Guatemala, Brazil, and Chile, as well as in the Caribbean. Courses can be taken in reference to the specific program types that Zumba Fitness offers, normally starting with Zumba Basic 1 and 2. The availability of instructor training courses in various cities in countries all over the world, their relative short duration of one or two days, together with the fact that participants don't need any prerequisites (at least to enter a Basic Course) surely help explain the global spread of Zumba classes. Furthermore, licensed instructors are provided with teaching material including a manual, music CDs and DVDs, and they get access to Zumba merchandise and clothing they can sell to students in their classes. According to Perlman, the Zumba business model has helped many people and their families to overcome difficult times in the recession, while the fact that instructors sell Zumba articles before and after their classes even helps them become entrepreneurs (Lapowsky 2010).

From Aerobics to Zumba: "It's Supposed to Be a Dance Party"[1]

Having myself participated in and watched classes in public places in Mexico, it soon became obvious that Zumba, first and foremost, attracts women. Performance coach Ronald Woods observes: "Its appeal is primarily to females who enjoy a vigorous, fun workout in one hour that is aerobic, toning and body sculpting" (2011, 41). As Woods's reference to its aerobic qualities suggests, Zumba directly builds on the same target audience aerobics relies on.[2] Zumba, which according to a British newspaper, is "hot, hot, hot" ("The secret to fitness craze Zumba's success?" 2011), even appears to have partly replaced the various forms of aerobics that played a central part in the fitness industry for about two or three decades. Being directed at participants of all different ages interested in an instructor-based workout to music, the differences between Zumba and some forms of aerobics, for example, so-called dance aerobics, are not always clear, as aerobics also has started to use different kinds of music from Latin American rhythms to hip hop. In fact, newspaper or magazine writers often describe Zumba as a special Latin American–inspired form of dance aerobics (see Parcher 2008). There nevertheless remains the licensing system for Zumba instructors, which clearly demarcates which classes can be called Zumba classes, though there might still be various individual approaches by Zumba instructors to organizing a fitness routine.

In the 1980s, a boom of aerobics started in the United States, which soon after also swept over Europe and other continents. Aerobics—combining cardiovascular training with strength and flexibility exercises to music in sessions of 40–60 minutes—opened the gym to women; until then it had been a very masculine space (Brabazon 2002, 63–64). Although aerobics seemed to expand women's role in sports as it steered more and more women into the fitness centers, feminist research on aerobics in the 1980s exposed its sexualizing character and thus its tendency to reproduce societal patterns that subjugate women. Due to its focus on outer appearance, its "preoccupation with beauty, glamour, and sex appeal as status symbols" (MacNeill 1988, 205–206), researchers underlined aerobics' role in developing "women's potential in the sexual marketplace, not in athletics" (Theberge 1987, 195), thus reinforcing women's oppression in a masculine society instead of empowering them by way of physical activity.

Later researchers though, while not completely dismissing earlier findings, added other aspects to this view of aerobics as a mere women's "body shaper." Pirkko Markula, a Finnish researcher in the United States, who herself participated actively in aerobics classes and interviewed many aerobicizers, points out meanings such as the pleasure and the fitness effects women experienced in aerobic classes. While questioning her own role as commenting from inside the system, she states that she

> felt true pleasure while moving through a clever new combination of steps. I also improved my physical fitness through aerobics. Consequently, I disagreed with the idea that aerobics only contributed to the dominance of patriarchy. Yet I, operating within the aerobics, could have been unaware how thoroughly patriarchal hegemony dictated the everyday practices in aerobics classes. (2003, 55)

In order to refute her doubts and support her thesis that women took aerobics classes not only out of concern for their outer appearance, as dictated by men, Markula started to conduct interviews with various female exercisers. According to her findings, women also participated for other reasons, such as enjoyment and long-term health effects—a view that also reflects my own experience gathered in various aerobics classes of all kinds during my university years. Her ethnographic fieldwork brought in a new aspect: the link between aerobics and dance elements. Following Markula's research and her interest in aerobicizers' own views, most women participating in aerobics classes emphasize the "dance-like qualities" (Markula 2003, 61) the workout offers them. While they surely differentiate between the exercise aspect of aerobics and dance classes, they welcome the incorporation of dance steps into their fitness routine, giving it the flair of dancing. Accentuating the fun aspect and group feeling of aerobics, which differentiates it from "serious" sports based on competition, Pirkko Markula concludes:

> The exercisers seemed to enjoy the feeling of dance as long as the moves did not get too complicated. The "dancy" feeling comes from small additions such as hip and shoulder movements, snapping and clapping, which make the exercise movements flow more gracefully. [For exercisers] these movements are the best part of aerobics. (2003, 62)

If one now looks at the descriptions, advertisements, as well as magazine and newspaper coverage on Zumba, it seems to be the dance elements, more particularly Latin American or other "exotic" international dance movements, that fascinate and attract more and more people, especially women, from all over the world. This aspect is thus emphasized by Zumba promoters and participants. As journalist Janice Lloyd (2011) writes, Zumba "is more like a wild party scene than a strict exercise regiment [*sic*]!" An instructor she interviewed accordingly announces that "Zumba is exercise in disguise. ... It's fun. When people hear the music, they get moving. They lose weight, too, and feel good about themselves" (2011). Issie Lapowsky (2010), writing for *Inc.* magazine, calls the hype around Zumba a "dance craze" and names it a "dance fitness program." Some writers stress the dance element in Zumba as being the distinguishing feature between Zumba and traditional aerobics: "Instructor Tanya Nuchols said Zumba is a fresh take on the monotony of traditional aerobics classes. It combines Latin-flavored music and traditional dance moves from salsa, tango and merengue with aerobics to keep people moving and shaking while they're body sculpting" (Parcher 2008). Although the dance element is supposed to be more apparent than in aerobics, participants still accentuate that there is no need to be trained in dancing in order to enjoy a Zumba class (Parcher 2008). Thus Zumba seems to build on aerobics' success as a workout, focusing on a distinct kind of music and allowing participants to let themselves be moved and motivated by dance elements while exercising their bodies.[3] The Hollywood actress Kirstie Alley, a Zumba fan, when asked about her reasons for choosing this fitness routine, is quoted as saying: "My resolution this year is to have fun when I work out" (fitsugar 2012).

Zumba around the World: The Global Success of a Latin American Dance Workout and Body Image

The observed relation between Zumba and aerobics, and the basis of both routines—to a greater or lesser extent—in dance movements, may be a starting point for understanding Zumba's success. But what is the distinctive feature of Zumba? What makes it different from aerobics and explains its new global success? What is, for example, a typical routine supposed to consist of? The company Zumba Fitness gives clear standards for its licensed instructors in whichever country they teach: Zumba basically consists of four Latin American rhythms and the accompanying dance steps, namely *merengue, salsa, cumbia,* and *reggaetón,* taught to instructors during the first training course, Zumba Basic 1. A second follow-up course, Zumba Basic

2, introduces instructors to four additional so-called rhythms: belly dance, flamenco, tango, and samba, thus (interestingly) including a more "oriental"[4] dance element, namely belly dance, as well as Spanish flamenco from outside the Latin American context.[5] Zumba Fitness provides its instructors worldwide with music recommended for use in class. My experience in northern Mexico, however, shows that instructors there tend to use only a small part of the music Zumba Fitness provides them with via Internet, instead making use of current hits in Latin American music, including more regional elements of *banda* and *norteña* music, in order to attract their local audiences.[6] Mexican instructors claim to find Zumba Fitness's music not Latin American enough, as it presents a mix of international or internationalized Latin American rhythms as well as hip hop and orientalized sounds linked with belly dance movements, applicable and accessible for a globalized audience. There thus exists an interesting area of tension between Zumba's Latin American global appeal and worldwide positioning and its ability, due to a rather loose licensing system, to allow more regional forms under the umbrella image of a Latin American dance fitness routine. This tension might be described with the help of the term "glocalization," a process by which "local cultures adapt and redefine any global cultural product to suit their particular needs, beliefs and customs" (Giulianotti and Robertson 2004, 546). Zumba thus must be investigated in regard to the specific interdependence between the local and the global or, in Giulianotti's and Robertson's words, the relationship between the particular and the universal, as "'the elemental form of global life' *per se*" (2004, 547).

The worldwide appeal of Zumba further builds on the global success of dance styles such as samba, salsa, and merengue and the music of international (Latin American) pop stars such as Ricky Martin or Shakira. These idols also brought with them and internationalized a certain idea of Latin American movements and maybe even a body image or ideal to strive toward, which appears to be distinct from the ideal that aerobics has been propagating. Whereas 1980s and '90s aerobics were associated with American and European top model idols such as Cindy Crawford or Claudia Schiffer, Zumba builds on the key Colombian figure of Beto Pérez as well as a few loosely associated Latino/a stars. Participants further stress Zumba's focus on hips and butts in the routine. While journalist Amber Parcher states that "exercisers don't have to swivel their hips and shake their buns to get a good workout," she continues that "it sure can be fun" and finally concludes: "[Zumba is] engaging and so exuberating. . . . You're shaking your hips, which you typically don't do" (Parcher 2008). For

global audiences, Zumba movements are often linked to the music
and the dancing of the Colombian music star Shakira: "If you haven't
tried it yet, you've no doubt seen fellow gym goers swivel their hips
to Shakira in group fitness studios or seen the infomercials on TV"
(Stevens 2012)—surely not only due to her music mixing Latin, rock,
and pop elements and sometimes even Middle Eastern influences,
but also due to her famous hip dance movements stressing her by
now famous backside (which even has its own page on Facebook).
Zumba thus might be associated not only with distinct movements,
but also with a more curvaceous body ideal than that represented by
key figures of aerobics.

The focus on hips and butts of Latin American music or dance stars
already has its history and has not only been linked to the dance movements, but has also been accentuated by way of costume or fashion.
A popular example from the beginning of the twentieth century is the
famous Carmen Miranda, one of the earliest examples of a globalized
and stereotyped image of a Latina woman (Baxmann 2007, 113) bringing with it a distinct image of the racialized and sexualized Latina
body. Although Carmen Miranda originally came from Portugal, she
soon became the Hollywood and, thus, the international icon of the
Brazilian or, more generally, Latin American woman marked by her
samba dancing and "performative hips" (Peña Ovalle 2011, 20). The
Hollywood depiction of Latin American women or Latinas as exotic
others, a depiction often linked to their dancing and bodily appearance and stressed by colorful and exotic costume, from the beginning
ascribed the Latin female body an in-between position. While a popular black star and dancer such as Josephine Baker clearly fit into the
traditional black/white binaries of Hollywood, the United States more
broadly, and the globalized media market, presenting the black female
body as linked to ideas of free movement and sexual liberation, the
Latina Hollywood star actress/dancer and her "brown body" take a
middle position in the continuum of black-white media representation. As Priscilla Peña Ovalle states, the "representational Latina bodies oscillate between the normalcy of whiteness and the exoticism of
blackness in visual culture" (2011, 127). A more current example of
the internationally famous Latina woman, whom Peña Ovalle discusses
in detail, is the singer, dancer, and actress Jennifer Lopez. While the
stage appearance of Carmen Miranda relied more on her colorful and
exotic costumes, which left her belly free and directed the viewer's gaze
to her hip movements—hips that in fact were quite small but got more
focus and shape by Miranda's use of extensive shoulder pads and deco-
rated big hats—Jennifer Lopez has surely become famous for her big

backside. Lopez not only sparked a media interest in female stars with curves, but probably helped boost the industry of bottom implants.[7] As discussed early on by Frances Negrón-Muntaner (1997), Jennifer Lopez had a prominent role in strengthening and updating the link between *latinidad*[8] and a distinct female body type: a curvaceous body with a big backside. The formation and expression of Latino/a identity thus strongly depends on Latino/a embodied experience with latinidad figured as "a fluid set of cultural boundaries that are consistently reinforced, challenged, or negotiated by and through Latina bodies" (Mendible 2007). "Lopez's gorgeous stereotypical Latina butt" (Molina and Valdivia 2004, 212) thus stands out, as María P. Figueroa suggests from reading Negrón-Muntaner, among the "identificatory markers from which to construct a pan-ethnic Latina identify [*sic*]" (2003, 269). Helped by Jennifer Lopez's global appeal, big buttocks and a curvaceous silhouette have become an international emblem of the "Latina body" (Mendible 2007).

Zumba directly or indirectly builds on this discourse of latinidad and stereotypical images of the Latina body. Zumba participants themselves stress the bottom-training aspect of Zumba classes, describing it, furthermore, as a movement program that can help women to feel good again about their backsides. A writer for the British *Observer*, for example, entitles her article "Big Bumba? Try Zumba" (Shaitly 2011), and on the Internet site *fitsugar* a female author by the name of Susi May recommends Zumba classes as they "will help you learn to love your butt." Describing the trouble she went through and the problems of self-confidence regarding her appearance, she recently found relief with the Zumba dance-fitness routine:

> These days, I'm coming to appreciate the size and shape of my backside, and I have Zumba to thank for my newfound derriere detente [*sic*]. The Latin-dance-inspired cardio class is full of rump shaking moves. Your hips lead in almost every step as you salsa and merengue to the syncopated steps. Sixty minutes of dancing to upbeat music is bound to make you feel happy anyway, but the bonus is loving your bum; it's central to almost every dance move and having a little extra flesh back there means you have a little more weight to throw around. If the soundtrack is full of Shakira tunes, your booty will be leading the way.(May2011)

Zumba thus breaks with the image of aerobics classes, usually identified with thin, tall top models, often making women feel bad about themselves as they perceive the apparent difference between these perfect bodies and their own appearance. Latin dance movement as the basis of Zumba is thus, once again, identified with hip and bottom movements and popular international stars like Shakira, leading to newly coined words such as the so-called Zumba butt (apparently a descendant of the term "yoga butt").[9] This also coordinates with the international success of songs such as "*Mueve la colita, mamita rica* (Move your butt, hot girl)" by the Soca Boys or "*A mover la colita* (Let's move the hips)" by La Sonora Dinamita in Zumba classes, songs that were not only featured prominently in classes I attended in Mexico, but also get numerous hits for Zumba videos on YouTube.

The close link of Zumba dance-fitness with hip and bottom movements due to its association with Latin American rhythms is further complemented by elements of hip hop and belly dance incorporated into the routine. An association with hip hop is especially stressed in the United States by the contributions of stars like Wyclef Jean, former member of the rap group The Fugees, and Pitbull, the rapper of Cuban descent, to Zumba programs and events. Thus Pitbull's tracks "Historia" and "Pause" are both part of the Zumba playlist and a video to the music of "Pause" can be found on the official Zumba website, featuring Beto and two female dancers dancing Zumba choreography. Both Pitbull and Jean performed at the Zumba Fitness convention in Orlando, Florida, in 2011. In an interview with *MTV News*, Pitbull explicitly stresses the intercultural aspect of Zumba incorporating musical and dance elements from various backgrounds into one global, accessible mix: "The way Zumba has done it is taking all those things that maybe we've all learned from different countries and put it into a form where it's global now" (Markman 2011). Wyclef Jean similarly stresses that "Zumba's many cultural elements adds to its strength" and further marks it as a universal phenomenon: "If it's hot in Brazil, it's hot in Afghanistan, it's hot in Jerusalem, it's hot in Flatbush [Brooklyn, New York]" (Markman 2011).

The incorporation of belly dancing and therewith a popular Middle Eastern element can be seen in a few of Zumba Fitness's promotional videos, though playing a less prominent part (Zumba Fitness 2012). Whereas Zumba wear itself features colorful, sporty clothing, such as Zumba cargo pants and tops—not too far from international aerobics wear—the Middle Eastern component is seen in the use of hip scarves in Zumba classes, as I observed in classes in Mexico. The fusion between Latin American music and dance with belly dancing, however, isn't exactly new, and has become more and more popular at least since Shakira and her hit single "Ojos Así." In the video for that song, the singer incorporates belly dance using a silver hip scarf. With its links to hip hop music and dancing as well as Middle Eastern elements, Zumba not only utilizes more current trends in popular music and dancing, but also combines various dance and music styles associated with the focus on female hips and bottoms. Whereas hip hop videos, mainly featuring black, but also some Latina women, tend to propagate a more sexualized, objectifying view of the female body (Perry 2003, 137), the Zumba video to Pitbull's "Pause" is a dance-fitness video that features a sporty, fun side of movement. It does put Beto Pérez in the center, accompanied by two trained, thin women, one blond and one dark-haired, in high heels, presenting a Zumba choreography to the song. With the steps presented in the various official videos from Zumba Fitness, Zumba draws on various culturally located music styles and movement catalogues, bringing together Mexican *quebradita*[10] with internationally popular Latin American salsa, American hip hop, and elements of Middle Eastern belly dancing. It thereby creates its own platform for being a global fitness routine, presenting a crossover of diverse cultural elements of movement on a very basic level, and thus in a way that is easily accessible and combinable for a global audience. Zumba's link with the various strands of music and dance popular in the international market can also be seen in its choice of music included on official Zumba-CDs, such as "Party Nation: World Music by Zumba Fitness" (2008), which, besides the song "Zumba Te Suelta" based on reggaetón and hip hop rhythms, and a track to be used for belly dancing entitled "Sahara Oasis," also presents an instrumental song named "African Dream." Zumba Fitness herewith not only aligns itself with the by-now well-known genre of "world music," but attempts to incorporate other movement and music traditions already established in the world market, here using the very generalizing label "African Beat." This concept also allows crossover versions, such as on the official Zumba album "Vibe Tribe" (2009), where one finds a mix of reggaetón with belly dance rhythms in the track "Echa Pa'lante," which is very popular among Zumba instructors, judging by the number of videos on YouTube. Furthermore, popular reggaetón artists cooperate with Zumba Fitness, as in the case of Puerto Rican Daddy Yankee, who participated in the Zumba Instructor Convention in Orlando, Florida, in August 2012 featuring his track "Lovumba." Daddy Yankee planned to use the opportunity to promote his new album *Prestige* in various American cities by building on the growing popularity of reggaetón in the United States, which is helped by Zumba ("Daddy Yankee, ¿Instructor de Zumba?" 2012).

ZUMBA IN MEXICO: A FITNESS-ROUTINE TO IDENTIFY WITH

In Mexico, as in other countries, Zumba has met with a lot of success. Besides classes registered on the website of Zumba Fitness, which are mainly those offered in gyms, there is a great flux of classes offered in public places, plazas, and parks as well as private neighborhoods, classes that start and disappear again depending on time of the year and demand. Whereas the licensing system of Zumba surely works in Mexico and is necessary for becoming an instructor in a gym, there might nevertheless be some uncertified instructors teaching Zumba in neighborhoods ettings.[11]

Descriptions of Zumba in Mexican health magazines tend to define it as a new Latin aerobics routine that combines cardiovascular training with simple dance steps to Latin rhythms. Stressing the fun aspect of Zumba as bringing together fitness with dance, Zumba is seen to be a routine mainly training bottom, legs and abdomen. It is furthermore understood to be for everyone, independent of age and level of fitness (see "Zumba" 2009; "Zumba" 2013). Zumba thus seems to be a fitness routine able to include every Mexican, women as well as men, in order to have fun and train oneself. Zumba's ability to animate the masses in Mexico is confirmed by various Zumba events organized in the country. In March 2012, for example, about 6,500 people came together in Mexico City on the famous Zócalo, the main square or plaza in the city's historic center, in order to break the current Guinness Book world record for the largest Zumba class, which had been established the year before in London ("New record for Zumba fitness class" 2012; Quintero 2012). During the last few years there have been so-called Zumba marathons in different Mexican cities, bringing together people in order to follow the fitness routine for up to five hours (see, e.g., Carbajal 2010). Zumba classes are even presented in penal institutions, as the Mexican news channel Televisa reported about a prison in Mérida, Yucatán, where Zumba is part of the regular physical education and is regarded as an important step in the male inmates' social reintegration process ("Mil internos bailan Zumba en Mérida" 2012).

Zumba's success in Mexico is surely helped by its governmental promotion, which started a few years ago. A report by the National Committee for Physical Culture and Sports (CONADE) in cooperation with the Office of Public Education (SEP) from 2008 includes Zumba among the physical activities promoted as part of the national governmental health initiative "Actívate, Vive Mejor (Activate Yourself,

Live Better)" initiated under President Felipe Calderón with the aim
to "diminish the accelerated occurrence of obesity and overweight in
the Mexican population which has placed us in second position in the
world"[12] (CONADE 2009). In Sonora, political candidates have also
taken up the initiative and extensively promoted Zumba in order to
enhance the regional population's health.[13] Some candidates here also
focus especially on the situation of women, stressing the importance of
public Zumba classes in Hermosillo (which are primarily attended by
women) due to the fact that Zumba "strongly increases woman's self-
esteem, who in general doesn't have time to look after herself, already
taking care of the children, working, taking care of her husband" ("La
zumba ayuda a transformar la vida de las mujeres" 2012).

But the Mexican government, political candidates, and civil organizations promoting low price or free classes alone wouldn't be able to
stir Zumba's continuing success in Mexico if there weren't sufficient
people participating enthusiastically. Following explanations about
Zumba published on www.zumbamexico.com.mx—although not an
official website of Zumba Fitness—the fitness-dance routine, despite
being a worldwide phenomenon, "has its roots in Latin America
and therefore has always found its place, inspiration and rhythm in
Mexico" ("Qué es zumba?" 2013). Beto Pérez, founding figure of
Zumba, is also quoted here, not only confirming the strong identification of Mexico with Latinness or latinidad, but further acknowledging
the leading position of Mexico regarding the spread of Zumba:

> Zumba® is for everybody, for people participating in the fitness world
> and those who aren't; it's a program that disseminates itself and Mexico
> is its most important home after the United States. It has been well
> received because Mexico needed a fitness movement with which it
> could identify itself and what is better than the Latin flavor of Zumba®.
> Over the years I became influenced by Mexican folklore, so much that
> in all my classes I can't leave my quebraditas and cumbias[14] outside the
> routine.("Quée szumba ?"2013)

According to this quote from Beto Pérez, Zumba owes a great deal
to Mexican music and dance and therefore is supposedly the first fitness routine Mexicans really feel at home with. Zumba's success and
steady promotion in Mexico speak to this. Zumba's link to Mexican
daily culture also becomes obvious by the fact that it has now entered
the field of the popular Mexican *telenovela* (soap opera).[15] Female
Zumba participants in Hermosillo, inviting me to classes in order for
me, the European, to learn more about their music and dance moves,

thus appear to typify the general trend in Mexico. Questioning neither the Latinness strongly promoted by Zumba Fitness[16] nor the Mexicanness of Zumba, Mexicans feel represented by and identify with Zumba dance and music despite its global (business) appeal. While the comments and reports on Zumba from the United States or European countries quoted before focus greatly on how Zumba as a dance-fitness routine is giving people (primarily women) the opportunity to learn how to move in a Latin way, thereby appreciating hip movements and their physical effects, Mexican announcements and comments seem to stress more of the positive health effects in general. These are, of course, bound up with the fun aspect, which seems to rest primarily on the dancing. One Mexican website, while explaining what Zumba is and stating its positive effects, mentions among them the following: "Improves physical coordination so that you will gradually turn yourself into an excellent dancer"; "You will learn the steps from popular songs"; and "Improves your self-esteem by changing you into a person that dances excellently and has a lot of strength" ("Zumba" 2013). Comments like these clearly reveal the prominent position dancing (or *baile*) holds in Mexican culture (see Hutchinson 2007; Nájera-Ramírez et al. 2009), and further confirms the link between Zumba practice and regional as well as popular Latin American music commonly listened to in Mexico. This is also acknowledged by a Zumba instructor in Sonora I interviewed, who mentions that he and other colleagues generally use songs currently popular in Mexico or the region in order to attract more participants who already know and love this music, with the music recommended by Zumba Fitness playing a very minor role. Similarly, my experience with Zumba classes shows that only very few songs published on official Zumba CDs are in fact used in public Zumba classes in northern Mexico, whereas my familiarity with the latest hits popular in Mexico (or Sonora) rapidly increased by attending the classes. Commentators' and politicians' focus on Zumba as a new Mexico-wide health practice in order to fight the population's overweight problems[17] thus seem to function in accordance with Mexican culture's basis in Latin American music and dance rhythms (see Sheehy 2008, 204–205). This also includes popular Latin American styles such as reggaetón, a mixture of various traditions such as reggae, hip hop, and different Latin American rhythms. As videos show, reggaetón's use of sexualized movements stressing the female body and especially the backside (known as *perreo*), rivals or even surpasses US hip hop videos' use of booty dancing, a style where the female rubs her buttocks against the male's groin (see Hanna 2012, 12).[18] While

Zumba promotion in the United States and in Europe often works in reference to stereotypical ideas about Latin American dance movements as centering on hip and bottom, the situation in Mexico is different. As was the case with rock 'n roll's arrival in Mexico in the middle of the twentieth century, when the rotating hips of "Elvis the Pelvis" didn't cause provocation to audiences used to mambo dancing and Caribbean-influenced rhythms (Baxmann 2007, 128), Zumba's success in Mexico doesn't need to be discussed in terms of hip and booty movements, as those applied are already practiced within common Latin American (popular) dancing.

CONCLUSION: MEXICAN QUEBRADITAS FOR THE WORLD

Investigating Zumba's trajectory all over the world and specifically in Mexico, success seems to be attributable to Zumba Fitness's ability to incorporate various Latin American as well as a few other music and dance styles into a global mix of "Latino" and Latino-compatible traditions (such as belly dance and hip hop, which had already appeared in Latino pop). This globally accessible mix builds on existing trends in the world music market, where regional dance and music traditions, such as salsa, flamenco, or belly dance, have met with success internationally. Zumba accordingly offers the possibility to identify with the practice beyond its center or origin in Latin American music and dance and movement cultures. By its continued focus on Latin American movement and music cultures, Zumba further builds on stereotyped movement and body images, such as the hot or sexually attractive Latina able to perform skillful hip movements and booty shakes. This image of Latina and Latin American women has been seen throughout Western performance history, from Carmen Miranda to Jennifer Lopez and Shakira. These stereotypes are further popularized and internationalized by affiliations with hip hop (such as joint projects with Pitbull and Wyclef Jean), reggaetón (with the artist Daddy Yankee as well as with Pitbull) and belly dance. These affiliations might work so well not only due to the fact that all these dance styles center on hip and bottom movements, but also because each artist has already appeared in crossover projects with Latin American music. Compared with reggaetón's *perreo* and its US equivalent, hip hop booty dancing, Zumba remains rather modest, building on the hot and sexy images, but still not incorporating them too much into the routine, a decision that might be explained by the business intention to appeal to the widest international audience possible. Furthermore, through their international availability, the body images and movements Zumba relies on are at the same time well-known (or exotic, depending on the locale) as well as basic enough not to discourage an international audience outside Latin America. And, as I showed with regard to the Mexican context, these images and movements are still relevant enough not to be dismissed by Latino participants. This is, of course, also due to Zumba Fitness's corporate strategy, specifically its license system, which is binding, but open enough to allow instructors to adjust their classes to regional conditions, music trends, and participants' movement abilities and customs. The global dance-fitness routine Zumba thus creates a platform of significance to identify with on a regional as well as a global level, as can be seen with this account of its success in Mexico. Zumba, probably the first aerobics practice able to connect with Mexican (Latino/a) participants on a grand scale, has been chosen by national and regional politicians and civil actors in order to train Mexican female (as well as male) bodies fighting overweight and other health problems. Zumba thus appears to be a fitness chameleon, oscillating between local regionalism and global homogenization, making its success story in Mexico only one example of how glocalization as the symbiosis of the local/particular and global/universal functions under distinct cultural circumstances (Guilianotti and Robertson 2004, 549). Thus Zumba is still seen as being distinctly Latin American and also Mexican. As a case in point, *quebraditas*, until recently a rather localized Northern Mexican phenomenon, have been included by Zumba's Beto into the league of internationally received Latin American dance and music culture.

NOTES

1. Parcher2008.
2. Pirkko Markula states that "aerobics are primarily a women's activity" (2003,61).
3. One Zumba instructor I interviewed in Hermosillo, Mexico stated that in his opinion Zumba *is* aerobics, only with more Latin American music and under a new name.
4. For further investigation on dance and Orientalism, Western conceptions of so-called Oriental dance, including its corresponding movements at the beginning of the twentieth century, see Brenscheidt gen. Jost 2011.
5. Zumba's association with Xbox as presented in their launch video instead introduces nine different rhythms and movements, which are mambo, salsa, merengue, hip hop, cumbia, calypso, flamenco, reggaetón, and rumba.

6. According to a German source, 70 percent of the songs used in Zumba classes have to be music provided by Zumba Fitness LLC (Gressmann 2011). Instructors, however, don't have to dispense with their favorite hits, as the latest official Zumba music compilation, *Zumba Fitness Dance Party 2012*, combines popular songs from artists such as Rihanna, Shakira, Pitbull, The Black Eyed Peas, and Jennifer Lopez with Zumba Fitness's own music productions.

7. As quoted by Myra Mendible, the London *Daily Mail* reported in 2003 that "Miss Lopez' rounded posterior is credited with making curvy bottoms trendy again as it is said by American plastic surgeons to have created a demand for silicone buttock implants" (Mendible 2007, 1).

8. The term *latinidad* (see Flores 2000, Dávila 2001) has mainly been discussed in US scholarship and met with a lot of criticism within Latina/o studies. Molina and Valdivia describe latinidad as a category constructed from the outside as well as from inside the Latino community. Latinidad is accordingly "a social construct informed by the mediated circulation of ethnic-specific community discourses and practices as well as mainstream economic and political imperatives through the cultural mainstream" (2004, 208) and thus negotiable, situated, contingent and always in-progress (Mendible 2007).

9. The denomination "yoga butt" is used rather informally referring to a perfectly trained, very tight bottom to be achieved only after years of hard (yoga) training. According to an entry from 2008 in the Internet slang word dictionary *Urban Dictionary*, a yoga butt is the "ultimate external sign of a strong and powerful body."

10. As an example of Zumba Fitness's incorporation of Mexican *quebradita*, see, for example, the song "Baila, Menea y Goza" on the album "Official 2008 Zumba Fitness Cardio Party Soundtrack." According to Sydney Hutchinson (2004), *quebradita* is a modern Mexican American dance popular in the border region and usually performed to Mexican *banda* or brass band music. The dance's name, literally "little break," refers to the back bends of the female dancers as well as to the movements' inspiration in the breaking of a wild horse (Hutchinson 2004, 651–652).

11. A certified Zumba instructor in Hermosillo I interviewed mentioned and strongly objected to the existence of uncertified instructors in public places and neighborhoods, whose training routines, at times, don't adhere to the necessary standard of health-conscious exercising methods.

12. This translation, as well as all translations from Spanish, is mine.

13. See, for example, the promotion of "Zumba por la salud" classes in Hermosillo as linked with the candidacy of Alejandro López Caballero for the city council ("Hermosillo en Zumba con López Caballero" 2012). Zumba also entered the arena of political campaigning in the United States when in 2010 "Michelle Obama incorporated it into her Get Moving campaign and a mass Zumba class was taught on the White House lawn at the launch" (Shaitly 2011).

14. While cumbia as a musical genre has its roots in Colombia, it first appeared in Mexico in the 1940s leading to the successful and wide proliferation of different cumbia styles in Mexico since the 1950s (Pacini Hernandez 2010,120) .

15. A scene with Zumba fitness-dancing appeared in May 2011 in the telenovela "Una familia con suerte," presented by the Mexican channel Televisa.

16. For another example of a company promoting Latinness as part of its international brand image, see Casanova (2011).

17. Even the Mexican coverage of Daddy Yankee's presence at the Zumba Instructor Convention 2012 is marked by comments on him planning to give speeches on the importance of exercise ("Daddy Yankee, a ritmo de Zumba"2012) .

18. See, for example, the official reggaetón video of "Báilame" from Reggaeton Boys featuring Franco el Gorila (2008).

BIBLIOGRAPHY

8-Uhr-Blatt(Berlin),3.2.1938.

Aapola, Sinikka, Marnina Gonick, and Anita Harris. 2005. *Young Femininity: Girlhood, Power and Social Change*. Basingstoke: Palgrave Macmillan.

Abrahamsen, Rita, and Michael C. Williams. 2007. "Securing the City: Private Security Companies and Non-State Authority in Global Governance." *International Relations* 21 (June): 237–253.

Acker, Joan. 2004. "Gender, Capitalism, and Globalization." *Critical Sociology* 30 (1): 17–41.

Adams, William Lee. 2008. "Dressed Not to Be Killed." *Time*, July 24. Accessed June 1, 2012. http://www.time.com/time/magazine article /0,9171,1826292,00.html.

Adey, Peter. 2009. "Facing Airport Security: Affect, Biopolitics, and the Preemptive Securitisation of the Mobile Body." *Environment & Planning D: Society & Space* 27 (2): 274–295.

AFP (Agence France Presse). 2006. "Vestidos de gala, camisetas y blusas a prueba de bala." AFP, March 23.

Ahmed, Leila. 2011. *A Quiet Revolution: The Veil's Resurgence from the Middle East to America*. New Haven, CT: Yale University Press.

Allen-Collinson, Jacquelyn. 2005. "Emotions, Interaction and the Injured Sporting Body." *International Review for the Sociology of Sport* 40 (2): 221–240.

Ames, Eric. 2009. *Carl Hagenbeck's Empire of Entertainments*. Seattle: University of Washington Press.

Amnesty International. 2004. *Colombia: Scarred Bodies, Hidden Crimes*. London: International Secretariat.

Andrews, David L., and George Ritzer. 2007. "The Global in the Sporting Glocal." In *Globalisation and Sport*, ed. Richard Giulianotti and Roland Robertson. Oxford: Blackwell Publishing.

Anzaldúa, Gloria. 2007. *Borderlands/La Frontera*. 3rd ed. San Francisco, CA: Aunt Lute Books.

Appadurai, Arjun. 1996. *Modernity At Large: Cultural Dimensions of Globalization*. Minneapolis: University of Minnesota Press.

Arburg, Hans-Georg von. 2003. "Archaeodermatologie der Moderne. Zur Theoriegeschichte der Tätowierung in der Architektur und Literatur zwischen 1830 und 1930." *Deutsche Vierteljahresschrift für Literaturwissenschaft und Geistesgeschichte* 3: 407–445.

Aris, Stephen. 1990. *Sportsbiz: Inside the Sports Business.* London: Hutchinson.

Aroneanu, Eugene. 1996. *Inside the Concentration Camps: Eyewitness Accounts of Life in Hitler's Death Camps.* Translated by Thomas Whissen. Westport, CT: Praeger.

Assía, Augusto. 2010. "Por la violencia, una feria de armas y seguridad tiene récord de visitas en México." *Clarín,* April 22. Accessed June 1, 2012. http://edant.clarin.com/diario/2010/04/22/elmundo/i-02185574.htm.

Atkinson, Michael. 2003. *Tattooed: A Sociogenesis of Body Art.* Toronto: University of Toronto Press.

Attwood, Feona. 2011. "Through the Looking Glass? Sexual Agency and Subjectification Online." In *New Femininities: Postfeminism, Neoliberalism and Subjectivity,* ed. Rosalind Gill and Christina Scharff, 203–214. Basingstoke: Palgrave Macmillan.

Ball, Hugo. 1974. *Die Kulisse: Das Wort und das Bild.* Einsiedeln: Benziger.

Banks, Ingrid. 2000. *Hair Matters: Beauty, Power, and Black Women's Consciousness.* New York: New York University Press.

Barber, Benjamin. 1996. *Jihad vs. McWorld: How Globalism and Tribalism Are Reshaping the World.* New York: Ballantine Books.

Barthwal-Datta, Monika. 2012. *Understanding Security Practices in South Asia: Securitization Theory and the Role of Non-State Actors.* New York: Routledge.

Basch, Linda. 1987. "The Politics of Caribbeanization: St. Vincentians and Grenadians in New York." In *Caribbean Life in New York City: Sociocultural Dimensions,* ed. Constance Sutton and Elsa Chaney. New York: The Center for Migration Studies.

Bauman, Zygmunt. 2006. *Liquid Fear.* Cambridge: Polity Press.

Baxmann, Inge. 2007. *Mayas, Pochos und Chicanos: Die transnationale Nation.* Munich: Wilhelm Fink.

Beasley, Barin. 2000. "Perceptions of Ideal Female Body Images: A Study of African American Student's Responses to Fashion Magazine Advertising." PhD diss., University of Southern Mississippi.

Beauboeuf-Lafontant, Tamara. 2009. *Behind the Mask of the Strong Black Woman: Voice and Embodiment of a Costly Performance.* Philadelphia: Temple University Press.

Beck, Ulrich. 2000. "What Is Globalisation?" In *Globalisation: The Reader,* ed. John Beynon and David Dunkerley. London: The Athlone Press.

Birke, Lynda I. A. 2000. *Feminism and the Biological Body.* New Brunswick, NJ: Rutgers University Press.

Blakely, Edward J., and Mary Gail Snyder. 1997. *Fortress America: Gated Communities in the United States.* Washington, DC: Brookings Institution Press.

Bloch, Ernst. 1959. *Das Prinzip Hoffnung.* Frankfurt am Main: Suhrkamp.

Bobel, Chris and Samantha Kwan, eds. 2011. *Embodied Resistance: Challenging the Norms, Breaking the Rules*. Nashville, TN: Vanderbilt University Press.

Böhme, Hartmut. 2000. "Fetischismus im neunzehnten Jahrhundert: Wissenschaftshistorische Analysen zur Karriere eines Konzeptes." In *Das schwierige 19. Jahrhundert*, ed. Jürgen Barkhoff, Gilbert Carr, and Roger Paulin, 445–464. Tübingen: Niemeyer.

Booth, Ken, ed. 2005. *Critical Security Studies and World Politics*. Boulder, CO: Lynne Rienner.

Botta, Renee. 2000. "The Mirror Image of Television: A Comparison of Black and White Adolescents' Body Image." *Journal of Communication* 50: 144–159.

Bourdieu, Pierre. 1977. *Outline of a Theory of Practice*. Translated by Richard Nice. Cambridge: Cambridge University Press.

———. 1984. *Distinction: A Social Critique of the Judgement of Taste*. Translated by Richard Nice. London: Routledge and Kegan Paul.

———. 1986. "The Forms of Capital." In *Handbook of Theory and Research for the Sociology of Education*, ed. John Richardson. New York: Greenwood.

———. 1990a. *In Other Words: Essays towards a Reflexive Sociology*. Translated by Matthew Adamson. Stanford, CA: Stanford University Press.

———. 1990b. *The Logic of Practice*. Stanford, CA: Stanford University Press.

———. 1998. *Practical Reason*. Cambridge: Polity Press.

Bourdieu, Pierre, and Loïc Wacquant. 1992. *An Invitation to Reflexive Sociology*. Cambridge: Polity Press.

Brabazon, Tara. 2002. *Ladies Who Lunge: Celebrating Difficult Women*. Sydney: University of New South Wales Press.

Brah, Avtar. 2001. "Difference, Diversity, Differentiation." In *Feminism and "Race,"* ed. Kum Kum Bhavnani. Oxford: Oxford University Press.

Brenscheidt gen. Jost, Diana. 2011. *Shiva Onstage: Uday Shankar's Company of Hindu Dancers and Musicians in Europe and the United States, 1931–38*. Berlin: LIT.

Brooks, Peter. 1989. "Storied Bodies, or Nana at Last Unveiled." *Critical Inquiry* 16 (1): 1–32.

Bruner, Edward M. 1994. "Abraham Lincoln as Authentic Reproduction: A Critique of Postmodernism." *American Anthropologist, New Series*, 96 (2): 397–415.

———. 2008. "Lincoln's New Salem as a Contested Site." *Museum Anthropology* 17 (3):14–24.

Budgeon, Shelley. 1994. "Fashion Magazine Advertising: Constructing Femininity in the 'Postfeminist' Era." In *Gender and Utopia in Advertising: A Critical Reader*, ed. Luigi Manca and Alessandra Manca, 55–70. Lisle, IL: Procopian Press.

———. 2011(a). "The Contradictions of Successful Femininity: Third-Wave Feminism, Postfeminism and 'New' Femininities." In *New Femininities: Postfeminism, Neoliberalism and Subjectivity*, ed. Rosalind Gill and Christina Scharff, 279–292. Basingstoke: Palgrave Macmillan.

———. 2011(b). *Third Wave Feminism and the Politics of Gender in Late Modernity*. Basingstoke: Palgrave Macmillan.

Buzan, Barry, Ole Wæver, and Jaap De Wilde. 1998. *Security: A New Framework for Analysis*. Boulder, CO: Lynne Rienner Publishers.

Caldeira, Teresa Pires do Rio. 2000. *City of Walls: Crime, Segregation, and Citizenship in São Paulo*. Berkeley: University of California Press.

Caplan, Jane, ed. 2000. *Written on the Body: The Tattoo in European and American History*. Princeton, NJ: Princeton University Press.

Carbajal, Karla. 2010. "Realizan Maratón de Zumba." *El Imparcial: Diario Independiente de Sonora*, October 30. Accessed May 23, 2013. http://www.elimparcial.com/EdicionEnLinea/Notas/Noticias/30102010/476519.aspx.

Casanova, Erynn Masi. 2004. "No Ugly Women: Concepts of Race and Beauty among Adolescent Women in Ecuador." *Gender and Society* 18 (3): 287–308.

———. 2011. *Making Up the Difference: Women, Beauty, and Direct Selling in Ecuador*. Austin, TX: University of Texas Press.

Casanova, Erynn Masi and Barbara Sutton. 2013. "Transnational Body Projects: Media Representations of Cosmetic Surgery Tourism in Argentina and the United States." *Journal of World-Systems Research* 19 (1): 57–81.

Cashmore, Ellis. 1998. "Between Mind and Muscle" (review article). *Body and Society* 4 (2): 83–90.

Chagüendo, Francy Elena. 2011. "En Colombia también se blindan blusas y camisas." *El País*, Mayo 15. Accessed June 1, 2012. http://www.elpais.com.co/elpais/economia/en-colombia-tambien-blindan-blusas-y-camisas.

Charmaz, Kathy. 2002. "Qualitative Interviewing and Grounded Theory Analysis." In *Handbook of Interview Research Context and Method*, ed. Jaber F. Gubrium and James A. Holstein. Thousand Oaks, CA: Sage.

Chew, Phyllis. 2008. "No Fire in the Belly: Women's Political Role in Singapore." In *Gender Politics in Asia: Women Manoeuvring in Dominant Gender Orders*, ed. Wil Burghoorn, Kazuki Iwanaga, Cecelia Milwertz, and Qi Wang, 185–216. Copenhagen: NIAS Press.

Chossudovsky, Michel. 2003. *The Globalization of Poverty and the New World Order*. 2nd ed. Montreal: Global Research.

Chua, Beng Huat, 1995. "That Imagined Space: Nostalgia for Kampungs." In *Portraits of Places: History, Community and Identity in Singapore*, ed. Brenda S. A. Yeoh and Lily Kong. Singapore: Times Edition.

CNN (Cable News Network). 2009. "The Armani of Bullet-Proof." *CNN*. Video File. March 16. Accessed June 21, 2012. http://edition.cnn.com/video/?/video/international/2009/03/13/biz.trav.caballero.range.cnn.

———. 2012. "¿Fácil ser empresario en América Latina?" Video File. April 25. Accessed June 21, 2012. http://edition.cnn.com/video/?/video/spanish/2012/04/25/exp-cnn-dinero-emprendimiento-industria-textil.cnn.

Cocteau, Jean. 1983. *Poésie Critique 1*. Paris: Gallimard.

Colley, Linda. 2004. *Captives: Britain, Empire and the World, 1600–1850*. New York: Anchor.

Colombiatravel. 2009. "Colombia, The Only Risk Is Wanting to Stay." *You Tube*. Video File. February 2. Accessed June 9, 2012. http://www.youtube.com/watch?feature=player_embedded&v=0me7t7wXKLw#!

CONADE (Comisión Nacional de Cultura Física y Deporte). 2009. "Feria de la Actividad Física para Vivir Mejor." Accessed May 23, 2013. http://www.ime.gob.mx/ime2/images/imenitas/feria_fisica.pdf.

Craig, Maxine Leeds. 2002. *Ain't I a Beauty Queen?: Black Women, Beauty, and the Politics of Race*. New York and Oxford: Oxford University Press.

Crais, Clifton and Pamela Scully. 2009. *Sara Baartman and the Hottentot Venus: A Ghost Story and a Biography*. Princeton, NJ: Princeton University Press.

Creswell, John W. 2003. *Research Design: Qualitative, Quantitative, and Mixed Methods Approaches*. Thousand Oaks, CA: Sage.

Currah, Paisley, and Tara Mulqueen. 2011. "Securitizing Gender: Identity, Biometrics, and Transgender Bodies at the Airport." *Social Research* 78 (2): 557–582.

"Daddy Yankee, a ritmo de zumba." 2012. *Ritmoson Latino / El Vocero*, July 10. Accessed August 5, 2012. http://www2.esmas.com/ritmosonlatino/noticias/468223/?page=undefined.

"Daddy Yankee, ¿Instructor de zumba?" 2012. *Ritmoson Latino / Notimex*, July 19. Accessed August 5, 2012. http://www2.esmas.com/ritmosonlatino/noticias/475644/daddy-y ankee-instructor-zumba/.

Darling-Wolf, Fabienne. 2004. "Sites of Attractiveness: Japanese Women and Westernized Representations of Feminine Beauty." *Critical Studies in Mass Communication* 21: 325–345.

Dávila, Arlene. 2001. *Latinos, Inc.: The Marketing and Making of a People*. Berkeley: University of California Press.

Dawe, Tracey. 2008. "Kafka's Penal Colony: Reflections of German Colonialism and National Identity." In *Reflections: New Directions in Modern Languages and Cultures*, ed. Sarah Buxton, Laura Campbell, Tracey Dawe, and Elise Hugueny-Léger. Foreword by Edward Welch, 129–143. Newcastle upon Tyne: Cambridge Scholars.

Dayal, Samir. 1996. "Diaspora and Double-Consciousness." *The Journal of the Midwest Modern Language Association* 29: 46–62.

Degener, Janna. 2010. "Wenn Sprachen sterben." www.goethe.de, January 7, 2010. Accessed November 24, 2012. https://www.goethe.de/ges/spa/sui/de5589701.htm.

Denzin, Norman K. 2003. *Performance Ethnography: Critical Pedagogy and the Politics of Culture*. Thousand Oaks, CA: Sage.

Dery, Mark. 1994. *Flamewars: The Discourse of Cyber Culture*. Durham, NC: Duke University Press.

Dewey, Susan. 2008. *Making Miss India Miss World: Constructing Gender, Power, and the Nation in Postliberalization India*. Syracuse, NY: Syracuse University Press.

Dickson-Swift, Virginia, Erica L. James, Sandra Kippen, and Pranee Liamputtong. 2009. "Researching Sensitive Topics: Qualitative Research as Emotion Work." *Qualitative Research* 9 (1): 61–79.

"Die Harald-Schmidt-Show." ARD/Das Erste. Cologne. Oct 22, 2010.

DiMaggio, Paul. J. and Walter W. Powell. 1983. "The Iron Cage Revisited: Institutional Isomorphism and Collective Rationality in Organizational Fields." *American Sociological Review* 48 (1): 147–160.

Donohue, John J. 1994. *Warrior Dreams: The Martial Arts and the American Imagination*. Westport, CT: Praeger.

Dreyfus, Hubert L., and Paul Rabinow. 1982. *Michael Foucault: Beyond Structuralism and Hermeneutics*. Chicago: The University of Chicago Press.

Drost, Nadja. 2009. "For Bullet-Proof Underwear, Miguel Caballero is Your Man." *The Global Post*, April 7. Accessed June 1, 2012. http://www.globalpost.com/dispatch/the-americas/090402/bullet-proof-underwear-miguel-caballero-your-man.

Du Bois, Christine M. 2000. "Race, Ethnicity, and Mass Media: Identities and Concerns about Reputation among Chesapeake-Area West Indians." PhD diss., The Johns Hopkins University.

Dueñas Villamil, Jairo. 2011. "La moda blindada de Miguel Caballero." *Cromos*, March 28. Accessed June 1, 2012. http://www.cromos.com.co/personajes/actualidad/articulo-140751-la-moda-blindada-de-miguel-caballero.

Dupuis, Ann, and David Thorns. 2008. "Gated Communities as Exemplars of 'Forting Up' Practices in a Risk Society." *Urban Policy & Research* 26 (2): 145–157.

Durham, Meenakshi. 2004. "Constructing the 'New Ethnicities': Media, Sexuality, and Diaspora Identity in the Lives of South Asian Immigrant Girls." *Critical Studies in Media Communication* 21:140–161.

Eco, Umberto. 1987. *Travels in Hyper-Reality*. London: Picador.

Edmonds, Alexander. 2010. *Pretty Modern: Beauty, Sex, and Plastic Surgery in Brazil*. Durham, NC: Duke University Press.

EFE. 2010. "El 'Armani' de los chalecos antibalas blinda a los reporteros mexicanos." August 28. Accessed June 1, 2012. http://www.abc.es/20100828/internacional/chalecos-blindados-mexico-201008281804.html.

Eicher, Joanne B. 2001. "Dress, Gender and the Public Display of Skin." In *Body Dressing*, ed. Joanna Entwistle and Elizabeth Wilson, 233–252. Oxford: Berg.

El Economista. 2012. "Eurocopter blindará sus aeronaves." April 24. Accessed June 1. http://eleconomista.com.mx/estados/2012/04/24/eurocopter-blindara-sus-aeronaves.

Elias, Norbert. 1971. "The Genesis of Sport as a Sociological Problem." In *The Sociology of Sport: A Selection of Readings*, ed. Eric Dunning. London: Frank Cass.

———. 1978. *The Civilising Process: The History of Manners.* New York: Urizen Books.

———. 1986. "An Essay on Sport and Violence." In *Quest for Excitement: Sport and Leisure in the Civilizing Process,* ed. Norbert Elias and Eric Dunning. Oxford: Basil Blackwell.

———. 2000. *The Civilising Process: Sociogenetic and Psychogentic Investigations.* Cornwall: Blackwell Publishers.

Enloe, Cynthia H. 2007. *Globalization and Militarism: Feminists Make the Link.* Lanham, MD: Rowman & Littlefield.

Espiritu, Yen L. 2001. "'We Don't Sleep Around Like White Girls Do:' Family, Culture, and Gender in Filipina American Lives." *Signs* 26: 415–440.

Evans, John, Brian Davies, and Jan Wright. 2003. *Bodies of Knowledge.* London: Routledge.

Ewen, Stuart. 1999 (1988). *All Consuming Images: The Politics of Style in Contemporary Culture.* New York: Basic Books.

Fanon, Frantz. 1991 (1967). *Black Skin, White Masks.* London: Pluto Press.

Featherstone, Mike. 2007. *Consumer Culture and Postmodernism.* 2nd ed. Thousand Oaks, CA: Sage.

Fees, Craig. 1996. "Tourism and Politics of Authenticity in a North Cotswold town." In *The Tourist Image: Myth and Myth Making in Tourism,* ed. Tom Selwyn. London: John Wiley and Sons.

Feige, Marcel. 2003. *Ein Tattoo ist für immer- Geschichte der Tätowierung in Deutschland.* Berlin: Schwartzkopf.

Figueroa, María P. 2003. "Resisting 'Beauty' and *Real Women Have Curves.*" In *Velvet Barrios: Popular Culture and Chicana/o Sexualities,* ed. Alicia Gaspar de Alba, 265–282. New York: Palgrave Macmillan.

FitSugar."Celebrity Fans of Zumba," 2012. *Shape.* Accessed May, 23, 2013. http://www.shape.com/celebrities/celebrity-workouts/celebrity-fans-zumba?page=2.

Flores, Juan. 2000. *From Bomba to Hip Hop: Puerto Rican Culture and Latino Identity.* New York: Columbia University Press.

Flynn, Kristin and Marian Fitzgibbon. 1996. "Beauty Ideal Ideals of Low Income African American Mothers and Their Pre-Adolescent Daughters." *Journal of Youth and Adolescence* 25: 615–630.

Flynn, Michael G. 1998. "Future Research Needs and Directions." In *Overtraining in Sport,* ed. Richard Kreider, Andrew Fry, and Mary L. O'Toole. Champaign, IL: Human Kinetics.

Foner, Nancy. 1997. "The Immigrant Family: Cultural Legacies and Cultural Changes." *International Migration Review* 31: 961–974.

———. 1998. "West Indian Identity in the Diaspora: Comparative and Historical Perspectives." *Latin American Perspectives* 25: 173–188.

———. 2001. "Introduction: West Indian Migration to New York: An Overview." In *Islands in the City: West Indian Migration to New York,* ed. Nancy Foner, 1–22. Berkeley: University of California Press.

Forster, Georg. 1983 (1782). *Reise um die Welt.* Berlin: Insel.

Fort, Meredith P., Mary Anne Mercer, and Oscar Gish. 2004. *Sickness and Wealth: The Corporate Assault on Global Health*. Cambridge, MA: South End Press.

Foster, George. M. 1986. "South Sea Cruise: A Case Study of a Short-lived Society." *Annals of Tourism Research* 13 (1): 215–238.

Foster, John Bellamy and Robert W. McChesney. 2012. *The Endless Crisis: How Monopoly-Finance Capital Produces Stagnation and Upheaval from the U.S.A. to China*. New York: Monthly Review Press.

Foucault, Michel. 1977. *Discipline and Punish: The Birth of the Prison*. Translated by Alan Sheridan. New York: Penguin.

———. 1990. *The History of Sexuality, Volume II*. New York: Vintage Books.

———. 1995 (1977). *Discipline and Punish: The Birth of the Prison*. New York: Vintage Books.

Fregoso, Rosa Linda, and Cynthia L. Bejarano, eds. 2010. *Terrorizing Women: Feminicide in the Américas*. Durham, NC: Duke University Press.

Friedman, Jonathan. 1992. "The Past in the Future: History and the Politics of Identity." *American Anthropologist* 94 (4): 837–859.

———. 1994. *Cultural Identity and Global Process*. London: Sage Publications.

Ganetz, Hillevi. 1995. "The Shop, the Home and Femininity as a Masquerade." In *Youth Culture in Late Modernity*, ed. Johan Fornas and Goran Bolin, 72–99. London: Sage.

García, Jacobo G. 2010. "Miguel Caballero, el 'Armani' del blindaje." *El Mundo*, April 24. Accessed June 21, 2012. http://www.elmundo.es /america/2010/04/23/mexico/1272026557.html.

García Canclini, Néstor. 2001. *Hybrid Cultures: Strategies for Entering and Leaving Modernity*. Minneapolis: University of Minnesota Press.

Gaspar de Alba, Alicia, with Georgina Guzmán, eds. 2010. *Making a Killing: Feminicide, Free Trade, and La Frontera*. Austin: University of Texas Press.

Gast, Nicole. 2010. "Giftige Autolacke in farbigen Tattoos." Bild Online. July 24, 2008. Accessed January 12, 2010. http://www.bild.de /ratgeber/gesundheit/tattoo/in-taetowierungen-kann-krebs-verursa-chen-5256686.bild.html.

Geibel, Emanuel. 1915(1861). "Deutschlands Beruf." *Gesammelte Werke*. Leipzig: Hesse und Becker.

Genz, Stephanie and Benjamin Brabon. 2009. *Postfeminism: Cultural Texts and Theories*. Edinburgh: Edinburgh University Press.

Geertz, Clifford. 2001 (1973). "Thick Description: Toward an Interpretive Theory of Culture." In *The American Tradition in Qualitative Research*, ed. Norman K. Denzin and Yvonna S. Lincoln. Thousand Oaks, CA: Sage.

Gentry, Clyde. 2001. *No Holds Barred: Evolution*. Richardson, TX: Archon Publishing.

Giddens, Anthony. 1984. *The Constitution of Society: Outline of the Theory of Structuration*. Berkeley: University of California Press.

————. 1991. *Modernity and Self-Identity: Self and Society in the Late Modern Age*. Cambridge: Polity Press.

Gill, Rosalind. 2003. "From Sexual Objectification to Sexual Subjectification: The Resexualisation of Women's Bodies in the Media." *Feminist Media Studies* 3 (1): 100–106.

————.2007. "Postfeminist Media Culture, Elements of a Sensibility." *European Journal of Cultural Studies* 10 (2): 147–166.

Giulianotti, Richard. 1999. *Football: A Sociology of the Global Game*. Cambridge: Polity Press.

Giulianotti, Richard and Roland Robertson. 2004. "The Globalization of Football: A Study in the Glocalization of the 'Serious Life.'" *The British Journal of Sociology* 55 (4): 545–568.

————. 2007. "Sport and Globalisation: Transnational Dimensions." In *Globalisation and Sport*, ed. Richard Giulianotti and Roland Robertson. Oxford: Blackwell Publishing.

Gleeson, Kate and Hannah Frith. 2004. "Pretty in Pink: Young Women Presenting Mature Sexual Identities." In *All About the Girl: Culture, Power and Identity*, ed. Anita Harris, 103–113. London and New York: Routledge.

Gómora, Doris. 2010. "Tecnología blindada se abre paso en el mercado mexicano." *El Universal*, August 17. Accessed July 16, 2012. http://www.eluniversal.com.mx/nacion/179761.html.

González Echevarría, Robert. 1999. *The Pride of Havana: A History of Cuban Baseball*. New York: Oxford University Press.

González Velázquez, Lilia. 2011. "Trajes a la medida en ropa blindada." *El Economista*, April 27. Accessed June 1, 2012. http://eleconomista.com.mx/industrias/2011/04/27/trajes-medida-ropa-blindada.

Goodman, J. Robyn. 2002. "Flabless Is Fabulous: How Latina and Anglo Women Read and Incorporate the Excessively Thin Body Ideal into Everyday Experience." *Journalism and Mass Communication Quarterly* 79: 712–727.

Goodman, J. Robyn, and K. Walsh-Childers. 2004. "Sculpting The Female Breast: How College Women Negotiate the Media's Ideal Breast Image." *Journalism and Mass Communication Quarterly* 81: 657–674.

Goodman, Leo A. 1961. "Snowball Sampling." *The Annals of Mathematical Statistics* 32: 148–170.

Greenblatt, Stephen. 1980. *Renaissance Self-Fashioning. From More to Shakespeare*. Chicago: University of Chicago Press.

Greider, William. 1997. *One World, Ready or Not: The Manic Logic of Global Capitalism*. New York: Simon & Schuster.

Gressmann, Nina. 2011. "Bei diesem Tanz-Workout wird sogar Shakira schwach." *Die Welt*, November 25. Accessed May 23, 2013. http://www.welt.de/lifestyle/article13698129/ Bei-diesem-Tanz-Workout-wird-sogar-Shakira-schwach.html.

Griebel, Bernd. 2001. "Ist die deutsche Sprache in Gefahr?" Accessed November 24, 2012. http://web.hszg.de/~bgriebel/goerlitz.html.

Griffin, Christine. 2004. "Good Girls, Bad Girls: Anglocentrism and Diversity in the Constitution of Contemporary Girlhood." In *All about the Girl: Culture, Power and Identity*, ed. Anita Harris, 29–44. London and New York: Routledge.

Guattari, Felix. 1992. "Regimes, Pathways, Subjects." In *Zone 6: Incorporations*, ed. Jonathan Crary and Sanford Kwinter, 11–24. Cambridge, MA: MIT Press.

Gubrium, Jaber F., and James A. Holstein. 2000. "Analysing Interpretive Practice." In *Handbook of Qualitative Research*. 2nd ed., ed. Norman K. Denzin and Yvonna S. Lincoln. London: Sage.

Gute Zeiten- Schlechte Zeiten. 2009. "Folge 4318". Prod. RTL Grundy. 26 August.

Guttmann, Allen. 1995. *Games and Empires*. New York: Columbia University Press.

Gwynne, Joel. 2013. "SlutWalk, Feminist Activism and the Foreign Body in Singapore." *Journal of Contemporary Asia* 43 (1): 173–185.

Hanna, Judith Lynne. 2012. *Naked Truth: Strip Clubs, Democracy, and a Christian Right*. Austin: University of Texas Press.

Hannerz, Ulf. 1996. *Transnational Connections: Culture, People, Places*. London: Routledge.

Hargreaves, Jennifer. 1994. *Sporting Females*. London: Routledge.

Hargreaves, John. 2002. "Globalisation Theory, Global Sport, and Nations and Nationalism." In *Power Games: A Critical Sociology of Sport*, ed. John Sugden and Alan Tomlinson. London and New York: Routledge.

Harris, Anita. 2004. *Future Girl: Young Women in the Twenty-First Century*. London: Routledge.

Harris-Lacewell, Melissa. 2001. "No Place to Rest: African American Political Attitudes and the Myth of Black Women's Strength." *Women and Politics* 23: 1–33.

Harvey, David. 1991. *The Condition of Postmodernity: An Enquiry into the Origins of Cultural Change*. Malden, MA and Oxford: Blackwell.

———. 2005. *A Brief History of Neoliberalism*. New York: Oxford University Press.

Harvey, Jean and Francois Houle. 1994. "Sport, World Economy, Global Culture, and New Social Movements." *Sociology of Sports Journal* 11 (4): 337–355.

Heath, Jennifer, ed. 2008. *The Veil: Women Writers on Its History, Lore and Politics*. Berkeley: University of California Press.

Held, David. 1999. *Global Transformations: Politics, Economics and Culture*. Cambridge: Polity.

"Hermosillo en zumba con López Caballero". 2012. *dossierpolitico.com*, May 19. Accessed May 23, 2013. http://www.dossierpolitico.com/ver-noticiasanteriores.php?artid= 112593&relacion=dossierpolitico&criterio =onde.

Hoberman, John. 1992. *Mortal Engines*. New York: The Free Press.

Hockey, John and Jacquelyn Allen-Collinson. 2007. "Grasping the Phenomenology of Sporting Bodies." *International Review for the Sociology of Sport* 42 (2): 115–131.

Holmes, Rachel. 2007. *African Queen: The Real Life of the Hottentot Venus.* New York: Random House.

Honold, Alexander. 2006. "Austellung des Fremden: Menschen- und Völkerschau um 1900. Zwischen Anpassung und Verfremdung: Der Exot und sein Publikum." In *Das Kaiserreich transnational: Deutschland in der Welt 1871–1914,* ed. Sebastian Conrad and Jürgen Osterhammel, 171–190. Göttingen: Vandenhoeck & Ruprecht.

Hood III, M. V., and Grant W. Neeley. 2009. "Citizen, Defend Thyself: An Individual-Level Analysis of Concealed Weapon Permit Holders." *Criminal Justice Studies* 22 (1): 73–89.

Hope, Donna. 2011. "From *Browning* to *Cake Soap*: Popular Debates on Skin Bleaching in the Jamaican Dancehall." *The Journal of Pan African Studies* 4: 165–194.

Houlihan, Barrie. 1994. *Sport and International Politics.* Hemel Hempstead: Harvester Wheatsheaf.

Howes, David. 2003. *Sensual Relations: Engaging the Senses in Culture and Social Theory.* Ann Arbor: University of Michigan Press.

———, ed. 2004. *Empire of the Senses: The Sensual Culture Reader.* Oxford and New York: Berg.

Huber, N. R.1910. "Ein Mittelalterliches Zeugnis über eine Tätowierung in religiöserE kstase." *Archiv für Kriminalanthropologie* 39: 34–35.

Hughes, Matt. 2008. *Made in America: The Most Dominant Champion in UFC History.* New York: Simon Spotlight Entertainment.

Human Rights Watch. 1992. *Human Rights Watch World Report 1992—Colombia.* Accessed July 15, 2012. http://www.unhcr.org/refworld/docid/467fca45c.html.

———. 2011. *Neither Rights Nor Security: Killings, Torture, and Disappearances in Mexico's "War on Drugs."* Accessed July 15, 2012. http://www.hrw.org/sites/default/files/reports/mexico1111webwcover_0.pdf.

Hunter, Margaret. 2005. *Race, Gender and the Politics of Skin Tone.* New York: Routledge.

Hutchinson, Sydney. 2004. "Quebradita." In *Encyclopedia of Latino Popular Culture,* ed. Cordelia Chávez Candelaria, Peter J. García, and Arturo J. Aldama, 651–654. Westport, CT: Greenwood Publishers.

———. 2007. *From Quebradita to Duranguense: Dance in Mexican American Youth Culture.* Tucson: University of Arizona Press.

Hyndman, Jennifer. 2008. "Whose Bodies Count? Feminist Geopolitics and Lessons from Iraq." In *Feminism and War: Confronting U.S. Imperialism,* ed. Robin L. Riley, Chandra T. Mohanty, and Minnie B. Pratt, 192–204. London: Zed Books.

Incite! Women of Color against Violence. 2006. *Color of Violence: The INCITE! Anthology.* Cambridge, MA: South End Press.

Jamail, Milton H. 2000. *Inside Cuban Baseball.* Carbondale: Southern Illinois University Press.

Jarvie, Grant. 2006. *Sports, Culture and Society: An Introduction.* London: Routledge.

Joest, Wilhelm. 1887. *Tätowieren, Narbenzeichnen, und Körperbemalen. Ein Beitrag zur vergleichenden Ethnologie.* Berlin: Asher.

Journeyman Pictures. 2008. "Bulletproof Fashion—Mexico." *YouTube.* Video File. March 31. Accessed June 1, 2012. http://www.youtube. com/watch?v=-Bxnc78psZA.

Justus, Joyce B. 1983. "West Indians in Los Angeles: Community and Identity." In *Caribbean Immigration to the United States,* ed. Roy Bryce-Laporte and Delores Mortimer, 130–148. Washington, DC: Research Institute on Immigration and Ethnic Studies, Smithsonian Institute.

Kaeppler, Adrienne Lois. 1999. "The Mystique of Fieldwork." In *Dance in the Field: Theory, Methods and Issues in Dance Ethnography,* ed. Theresa J. Buckland. Basingstoke: Macmillan Press Ltd.

Kapur, Jyostna and Keith B. Wagner. 2011. "Neoliberalism and Global Cinema: Subjectivities, Publics and New Forms of Resistance." In *Neoliberalism and Global Cinema: Capital, Culture, and Marxist Critique,* ed. Jyostna Kapur and Keith B. Wagner, 1–16. London and New York: Routledge.

Kawash, Samira. 2000. "Safe House? Body, Building, and the Question of Security." *Cultural Critique* 45: 185–221.

Kershaw, Baz with Lee Miller/Joanne "Bob" Whalley and Rosemary Lee /Niki Pollard. 2011. "Practice as Research: Transdisciplinary Innovation in Action." In *Research Methods in Theatre and Performance,* ed. Baz Kershaw and Helen Nicholson. Edinburgh: Edinburgh University Press.

Killian, Caitlin. 2003. "The Other Side of the Veil: North African Women in France Respond to the Headscarf Affair." *Gender & Society* 17 (4): 567–590.

Kitchin, Phil. 1998. *Cyberspace.* New York: John Wiley & Sons.

Klein, Naomi. 2001. *No Logo.* London: Flamingo.

Kosut, Mary and Lisa Jean Moore, eds. 2010. *The Body Reader: Essential Social and Cultural Readings.* New York: New York University Press.

Krahmann, Elke, ed. 2005. *New Threats and New Actors in International Security.* New York: Palgrave Macmillan.

Krauss, Erich, and Bret Aita. 2002. *Brawl: A Behind the Scenes Look at Mixed Martial Arts Competition.* Toronto: ECW Press.

Kubisch, Bernd. 2009. "'Moda blindada' desde Colombia para el mundo." *El Periódico de Aragón,* February 11.

"La zumba ayuda a transformar la vida de las mujeres, por eso la seguiremos impulsando: Epifano 'Pano' Salido." 2012. *En Equipo: El México del Noroeste,* April 4. Accessed May 23, 2013. http://www.revistaenequipo. com/sonora/2541-la-zumba-ayuda-a-transformar-la-vida-de-las-mujeres-por-eso-la-seguiremos-impulsando-epifanio-pano-s alido.

LaBennett, Oneka. 2011. *She's Mad Real: Popular Culture and West Indian Girls in Brooklyn.* New York: New York University Press.

Lacey, Marc. 2008. "Right Thing to Wear at the Wrong End of a Gun." *The New York Times*, October 5. Accessed May 15, 2013 http://www. nytimes.com/2008/10/06/world/americas/06mexico.html?_r=1.

Lapowsky, Issie. 2010. "Zumba Turns Dancers into Entrepreneurs." *Inc. Magazine*, May 26. Accessed May 23, 2013. http://www.inc.com /articles/2010/05/zumba-fitness-entrepreneurs.html.

Lau, Kimberly. 2011. *Body Language: Sisters in Shape, Black Women's Fitness and Feminist Identity Politics*. Philadelphia, PA: Temple University Press.

Lazar, Michelle. 2011. "The Right to Be Beautiful: Postfeminist Identity and Consumer Beauty Advertising." In *New Femininities: Postfeminism, Neoliberalism and Subjectivity*, ed. Rosalind Gill and Christina Scharff, 37–51. Basingstoke: Palgrave Macmillan.

Lechner, Frank J. and John Boli, eds. 2011. *The Globalization Reader*. Malden, MA: Wiley- Blackwell.

Lees, Andrew. 2009. "Moral Discourse and Reform in Urban Germany, 1880–1914." In *Criminals and Their Scientists: The History of Criminology in International Perspective* ed. Richard Wetzell and Peter Becker, 85–104. Cambridge: Cambridge University Press.

Leigh Foster, Susan. 2003. "The Ballerina's Phallic Pointe." In *The Feminism and Visual Cultural Reader*, ed. Amelia Jones. London and New York: Routledge.

Leiter, Jeffrey. 2005. "Structural Isomorphism in Australian Nonprofit Organisations." *International Journal of Voluntary and Nonprofit Organisation* 16 (1): 1–31.

Levin, Daniel T. 2000. "Race as a Visual Feature: Using Visual Search and Perceptual Discrimination Tasks to Understand Face Categories and the Cross-Race Recognition Deficit." *Journal of Experimental Psychology* 129 (4): 559–574.

Lim, Serene. 2011. "Jetsetting with Chatri Sityodtong." In *Today*, August 27. Singapore: Mediacorp Press Ltd.

Lloyd, Janice. 2011. "Zumba Brings the Dance Party into the Health Club." *USA Today*, October 27. Accessed June 10, 2012. http://yourlife.usato-day.com/fitness- food/exercise/story/2011–10–27/Zumba-brings-the-dance-party-into-the-health-c lub/50940786/1.

Loland, Sigmund, Berit Skirstad, and Ivan Waddington. 2006. *Pain and Injury in Sports: Social and Ethical Analysis*. London: Routledge.

Lombroso, Cesare. 1911. *Criminal Man: According to the Classification of Cesare Lombroso*. New York and London: G. P. Putnam and Sons.

Loos, Adolf. 1997 (1908). *Ornament and Crime*. Translated by Michael Mitchell. Riverside: Ariadne Press.

Lorber, Judith and Lisa Jean Moore. 2010. *Gendered Bodies: Feminist Perspectives*. New York: Oxford University Press.

Lovejoy, Meg. 2001. "Disturbances in the Social Body: Differences in Body Image and Eating Problems among African American and White Women." *Gender and Society* 15 (2): 239–261.

Luedecke, Hugo Ernest. 1907. "Erotische Tätowierungen." *Anthropophyteia. Jahrbücher für folklorischische Erhebungen und Forschungen zur Entwicklungsgeschichte der geschlechtlichen Moral*, ed. Friedrich Krauss, IV. Band. Leipzig: Deutsche Verlagsactiengesellschaft.

MacLeish, Kenneth T. 2012. "Armor and Anesthesia: Exposure, Feeling, and the Soldier's Body." *Medical Anthropology Quarterly* 26 (1): 49–68.

MacNeill, Margaret. 1988. "Active Women, Media Representations, Ideology." In *Not Just a Game*, ed. Jean Harvey and Hart Cantelon, 195–212. Altona, Canada: University of Ottawa Press.

Maguire, Joseph. 1999. *Global Sport: Identities, Societies, Civilisations.* Cambridge: Polity.

Malacrida, Claudia and Jacqueline Low, eds. *Sociology of the Body: A Reader.* New York: Oxford University Press.

Mangan, James Anthony. 1987. *The Games Ethic and Imperialism.* London: Viking.

Manila Bulletin. 2011. "2 Filipino URCC Champions Featured in Biggest MMA Event in Asia" in *Manila Bulletin*, July 22. Philippines: Manila Bulletin Publishing Corp.

Markman, Rob. 2011. "Pitbull And Wyclef Get Fit With Zumba." *MTV News*, July 15. Accessed May 23, 2013. http://www.mtv.com/news /articles/1667348/pitbull-wyclef-zu mba.jhtml.

Markula, Pirkko. 2003. "Postmodern Aerobics: Contradiction and Resistance." In *Athletic Intruders: Ethnographic Research on Women, Culture, and Exercise*, ed. Anne Bolin and Jane Granskog, 53–78. Albany: State University of New York Press, 2003.

Martin, Emily. 1994. *Flexible Bodies: Tracking Immunity in American Culture from the Days of Polio to the Age of AIDS.* Boston, MA: Beacon Press.

Mauss, Marcel. 2006 (1935). "Techniques of the Body." In *Techniques, Technology and Civilisation,* edited and introduced by Nathan Schlanger. New York: Durkheim Press.

May, Susi. 2011. "Learn to Love Your Booty." *fitsugar*, February 8. Accessed May 23, 2013. http://www.fitsugar.com/Zumba-Dance-Class-Help-You-Learn-Love-Your-Butt-13789994 .

Mayeda, David T. and David E. Ching. 2008. *Fighting for Acceptance: Mixed Martial Arts and Violence in American Society.* New York: iUniverse Inc.

Mazzarella, Sharon R. 2005. "Introduction: It's a Girl Wide Web." In *Girl Wide Web: Girls, the Internet and the Negotiation of Identity*, ed. Sharon R. Mazzarella, 1–12. New York: Peter Lang.

McColl, Richard. 2009. "Bulletproof Kimono: An Interview with Miguel Caballero." *Matador.* March 3. Accessed July 22, 2012. http://matadornetwork.com/bnt/bulletproof-kimono-an-interview-with-miguel-caballero/.

McCormick, Naomi and John Leonard. 2004. "Gender and Sexuality in the Cyberspace Frontier." In *net.seXXX: Readings on Sex, Pornography and the Internet*, ed. Dennis S. Waskell, 183–191. New York: Peter Lang,

McMichael, Philip. 2011. *Development and Social Change: A Global Perspective.* 5th ed. Thousand Oaks, CA: Sage.

McMillan, Sally J. 2000. "The Microscope and the Moving Target: The Challenge of Applying Content Analysis to the World Wide Web." *Journalism and Mass Communication Quarterly* 77 (1): 80–98.

McRobbie, Angela. 2000. *Feminism and Youth Culture.* London: Macmillan.

Melzack, Ronald. 2001. "Pain and the Neuromatrix in the Brain." *Journal of Dental Education* 65 (12): 1378–1382.

Mendible, Myra, ed. 2007. *From Bananas to Buttocks: The Latina Body in Popular Film and Culture.* Austin: University of Texas Press.

Merleau-Ponty, Maurice. 1962. *Phenomenology of Perception.* 6th ed. Translated by Colin Smith, with translation revisions supplied by Forrest Williams and David Guerriere. London: Routledge and Kegan Paul.

Messner, Michael. 1990. "Boyhood, Organized Sports, and the Construction of Masculinities." *Journal of Contemporary Ethnography* 18 (1): 416–444.

Metropolis. 2009. "Bulletproof Clothing in Colombia." *YouTube.* Video File. January 15. Accessed June 1, 2012. http://www.youtube.com /watch?v=Tp0At-a-_TQ.

Meyer, John W., John Boli, George M. Thomas, and Francisco O. Ramírez. 1997. "World Society and the Nation-State." *American Journal of Sociology* 193 (1): 144–181.

Mifflin, Margot. 1997. *Bodies of Subversion: A Secret History of Women and Tattooing.* New York: Power House Books.

"Mil internos bailan Zumba en Mérida." 2012. *Televisa,* July 12. Accessed May 23, 2013. http://tvolucion.esmas.com/noticieros/primero-noticias/180707/mil-internos-bailan-z umba-merida/.

Miller Tricia, Geoffrey Lawrence, Jim McKay, and David Rowe. 2001. *Globalisation and Sport: Playing the World.* London: Sage.

Mödersheim, Sabine. 2002. "Skin Deep—Mind Deep. Emblematics and Modern Tattoos." In *Emblems from Alciato to the Tattoo. Selected Papers of the Leuven International Emblem Conference 18–23 August, 1996,* ed. Peter M. Daly, John Manning, and Marc van Vaeck, 309–333. Turnhout: Brepols.

Moghadam, Valentine M. 2005. *Globalizing Women: Transnational Feminist Networks.* Baltimore, MD: The Johns Hopkins University Press.

Mohanty, Chandra Talpade. 2003. *Feminism without Borders: Decolonizing Theory, Practicing Solidarity.* Durham, NC: Duke University Press.

Molina Guzmán, Isabel, and Angharad N. Valdivia. 2004. "Brain, Brow, and Booty: Latina Iconicity in U.S. Popular Culture." *The Communication Review* 7: 205–221.

Morgan, David. 1997. *Focus Groups as Qualitative Research.* Thousand Oaks, CA: Sage.

Morley, David, and Kevin Robins. 1995. *Spaces of Identity: Global Media, Electronic Landscapes and Cultural Boundaries.* London: Routledge.

Muchhala, Bhumika, ed. 2007. *Ten Years After: Revisiting the Asian Financial Crisis.* Washington, DC: Woodrow Wilson International Center for Scholars Asia Program.

Nader, Ralph, William Greider, Margaret Atwood, Vandana Shiva, Mark Ritchie, Wendell Berry, Jerry Brown, Herman Daly, Lori Wallach, Thea Lee, Martin Khor, David Phillips, Jorge Castañeda, Carlos Heredia, David Morris, and Jerry Mander. 1993. *The Case against "Free Trade": GATT, NAFTA, and the Globalization of Corporate Power.* San Francisco, CA: Earth Island Press.

Nájera-Ramírez, Olga, Norma E. Cantú, Brenda M. Romero, eds. 2009. *Dancing across Borders: Danzas y Bailes Mexicanos.* Urbana and Chicago: University of Illinois Press.

Neely, Sarah. 2012. "Making Bodies Visible: Post-Feminism and the Pornographication of Online Identities." In *Transgression 2.0: Media, Culture and the Politics of a Digital Age,* ed. David J. Gunkel and Ted Gournelos, 101–117. London: Continuum.

Negrón-Muntaner, Frances. 1997. "Jennifer's Butt." *Aztlán* 22 (2): 181–194.

"New record for Zumba fitness class." 2013. *BBC News,* March 26. Accessed May 23, 2013. http://www.bbc.co.uk/news/world-latin-america-17511694.

New York City Department of City Planning. 2012. "Population Facts." Accessed July 2012. http://www.nyc.gov/html/dcp/html/census/pop_facts.shtml.

Ng, Jenna. 2011. "Neoliberalism and Authoritarianism in Singaporean Cinema: A Case Study of Perth." In *Neoliberalism and Global Cinema: Capital, Culture, and Marxist Critique,* ed. Jyostna Kapur and Keith B. Wagner, 261–278. London and New York: Routledge.

Oates, Joyce Carol. 1987. *On Boxing.* Garden City, New York: Doubleday.

Oettermann, Stephan. 1975. *Zeichen auf der Haut. Die Geschichte der Tätowierung in Europa.* Hamburg: Syndikat.

Okely, Judith. 2007. "Fieldwork Embodied." In *Embodying Sociology: Retrospect, Progress and Prospects,* ed. Chris Shilling. Malden, MA: Blackwell.

Ong, Aiwha. 1996. "Cultural Citizenship as Subject-Making: Immigrants Negotiate Racial and Cultural Boundaries in the United States." *Current Anthropology* 37: 737–762.

———. 1999. *Flexible Citizenship: The Logic of Transnationality.* Durham, NC: Duke University Press.

———. 2006. *Neoliberalism as Exception: Mutations in Citizenship and Sovereignty.* Durham, NC: Duke University Press.

Orgel, Stephen. 2002. *The Authentic Shakespeare.* New York: Routledge.

O'Toole, Mary Louise. 1998. "Overreaching and Overtraining in Endurance Athletes." In *Overtraining in Sport,* ed. Richard Kreider, Andrew Fry, and Mary L. O'Toole. Champaign, IL: Human Kinetics.

Oxford Dictionaries. 2013. *Oxford Dictionaries: The World's Most Trusted Dictionaries.* Accessed May 15, 2013. http://oxforddictionaries.com/

Owen, David. 2011. "Survival of the Fitted." *The New Yorker,* September 26: 69–73.

Pacini Hernandez, Deborah. 2010. *Oye como va! Hybridity and Identity in Latino Popular Music.* Philadelphia: Temple University Press.

Parcher, Amber. 2008. "Zumba Shakes the Monotony out of Ordinary Aerobics Classes." *The Washington Post,* July 31. Accessed May 23, 2013. http://www.washingtonpost.com/wp-dyn/content/article/2008/07/30/ AR2008073001580.html.

Parker-Starbuck, Jennifer and Roberta Mock. 2011. "Researching the Body in/as Performance." In *Research Methods in Theatre and Performance,* ed. Baz Kershaw and Helen Nicholson. Edinburgh: Edinburgh University Press.

Patton, Tracey O. 2006. "'Hey Girl, Am I More Than My Hair?' African American Women and Their Struggles with Beauty, Body Image, and Hair." *NWSA Journal* 18: 24–51.

Paulse, Michelle. 1994. "Commingled." In *Miscegenation Blues: Voices of Mixed Race Women,* ed. Carol Camper, 43–51. Toronto: Sister Vision.

Peña Ovalle, Priscilla. 2011. *Dance and the Hollywood Latina: Race, Sex, and Stardom.* New Brunswick, NJ: Rutgers University Press.

Peoples, Columba and Nick Vaughan-Williams. 2010. *Critical Security Studies: An Introduction.* New York: Routledge.

Pérez, Louis A. Jr. 1994. "Between Baseball and Bullfighting: The Quest for Nationality in Cuba, 1868–1898." *The Journal of American History* 81 (2): 493–517.

Perry, Imani. 2003. "Who(se) am I? The Identity and Image of Women in Hip-Hop." In *Gender, Race, and Class in Media: A Text-Reader,* ed. Gail Dines and Jean M. Humez, 136–148. Thousand Oaks, CA: Sage.

Polanyi, Michael. 1983. *The Tacit Dimension.* New York: Doubleday and Company, Inc.

Portes, Alejandro and Bryan R. Roberts. 2005. "The Free-Market City: Latin American Urbanization in the Years of the Neoliberal Experiment." *Studies in Comparative International Development* 40 (1): 43–82.

Portillo, Lourdes, dir. 2001. *Señorita Extraviada. Missing Young Woman.* VHS Video. New York, NY: Women Make Movies.

Poster, Mark. 1995. *The Second Media Age.* Oxford: Polity Press.

Potter, Caroline. 2008. "Sense of Motion, Senses of Self: Becoming a Dancer," *Ethnos* 73 (4): 444–465.

Pratt, Sarah. 2005. "Miguel Caballero." *Rolling Stone,* October 6, Issue 984, p. 100.

Proexport Colombia. 2012. "Estrategias." Accessed July 24, 2012. http://www.colombia.travel/es/prensa/campana-del-riesgo/estrategias.

"Qué es Zumba?" 2013. Accessed May 23. http://www.zumbamexico.com.mx/zumbamex/ queeszumba.html.

Quintanilla, Michael. 2003. "Fashion Security: Air Travelers Dress to Avoid the 'Buzz.'" *Orlando Sentinel*, February 23. Accessed April 2, 2012. http://articles.orlandosentinel.com/2003-02-23/travel/0302200375_1_airport-security-metal-sensors-detector.

Quintero M., Josefina. 2012. "Logran itztpalapenses el record Guinness de gente haciendo *aeróbics*." *La Jornada*, March 26. Accessed August 2, 1012. http://www.jornada.unam.mx/2012/03/26/capital/037n2cap.

Qureshi, Sadiah. 2011. *Peoples on Parade: Exhibitions, Empire and Anthropology in Nineteenth-Century Britain*. Chicago: University of Chicago Press.

Radner, Hilary. 2011. *Neo-Feminist Cinema: Girly Films, Chick Flicks and Consumer Culture*. London and New York: Routledge.

Redfern, Catherine and Kristen Aune. 2010. *Reclaiming the F Word: The New Feminist Movement*. London: Zed Books.

Rheingold, Howard. 1994. *The Virtual Community: Surfing the Internet*. London: Minerva.

Richtel, Matt. 2012. "New Fashion Wrinkle: Stylishly Hiding the Gun." *The New York Times*, April 23. Accessed July 24, 2012. http://www.nytimes.com/2012/04/24/us/fashion-statement-is-clear-the-gun-isnt.html.

Riley, Robin L., Chandra T. Mohanty, and Minnie B. Pratt, eds. 2008. *Feminism and War: Confronting U.S. Imperialism*. London: Zed Books.

Robertson, Roland. 1995. "Glocalisation: Time-Space and Homogeneity-Heterogeneity." In *Global Modernities*, ed. by Mike Featherstone, Scott M. Lash, and Roland Robertson. London: Sage.

Rock, Chris, producer, and Jeff Stilson, director. 2009. *Good Hair: Sit Back and Relax* (Documentary). USA: HBO Films.

Rodríguez, Dennis. 2011. "La ropa antibalas se hace en Bogotá." *El Comercio*, June 19. Accessed June 1, 2012. http://www.elcomercio.com/mundo/ropa-antibalas-hace-Bogota_0_501549925.html.

Rooke, Alison and Monica Moreno Figueroa. 2006. "Identity Parade." *Research Newsletter*, Sociology Department, Goldsmiths, University of London, 21: 18–21.

Rose, Nikolas. 1992. *Governing the Soul: The Shaping of the Private Self*. London: Routledge.

Rothfels, Nigel. 2002. *Savages and Beasts: The Birth of the Modern Zoo*. Baltimore, MD: The Johns Hopkins University Press.

Saad, Lydia. 2011. "Self-Reported Gun Ownership in U.S. is Highest Since 1993." Accessed July 24, 2012. http://www.gallup.com/poll/150353/self-reported-gun-ownership-highest-1993.aspx.

Said, Edward. 2001. "The Clash of Ignorance." *The Nation*, October 4, 2001. Accessed June 6, 2013. http://www.thenation.com/article/clash-ignorance.

Saltarino, Signor. 1974 (1895). *Fahrend Volk. Abnormitäten, Kuriositäten und interessante Vertreter der wandernden Künstlerwelt. Mit 135 in den Text gedruckten authentischen Abbildungen*. Berlin: Brinkmann und Bose.

Sarrazin, Thilo. 2010. *Deutschland schafft sich ab. Wie wir unser Land aufs Spiel setzen*. Munich: DVA.

Sassen, Saskia. 2007. "Introduction: Deciphering the Global." In *Deciphering the Global: Its Scales, Spaces, and Subjects*, ed. Saskia Sassen, 1–18. New York: Routledge.

Samudra, Jaida Kim. 2008. "Memory in Our Body: Thick Participation and the Translation of Kinesthetic Experience." *American Ethnologist* 35 (4): 665–681.

Sax, Benjamin and Dieter Kuntz. 1992. *Inside Hitler's Germany: A Documentary History of Life in the Third Reich*. Lexington, MA: Heath and Company.

Scarry, Elaine. 1985. *The Body in Pain: The Making and Unmaking of the World*. New York and Oxford: Oxford University Press.

Schatzki, Theodore R., Karin Knorr Cetina, and Eike von Savigny, eds. 2000. *The Practice Turn in Contemporary Theory*. Edinburgh: Edinburgh University Press.

Scheugl, Hans. 1974. *Show Freaks und Monster. Sammlung Felix Adanos*. Cologne: DuMont.

Schiefenhövel, Wulf. 1995. "Perception, Expression, and Social Function of Pain: A Human Ethological View." *Science in Context* 8(1): 31–46.

Schönfeld, Walther. 1960. *Körperbemalen, Brandmarken, Tätowieren. Nach griechischen, römischen Schriftstellern, Dichtern, neuzeitlichen Veröffentlichungen und eigenen Erfahrungen, vorzüglich in Europa*. Heidelberg: Dr. Alfred Hüthig.

Schooler, Deborah L., Monique Ward, Ann Merriwether, and Allison Caruthers. 2004. "Who's That Girl: Television's Role in the Body Image Development of Young White and Black Women." *Psychology of Women Quarterly* 28: 38–47.

Schultz, Emily, and Robert H. Lavenda. 1990. *Cultural Anthropology: A Perspective on the Human Condition*. St Paul, MN: West Publishing Company.

Seymour, Wendy. 2007. "Exhuming the Body: Revisiting the Role of the Visible Body in Ethnographic Research" *Qualitative Health Resource* 17 (9): 1188–1197.

Shaitly, Shahesta. 2011. "Big Bumba? Try Zumba." *The Observer*, March 27. Accessed May 23, 2013. http://www.guardian.co.uk/lifeandstyle/2011/mar/27/big-bumba-try-zumba .

Shakespeare, William. 1942. *The Complete Plays and Poems of William Shakespeare*, ed. William Neilson and Charles Hill. The New Cambridge edition. Cambridge, MA: Houghton Mifflin Company.

Shapiro, Michael. 2005. "Every Move You Make: Bodies, Surveillance, and Media." *Social Text* 23 (2): 21–34.

Shaw, Andrea. 2006. *The Embodiment of Disobedience: Fat Black Women's Unruly Political Bodies*. Oxford, UK: Lexington Books.

Sheehy, Daniel E. 2008. "Mexico." In *The Garland Handbook of Latin American Music*, ed. Dale A. Olsen and Daniel E. Sheehy, 181–208. New York: Routledge.

Sherman, Yael D. 2011. "Neoliberal Femininity in Miss Congeniality." In *Feminism at the Movies: Understanding Gender in Contemporary Popular Cinema*, ed. Hilary Radner and Rebecca Stringer, 80–92. London and New York: Routledge.

Shilling, Chris. 1991. "Educating the Body: Physical Capital and the Production of Social Inequalities." *Sociology* 25: 653–672.

———. 2004. "Physical Capital and Situated Action: A New Direction for Corporeal Sociology." *British Journal of Sociology of Education* 25: 473–487.

———. 2005. *The Body in Culture, Technology and Society*. London: Sage.

Shiva, Vandana. 2005. *Earth Democracy: Justice, Sustainability, and Peace*. Cambridge, MA: South End Press.

Sitrin, Marina. 2012. *Everyday Revolutions: Horizontalism and Autonomy in Argentina*. London; New York: Zed Books.

Sklair, Leslie. 2000. *The Transnational Capitalist Class*. Malden, MA: Wiley-Blackwell.

Smart, Barry. 2005. *The Sport Star: Modern Sport and the Making of Modern Sport*. London: Allen Lane.

———. 2007. "Not Playing around: Global Capitalism, Modern Sport and Consumer Culture." In *Globalisation and Sport*, ed. Richard Giulianotti and Roland Robertson. Oxford: Blackwell Publishing.

Smith, Robert Courtney. 2005. *Mexican New York: Transnational Lives of New Immigrants*. Berkeley: University of California Press.

Social Movement Studies. 2012. Special Issue: Occupy! 11 (3–4).

Sontag, Susan. 1983. *A Susan Sontag Reader*. 1st Vintage Books edition. New York: Vintage.

Sparkes, Andrew. 1999. "The Fragile Body-Self." In *Talking Bodies: Men's Narratives of the Body and Sport*, ed. Andrew Sparkes and Martti Silvennoinen. Jyvaskyla, Finland: SoPhi.

Sparkes, Andrew and Brett Smith. 2003. "Men, Sport, Spinal Cord Injury and Narrative Time." *Qualitative Research* 3 (3): 295–320.

Spencer, Dale C. 2009. "Habit(us), Body Techniques and Body Callusing: An Ethnography of Mixed Martial Arts." *Body and Society* 15 (4): 119–143.

———. 2012. *Ultimate Fighting and Embodiment. Violence, Gender, and Mixed Martial Arts*. New York: Routledge.

———. 2013. "Sensing Violence: An Ethnography of Mixed Martial Arts." *Ethnography*.doi:10.1177/14661381124711 08.

Stiglitz, Joseph E. 2003. *Globalization and its Discontents*. New York: W.W. Norton and Company.

Stern, Susannah. 2008. "Producing Sites, Exploring Identities: Youth Online Authorship." In *Youth, Identity and Digital Media*, ed. David Buckingham, 95–117. Cambridge, MA: MIT Press.

Stevens, Carrie. 2013. "Why You Should Give In to the Zumba Craze." *Fitbie.* Accessed May 23, 2013. http://fitbie.msn.com/get-fit/why-you-should-give-zumba-craze.

Stokes, Doug. 2005. *America's Other War: Terrorizing Colombia.* New York: Zed Books.

Straubhaar, Joseph D. 1997. "Distinguishing the Global, Regional and National Levels of World Television." In *Media in a Global Context: A Reader,* ed. Annabelle Sreberny- Mohammadi, Dwayne Winseck, Jim McKenna, Jim and Oliver Boyd-Barrett, 34–56. New York: Edward Arnold.

Strong, Pauline Turner. 1999. *Captive Selves, Captivating Others: The Politics and Poetics of Colonial American Captivity Narratives.* Boulder, CO: Westview Press.

Sutton, Barbara. 2010. *Bodies in Crisis: Culture, Violence, and Women's Resistance in Neoliberal Argentina.* New Brunswick, NJ: Rutgers University Press.

———. 2012. "Body." In *Encyclopedia of Globalization,* ed. George Ritzer, 111–116. Malden, MA: Wiley-Blackwell.

Sutton, Barbara, Sandra Morgen, and Julie Novkov, eds. 2008. *Security Disarmed: Critical Perspectives on Gender, Race, and Militarization.* New Brunswick, NJ: Rutgers University Press.

Sutton, Constance and Susan R. Makiesky-Barrow. 1987. "Migration and West Indian Racial and Ethnic Consciousness." In *Caribbean Life in New York City: Sociocultural Dimensions,* ed. Constance Sutton and Elsa Chaney. New York: The Center for Migration Studies.

Tan, Kenneth P. 2012. "The Ideology of Pragmatism: Neo-liberal Globalisation and Political Authoritarianism in Singapore." *Journal of Contemporary Asia,* 42(1): 67–92.

The Global Trip. 2008. "The Global Trip: Erik Gets Shot In Colombia." *YouTube.* Video File. January 10. Accessed June 1, 2012. http://www.youtube.com/watch?v=-SJ33qMRKFY.

"The Secret to Fitness Craze Zumba's Success?" 2011. *The Independent,* September. Accessed May 23, 2013. http://www.independent.co.uk/life-style/health-and-families/the-secret-to-fitness-craze-zumbas-success-2350675.html#.

The World. 2011. "Colombian Designer Takes Bulletproof to New Level." September 22. Accessed July 24, 2012. http://www.theworld.org/2011/09/slideshow-colombian-designer-takes-bulletproof-to-new-level/.

Theberge, Nancy. 1987. "Sport and Women's Empowerment." *Women's Studies International Forum* 10: 387–393.

Thompson, Margo Hobbs. 2009. "Body-Swapping, Empowerment and Empathy: Linda Stein's Recent Sculpture." Accessed July 24, 2012. http://www.lindastein.com/home/BSACat_LoRes.pdf.

Thompson, Sharon, and Sara Corwin. 1997. "Ideal Body Size Beliefs and Weight Concerns of Fourth-Grade Children." *International Journal of Eating Disorders* 21: 279–284.

Tilly, Richard. 1993. *Geschichte der Wirtschaft: Vom Merkantilismus zur totalen Marktwirtschaft.* Oldenbourg: Wissenschaftsverlag.

Today. 2011. "SportsZone Ventures into the Fighting Cage." In *Today,* September 3. Singapore: Mediacorp Press Ltd.

Treat, John W. 1996. "Yoshimoto Banana Writes Home." In *Contemporary Japan and Popular Culture,* ed. John W. Treat, 275–308. Honolulu: University of Hawai'i Press Curzon.

Tucholsky, Kurt. 1978(1928). "So verschieden ist es im menschlichen Leben." *Die Weltbühne. Vollständiger Nachdruck der Jahrgänge 1918–1933.*Koe nigstein:Athe näum.

Tudor, Deborah. 2011. "Twenty First Century Neoliberal Man." In *Neoliberalism and Global Cinema: Capital, Culture, and Marxist Critique,* ed. Jyostna Kapur and Keith B. Wagner, 59–75. London and New York: Routledge.

Turner, Bryan S. 2006. *Vulnerability and Human Rights.* University Park: Pennsylvania State University Press.

Turner, Victor Witter. 1969. *The Ritual Process: Structure and Anti-Structure.* Chicago: Aldine.

TVE (*Televisión Española*). 2010. "Miguel Caballero—Reportaje por TVE." *YouTube.* Video File. September 8. Accessed June 1, 2012. http://www. youtube.com/watch?v=7tBQC8oD7q4&list=UUWdCrHtg_RwSqkP3j mZKRWQ&index=10&feature=plcp.

UNDP (United Nations Development Programme). 1994. *Human Development Report.* New York: Oxford University Press.

U.S. Census Bureau. 2010. "Place of Birth for Foreign-Born Population." Accessed July 2012. http://factfinder2.census.gov/faces/tableservices/jsf /pages/ productview.xhtml?pid=ACS_10_SF4_B05006&prodType=table.

Van Bottenburg, Maarten and Johan Heilbron. 2006. "De-sportization of Fighting Contests: The Origins and Dynamics of No Holds Barred Events and the Theory of Sportization." *International Review for the Sociology of Sports* 41 (3): 259–282.

Van Bottenburg, Maarten. 2001. *Global Games.* Urbana: University of Illinois Press.

VICE (Vice Media Inc.). 2007. "Bogota's Bulletproof Tailor." *VICE.* Video File. Accessed June 1, 2012. http://www.vice.com/es_mx/video/watch /behind-the-seams/bogota-s-bulletproof-tailor.

Villagran, Lauren. 2012. "Beyond the Vest: Bulletproof Clothing Finds a Fashion Sense." January 19. Accessed July 22. http://www.smartplanet. com/blog/global-observer/beyond-the-vest-bulletproof-clothing-finds-a-fashion-sense/2981.

Volkery, Carsten, and Herwig Birg. 2000. "Sterben die Deutschen aus?" *Spiegel Online.* January 6, 2000. Accessed November 28, 2012. http: //www.spiegel.de/politik/ausland/interview-sterben-die-deutschen-aus-a-58855.html.

Wacquant, Loïc. 2004. *Body and Soul: Notebooks of an Apprentice Boxer.* Oxford: Oxford University Press.

Wade, Robert Hunter. 2004. "Is Globalization Reducing Poverty and Inequality?" *World Development* 32 (4): 567–589.

Wagner, Richard. 2010. "Wulffs präsidiales Tattoo. Die perforierte Republik."Frankfurter Allgemeine FAZ.net. July 4, 2010. Accessed March 23, 2011. http://www.faz.net/aktuell/politik/wulffs-praesidiales-tattoo-die-perforierte-republik-11010921.html.

Waldby, Catherine. 1995. "Destruction: Boundary Erotics and Refiguration of the Heterosexual Male Body." In *Sexy Bodies: The Strange Carnalities of Feminism*, ed. Elizabeth Grosz and Elspeth Probyn, 266–278. New York: Routledge.

Walde, Gabriela. 2007. "Das Ende eines Körperkultes." Die Welt Online. June 7, 2007. Accessed January 12, 2010. http://www.welt.de/wissenschaft/article927942/Das-Ende-eines-Koerperkultes.html.

Walker Rettberg, Jill. 2008. *Blogging*. Cambridge: Polity Press.

Wallerstein, Immanuel. 2000. "Globalization or the Age of Transition? A Long-Term View on the Trajectory of the World-System." *International Sociology* 15 (2): 249– 265.

Waters, Mary. 1999. *Black Identities: West Indian Immigrant Dreams and American Realities*. Cambridge, MA and London: Harvard University Press.

Watson Andaya, Barbara, and Leonard Andaya. 2001. *A History of Malaysia*. Basingstoke: Palgrave Macmillan.

WCRC (Women of Color Resource Center). 2006. *Fashion Resistance to Militarism*. Video DVD. Directed and ed. Kimberly Alvarenga; Executive Producer Christine Ahn. Oakland, California.

Weber, Sandra, and Claudia Mitchell. 2008. "Imaging, Keyboarding and Posting Identities: Young People and New Media Technologies." In *Youth, Identity and Digital Media*, ed. David Buckingham, 25–47. Cambridge: MIT Press.

Wehler, Ulrich. 1995. *Deutsche Gesellschaftsgeschichte*. Bd. 3: *Von der Deutschen Doppelrevolution bis zum Beginn des ersten Weltkrieges*. Munich: C. H. Beck.

Weiss, Robert. 1994. *Learning from Strangers*. New York: The Free Press.

Weitz, Rose, ed. 2009. *The Politics of Women's Bodies: Sexuality, Appearance, and Behavior*. New York: Oxford University Press.

Wetzell, Richard and Peter Becker, eds. 2009. *Criminals and Their Scientists: The History of Criminology in International Perspective*. Cambridge: Cambridge University Press.

Whitlock, Flint. 2011. *The Beasts of Buchenwald: Karl and Ilse Koch, Human-Skin Lampshades, and the War-Crimes Trial of the Century*. Brule, WI: Cable Publishing.

Willett, Rebekah. 2008. "Consumer Citizens Online: Structure, Agency and Gender in Online Participation." In *Youth, Identity and Digital Media*, ed. David Buckingham, 49–69. Cambridge: MIT Press.

Wilson, Ara. 2004. *The Intimate Economies of Bangkok: Tomboys, Tycoons, and Avon Ladies in the Global City*. Berkeley: University of California Press.

Winter, Bronwyn. 2008. *Hijab and the Republic: Uncovering the French Headscarf Debate.* Syracuse, NY: Syracuse University Press.

Woods, Ronald B. 2011. *Social Issues in Sport.* Champaign, IL: Human Kinetics.

Wuttke, Heinrich. 1877. *Die Entstehung der Schrift, die verschiedenen Schriftsysteme und das Schrifttum der nicht alfabetarisch schreibenden Völker.* Leipzig: L. D. Weigel.

Wyss, Jim. 2012. "Fashionable Bullet-Proof Wear Finds Growth Abroad." *The Miami Herald*, March 5.

Yazbeck Haddad, Yvonne. 2007. "The Post-9/11 *Hijab* as Icon," *Sociology of Religion* 68 (3): 253–267.

Young, Katharine. 1997. *Presence in the Flesh: The Body in Medicine.* Cambridge, MA: Harvard University Press.

Zantop, Susanne. 1997. *Colonial Fantasies: Conquest, Family and Nation in Precolonial Germany, 1770–1870.* Durham, NC: Duke University Press.

Zaslow, Emilie. 2009. *Feminism, Inc.* Basingstoke: Palgrave Macmillan.

"Zumba." 2009. *Revista Femenina*, March 27. Accessed May 23, 2013. http://revistafemenina.com/zumba/.

"Zumba." 2013. Accessed May. http://www.consejos.com.mx/zumba.htm.

Zumba Fitness, LLC. 2012. Accessed November 23, 2012. http://www.zumba.com.

Zumba Fitness, LLC. 2013. Latest modified version. Accessed May 23, 2013. http://www.zumba.com.

CONTRIBUTORS

Thomas J. D. Armbrecht is an associate professor of French at the University of Wisconsin-Madison. He specializes in theater as literature and dramatic art, and in twentieth-century French philosophy. Previous publications include a monograph about the relation of literary genre to sexuality in the works of Marguerite Yourcenar and Julien Green, as well as articles about the intersections of art and literature. He is currently writing a book about polymathy and polyphony in the works of French authors Pierre Loti, Jean Cocteau, and Hervé Guibert.

Diana Brenscheidt gen. Jost teaches at the University of Sonora, Mexico, in the department of music and the university's graduate program of humanities and fine arts. In 2011 she received her PhD in ethnomusicology from the University of Cologne in Germany. She is author of the book *Shiva Onstage: Uday Shankar's Company of Hindu Dancers and Musicians in Europe and the United States, 1931–38* (LIT, 2011). Her current research focuses on local music, dance, and body cultures in (northern) Mexico. She has also published work on topics related to the history of ethnomusicology.

Erynn Masi de Casanova is assistant professor of Sociology at the University of Cincinnati, where she is also a faculty affiliate of the Department of Women's, Gender, and Sexuality Studies and the Department of Romance Languages and Literatures. She is the author of *Making Up the Difference: Women, Beauty, and Direct Selling in Ecuador* (University of Texas Press, 2011), which won the National Women's Studies Association's Sara A. Whaley Book Prize. Her research focuses on issues of gender, bodies, and identity, and has been published in journals such as *Gender & Society, Feminist Economics, Sociological Forum, Latino Studies, Women's Studies Quarterly,* and *Ethnography.* Her work has been featured in mainstream media outlets such as *The New York Times* and *The Huffington Post,* as well as international newspapers. She is currently conducting research on paid domestic work in Latin America and white-collar men and dress inc orporateAme rica.

Nahed Eltantawy is an assistant professor of Journalism at High Point University, North Carolina. She completed her PhD in Public Communication at Georgia State University. Her MA and BA in Political Science were completed at the American University in Cairo. She has worked as a journalist in Cairo, Egypt, and as a freelancer in Atlanta, Georgia. Her research interests focus on media representations of Arabs and Muslims in general, and Arab and Muslim women in particular, as well as the impact of global capitalism on women in the developing world. With recent events in Egypt and other Arab countries, she has also published work on the Arab Spring and social media in the Arab world.

Anisha Gautam is a PhD candidate in Women's and Gender Studies at the University of New South Wales (Australia). Her work interrogates the question of identity through a postcolonial, phenomenological framework. Specifically, she is interested in how raced, gendered, and queer subjects understand and articulate their understandings of the self in relation to time and history. She is also, on occasion, a short story and creative nonfiction writer.

Kamille Gentles-Peart is an associate professor of Global Communication at Roger Williams University. She holds a PhD in Communication from the University of Michigan, Ann Arbor. Her scholarship addresses intercultural and mediated communication practices within diasporic populations. Her current research project explores the significance of body politics in the negotiation of cultural citizenship by West Indian immigrant women in the United States. Her most recent publication is a coedited volume titled *Re-Constructing Place and Space: Media, Power, and Identity in the Constitution of Caribbean Diasporas* (Cambridge Scholars Press, 2012), which won the 2012 Outstanding Book Award from the African American Communication and Culture Division of the National Communication Association.

Joel Gwynne is an assistant professor of English at the National Institute for Education, Nanyang Technological University, Singapore, where he teaches contemporary literature and feminist studies. His research focuses on the relationship between feminism and globalization, particularly in the context of postfeminism and sexuality studies. He has published articles on film, literature, and media studies in the *Journal of Postcolonial Writing, Journal of Gender Studies, Journal of Contemporary Asia* and *Film, Fashion and Consumption.*

He is coeditor of the collections *Sexuality and Contemporary Fiction* (Cambria Press, 2012) and *Postfeminism and Contemporary Hollywood Cinema* (Palgrave Macmillan, 2013). He is currently writing a monograph on young women's fashion blogs in Singapore and Malaysia, to be published by NIAS Press in 2016.

Verena Hutter is a visiting assistant professor at DePauw University, Indiana. She holds a PhD from the University of California, Davis. Her current research explores tattoos as literary, social, and political practice in Germany from the nineteenth century to today, and focuses on how notions of deviance intersect with discourses of identity,ge nder,na tion,a ndOthe rness.

Afshan Jafar is an assistant professor of Sociology at Connecticut College. Her research and teaching interests are globalization, transnational women's movements, fundamentalist and nationalist movements, gender, and the body. Her first book, *Women's NGOs in Pakistan* (Palgrave Macmillan, 2011), uncovers the overwhelming challenges facing women's NGOs and examines the strategies used by them to ensure not just their survival but an acceptance of their messages by the larger public. Her research has been published in journals such as *Social Problems, Gender Issues, Critical Half* and *Sexuality and Culture*. She is also a regular contributing editor for the University of Venus blog at InsideHigherEd.com and has also published career advicec olumnsf orIns ideHigherEd.

Lionel Loh Han Loong graduated from the University of Singapore (NUS) with a degree in social sciences and is currently pursuing his masters in social sciences at NUS. His areas of interest include the sociology of the body, social memory, gender and sexuality, sports and martial arts. For his masters thesis, he is researching the intersections between Muay Thai, masculinities, performativity, and transnationalism in a Thailand martial arts gym. He is affiliated with the National University of Singapore as a research scholar, and is also a research affiliate of Ubon Ratchathani University.

Mónica G. Moreno Figueroa is a lecturer (assistant professor) in Sociology at Newcastle University (UK) in the School of Geography, Politics and Sociology. With a PhD in Sociology from Goldsmiths, University of London, Mónica has taught at Goldsmiths and Birkbeck College, University of London, University of Nottingham, Princeton University, and El Colegio de México. Her research and teaching has been concerned with contemporary practices of racism, *mestizaje*, feminist theory, beauty, embodiment, visibility, and emotions. She is currently completing a book on the everyday life of racism in Mexico and has just published a coedited special issue for *Feminist Theory* on beauty, race and feminist theory (2013). Mónica has published in *Ethnicities* (2010); *Journal of Cultural Research* (2010); *Journal of Intercultural Studies* (2008); and *History of the Human Sciences* (2008); as well as in the edited collections *Racismos y otras formas de intolerancia* (2012); *Cultures of Colour* (2012); *Contesting Recognition* (2011); *Hope and Feminist Theory* (2010); *Mestizaje, Diferencia y Nación* (2010); and *Raza, Etnicidad y Sexualidades* (2008).

Barbara Sutton is an associate professor of Women's, Gender, and Sexuality Studies at the University at Albany, SUNY. She is affiliated with the departments of Sociology and of Latin American, Caribbean, and US Latino Studies. Sutton's scholarly interests include globalization, body politics, human rights, and women's movements, particularly in Latin American contexts. She coedited *Security Disarmed: Critical Perspectives on Gender, Race, and Militarization* (with Sandra Morgen and Julie Novkov; Rutgers University Press, 2008) and is the author of *Bodies in Crisis: Culture, Violence, and Women's Resistance in Neoliberal Argentina* (Rutgers University Press, 2010), winner of the 2011 Gloria E. Anzaldúa Book Prize from the National Women's StudiesAs sociation.

INDEX

Abdullah II of Jordan, 90
advertising, tattoos in, 130–2
aerobics classes
    body type associated with, 152–3
    critiques of, 147–8
    Zumba and, 149
"affective wall," Elias's concept of, 9
African diaspora, xix, 34
agency. *See also* individual agency
    bodily presentation and, 68–9
    consumption and, 55, 57
    female, 52
    imagination and, 21
    neoliberal discourse and, 52
    online, 56, 62, 68–9 (*see also*
        identity[ies], online)
    sexual, 65–6
    social/cultural, 29
Aghioni, Alberto, 145
Ahmed, Leila, xvii
Alley, Kirstie, 149
American women, thin ideal of,
    32–5
America's Next Top Model, 30
Ames, Eric, 121
Anglo beauty ideals, black women
    and, 26
Anzaldúa, Gloria, 141
Appadurai, Arjun, 7, 57
Armbrecht, Thomas J. D., xx, 187
    personal reflection of, 107–2
armored clothing. *See* bulletproof/
    bullet-resistant clothing
Aryan body, La Belle Irene and, 114
Asian financial crisis, Malaysia and,
    54

Attwood, Feona, 65
Audrey's blog, 58
    and corporeal perfectibility, 65–6
    female bodily management and, 64
    female friendship and, 63–4
    globalization impacts and, 70
    motivations for, 58–60
    new femininity and, 65–7
    selection for study, 57–8
    self-reflection in, 61–2
Aune, Kristin, 64
authenticity
    as fluid concept, 22–3
    martial arts training and, 4, 7, 13,
        17, 21–2
    of nonprofessional bloggers, 58,
        62, 69

Baartman, Sarah, 116, 134n.4
Baker, Josephine, 151
Balanchine, George, xiii
Ball, Hugo, 122
ballet dancers, body ideal of, xiii–xiv
ballet, styles of, xii–xiii
Banks, Tyra, 28
baseball, in Cuba, 6
Bauman, Zygmunt, 86
beauty ideal
    Anglo, black women and, 26
    black/white binary of, 35, 151
      (*see also* body type, black/
      non-white; body type, white/
      Caucasian)
    dialogic approach to, 27
    dominant, 26
    negotiating with, 28

CPI Antony Rowe
Chippenham, UK
2016-12-30 12:11